LAND, SEA & TIME

Book One

LAND, SEA & TIME

Book One

EDITORS

Edward A. Jones

Shannon M. Lewis

Pat Byrne

Boyd W. Chubbs

Clyde Rose

BREAKWATER

BREAKWATER
100 Water Street
P.O. Box 2188
St. John's, NF
A1C 6E6

Front, back cover and page bars from a painting by Anne Meredith Barry entitled Early September, Bonne Bay. *Collection of Breakwater.*

Series motif by Boyd W. Chubbs, featuring Avalon *an original typeface by Boyd W. Chubbs.*

Design and layout: Nadine Osmond
Production Co-ordinator: Carla Kean

Canadian Cataloguing in Publication Data

Main entry under title:

Land, sea and time

    ISBN 1-55081-160-6

1. Canadian literature (English) — Newfoundland.*   2. Canadian literature (English) — 20th century.*   3. Art, Canadian — Newfoundland   4. Art, Modern — 20th century — Newfoundland.
I. Jones, Edward, 1939-

NX513.A3N45 2000   C810.8'09718   C00-95005405

Copyright © 2000 Breakwater Books Ltd.

ALL RIGHTS RESERVED. No part of this work covered by the copyright hereon may be reproduced or used in any form or by any means—graphic, electronic or mechanical—without the prior written permission of the publisher. Any request for photocopying, recording, taping or storing in an information retrieval system of any part of this book shall be directed in writing to the Canadian Reprography Collective, 6 Adelaide Street East, Suite 900, Toronto, Ontario, M5C 1H6. This applies to classroom usage as well.

Every reasonable effort has been made to find copyright holders for material contained in this book. The publishers would be pleased to have any errors or omissions brought to their attention. Credits appear on pages 274-276.

Breakwater wishes to thank the Department of Education whose cooperation on this project is much appreciated. In particular we wish to express our indebtedness to Eldred Barnes, Language Arts Consultant, all the pilot teachers and the school boards in Newfoundland and Labrador who worked with us on this educational venture. Best wishes to you all.

 We acknowledge the financial support of the Government of Canada through the Book Publishing Industry Development Program (BPIDP) for our publishing activities.

Land, Sea & Time is a three-volume collection of a variety of Newfoundland and Labrador texts.

Text is defined as any language event, whether oral, written, or visual. In this sense, a conversation, a poem, a poster, a story, a photograph, a tribute, a music video, a television program, a radio documentary, and a multi-media production, for example, are all texts.

The series, *Land, Sea & Time, Book One, Book Two,* and *Book Three* offers a blend of previously neglected voices, new voices, and those often found in anthologies. Together, these books give readers an opportunity to explore the literary and cultural heritage of Newfoundland and Labrador.

Table of Contents

Erosion	E. J. Pratt	1
Violet Hovering	Tara T. Bryan	1
New facts for old	Wade Kearley	2
Wanderings	Robert Burt	2
Evelyn (short story)	Al Pittman	3
Evelyn (poem)	Al Pittman	6
Untitled	Michael Cook	6
Ancestors	Tom Moore	7
The Foure Elements in Newfound-land	Robert Hayman	7
Map of Newfoundland, 1616	John Mason	8
Excerpt from a Letter	Warrick Smith	8
Finos Mapas / Fine Maps	Jorge Luis Camacho	9
Introduction to *The Winds Softly Sigh*	R. F. Sparkes	10
Good Times	Danielle Loranger	12
Independence	Richard Greene	13
Tickle Cove Pond	Mark Walker	14
Newfoundland	Robert Lowell	16
The Founding of The Newfoundland Genealogical Society	Janet Miller Pitt	17
A Motif for Genealogy from a Tombstone	Boyd Chubbs	18
Beyond the Obvious	John F. O'Mara	19
Researching Your Family History in Newfoundland	Dianne C. Jackman	20
Epitaphs or Tombstone Inscriptions	Otto Tucker and Leo Moakler	21
Genealogy One-Liners	The Ancestor	23
My Grandmother and Knowlton Nash	Carl Leggo	24
Camay Soap Advertisement	Devine's Folklore	26
Foremother	Lillian Bouzane	27
Grandmother Figure I	Scott Fillier	29
Paddy with the Maul	Don Wright	30
Don Wright	Editors	31
Walking	Helen Porter	32
A New Name	Jim Wellman	33
Names and Souls	F. W. Peacock	34
Fumigating the Map	Harold Horwood	35
Avery's Mill	Walt Pinsent	37
Newfoundland Name Frequency List in *Gazetteer*	Mobilewords Ltd.	38
Photograph, Relocating from Silver Fox Island to Dover	B. Brooks	39
Places That Were	Geraldine Rubia	40
West Moon	Pat Byrne	43

Looking Back	*Enos D. Watts*	44
St. Leonard's Revisited	*Al Pittman*	45
An Off-Shore Wind	*Tom Dawe*	46
Cocomalt Advertisement	*Devine's Folklore*	51
It's a Glacial Sound That Quiets the House	*Boyd Chubbs*	52
Birthday Voyage (for B. W.)	*Pat Byrne*	53
West Moon Cover illustration	*Breakwater*	54
Excerpt from *West Moon*	*Al Pittman*	55
The Road Home	*Michael Crummey*	75
Quoth the Raven	*Angela Mercer*	76
The Monologue in Newfoundland	*Wilfred W. Wareham*	80
The Lobster Salad	*Traditional*	81
The Prince of Wales	*Traditional*	83
Smokeroom on the *Kyle*	*Ted Russell*	85
A Tall Tale: My Adventure with a Giant Squid	*T. E. Tuck*	87
Kraken or Giant Squid Advertisement	*Memorial University*	89
The Terror of Quidi Vidi Lake	*Otto Kelland*	90
The All 'Round Newfoundlander	*P. C. Mars*	95
The Cliffs of Baccalieu	*Jack Withers*	97
My Political Career	*Art Scammell*	98
Lighthouse—*Cabot Island* and *E. & S. Barbour Store*	*Carl Barbour*	102
Captain Carl Barbour (1908-1990)	*David Blackwood*	103
Inuit in Labrador: The Old Way of Life	*Brenda Clark*	104
The "Kimatullivik Exhibit"	*Newfoundland Museum*	107
Common Threads in Inuit Culture	*Enoch Obed*	108
Depiction of Inuit Hunters	*Keld Hansen*	110
Photograph, Inuit Family in Summer Camp	*Them Days*	111
High Water, Eagle River	*Scott Goudie*	112
Artist's Statement	*Scott Goudie*	113
We, the Inuit, Are Changing	*Martin Martin*	114
Portrait of Martin Martin and Family	*Them Days*	115
The Northern Lights of Labrador	*Don Fulford*	116
Mother Boggan	*Margaret Duley*	117
The St. John's Balladeers	*George Story*	124
Betsy Brennan's Blue Hen	*Johnny Burke*	132
Last Words of a Dying Man	*Johnny Burke*	134
Report of the South Coast Disaster Committee	*R. F. Horwood*	134
Summary of *Highway to Valour*	*Lisa de Leon*	135
Excerpt from *Highway to Valour*	*Margaret Duley*	135
Letter to Earthquake Relief Committee	*R. F. Horwood*	137
Photograph, The Tidal Wave Disaster	*Provincial Archives*	139

The Recitation	Lucy McFarlane	140
Photograph, Typical Scene in a One-Room Schoolhouse	Breakwater Archives	143
Cod Liver Oil Advertisement	Devine's Folklore	147
The Mummer	Tom Dawe	148
Motif for "The Mummer"	Boyd Chubbs	149
Any Mummers Allowed In?	Bud Davidge	150
Three Mummers at Winsor's Point	David Blackwood	151
Excerpts from *The Winds Softly Sigh*	R. F. Sparkes	152
Photograph of the *Kyle*	Breakwater Archives	158
Untitled	Rosalie Fowler	159
The Tangled Forest	William B. Ritchie	160
Artist's Statement	William B. Ritchie	161
Gilbert Hay	Inuit Art Quarterly	162
Nuikkusemajak	Gilbert Hay	162
Tuckamore Festival of the Arts: Songwriting	Shirley Montague	164
There is This Photograph	Carmelita McGrath	166
Percy Janes Boarding the Bus	Agnes Walsh	168
Beneath the Dust and Stars	Boyd Chubbs	169
Teenagers	Aubrey M. Tizzard	170
Pleasant Afternoon	Brad Reid	171
Miniskirt	Alastair Macdonald	174
Halfway up the Mountain	Harry Martin	176
Jim Wilson's Chum	Wilfred Grenfell	177
First Fruit of the Tree	Irving Fogwill	182
The Little Girl Learns to Swim, I, II and III	Sharon Puddester	184
Artist's Statement	Sharon Puddester	185
The Death of a Tree	Gary Saunders	186
Photograph of a Tree	Stewart Churchill	191
The Death of an Elm	Herbert Pottle	192
Alder Music	Gary Saunders	193
Talking to Trees	David Elliott	195
Julie-Ann	David Pitt	196
Photograph, Yaffling Fish on a Rooftop	Breakwater Archives	197
Barrens (for three Dylans)	Jeff Baggs	203
The Great Fire of '92	W. J. Kent	204
Photograph, St. John's After the Fire of 1892	Provincial Archives	208
The 1921 Fire at Nain	Martin Martin	209
Letter Written by Torsten Andersen, 1901	Torsten Andersen	210
Letter Written by Catherine O'Dell	Catherine O'Dell	211
Troubled Waters	H. M. Heather	212
Brick's Tasteless Advertisement	Devine's Folklore	216

Squarin' Up	A. R. Scammell	217
Newfoundland Paper Money, 1857-1882	Breakwater Archives	219
The Coil That Bends, The Line That Binds	Pam Hall	220
Depictions of *The Coil*	Pam Hall	221
Come In	Grace Butt	222
Full Circle	Nadine Browne	222
Eye	Mary Dalton	222
Praise	Boyd Chubbs	223
Lies for the Tourists	Mary Dalton	223
Photograph, Brigus, circa 1915	Mary Schwall	223
Vocabulary	Alastair Macdonald	224
Al Pittman and Tom Dawe: Island Poems	Terry Goldie	225
Excerpts from *No Man's Land*	Kevin Major	236
Beaumont Hamel	Frederick Andrews	240
The Ballad of Beaumont Hamel	Jim Fidler	241
Romance in the Twentieth Century	Robert G. MacDonald	242
Prelude to Doom	Irving Fogwill	243
Bill	Jack Turner	244
Seeking Recruits	Fred Adams	247
The Chance of Your Lifetime	Fred Adams	250
A Letter to Will	Stephen Walsh	251
Inscription	Robert G. MacDonald	253
Snaps from the War	Frances Cluett	254
Excerpt From a Letter Written by Frances Cluett	Frances Cluett	255
Letter Written by Frances Cluett to her Mother, Martha	Frances Cluett	256
Three O'Clock	Christopher Pratt	258
Artist's Statement	Christopher Pratt	259
The Master	Herbert Pottle	260
Photographs, Emile Benoit and Rufus Guinchard	Breakwater/The Telegram	261
Facing the Gale	Geoff Meeker	262
Cover of *II:II, Newfoundland Women Sing*	Connie Hynes	265
Sonny's Dream	Ron Hynes	266
Photograph, Buttercups	Dennis Minty	268
A Bouquet for Emily	Al Pittman	269
Author Index		271
Title Index		272
Text Credits		274
Visual Credits		276

Erosion

E. J. Pratt

It took the sea a thousand years,
A thousand years to trace
The granite features of this cliff,
In crag and scarp and base.

It took the sea an hour one night,
An hour of storm to place
The sculpture of these granite seams
Upon a woman's face.

Violet Hovering, Tara T. Bryan, oil on canvas

New facts for old

Wade Kearley

Who with lunar raving
obscures for word-blind children
the language of their senses?
All lies are broken and yield in time
to the violent questioning of age.

Those children with the power
to act do not long refuse;
curious fingers will find the braille,
decipher the image
on the paper retina.

No amount of shouting can conceal
those fingered pages, no moonshadow
can erase old scars or bind the hands
of children who feel your transparency.

Wanderings

Robert Burt

We threw our adolescence on the driftwood pyre,
Singing as the ashes blew away over the bold sea.
Only then could I escape from my locked vision—
The wanderings finally had shape and meaning.

I turned my back on my fantasy,
Which is what my youth was all about.
I now find it is my life—
The wanderings finally defined the dream.

The woodland paths branch out before us,
Fear not which one you take or leave.
Each one will hold its own adventure—
Wanderings, love, wanderings.

The wanderings have finally led me here again;
I knocked on your door as before.
But this time I entered—
And that has made all the difference.

Evelyn
Al Pittman

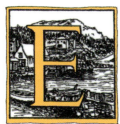

Evelyn must have been sixteen or so, older than us but not as old as married women or mothers. Though she lived in Borden's house, no one ever called her Evelyn Borden. She was simply Evelyn to everyone, one more person on the road who had always been there and always would be.

In her own mysterious way, she was an attractive girl with dark hair, long to her waist almost, a slender girl, dreamlike.

She had no friends. Our parents, when they spoke of her at all, spoke in whispers, and we were warned always to leave her alone.

She spent much of her time swinging high in the sky on a mill-rope swing that hung from a plank nailed to two poplars in a far corner of Borden's back yard.

Whenever I went by and saw her there, it seemed to me as though, at each extremity of the arc the swing inscribed, she might let go and take leave of the yard, the road, and the very earth below her.

I'd want to stop then and watch her. But because it was forbidden and because I was afraid of her, I'd pass on in the road taking with me, for as long as I could, the elusive images of her bare legs slanting smoothly skyward, her dark hair streaming behind her, her breasts straining against the thin fabric of her dress.

One morning after Mass, early that summer, my gaze concealed behind the crocheted curtain in the front room window, I watched her walking in the fields across the road from our house. She was wandering aimlessly through the knee-deep grass, her hair blowing in the breeze and she looked so lonely and unloved, I wondered why I had ever been afraid of her. What if I had the nerve to go out to her, I wondered, speak to her, say hello. Would she smile at me, take my hand perhaps? She'd laugh at me more than likely. Or claw my eyes out.

Maybe it would have been easy enough to ignore her, to have none of my confused feelings for her, had it not been for the way she dressed. Her dresses were always too long or too short and never nearly in fashion. Yet there was always something about the way they clung to her that bestowed upon her a sensuality that shocked the eye with its innocence and grace.

Summer evenings when we were hot at hockey with a sponge ball for a puck and birch junks for goal posts, she'd come strolling up the road. As she approached, the players would fall silent and the game would cease. Down the centre of our imaginary rink she'd stroll, her eyes dead-ahead or downcast, never a glance at either side of the nervous gauntlet she walked. Oh, the unspoken relief when she had passed and proceeded on her way. What a sudden flurry of skill on the road then!

Sometimes, in the privacy of his boughwolfen, Malcolm would tell us what he'd like to do with Evelyn. My ears burned when I heard and I despised Malcolm for profaning my images of her with his carnal vulgarity.

I could not, even in the heat of my bed at night, be comfortable with such thoughts of Evelyn. It was easy to think that way of Doris or Marlene or Hilda or

Beulah. But with Evelyn, something other than morality got in the way of it, some sense of violation more serious than sin.

The first time I stumbled upon her standing naked beneath the falls, the shimmering sheet of white water revealing her to my sight in the most startling garment of all, I stole away into the woods as quick as I could and waited all the way home for God to strike me dead.

He did not strike me dead though. Not then, nor any of the days after when I'd follow her to the falls, watch as she discarded her dress, always on the same rock, and look on trembling from my place in the alders as she climbed the low slippery slope to where the falling water splashed in an array of rainbows at the foot of the cliff.

The sight of her there, her arms stretched up into the cone of translucent white water, her thighs and stomach glistening like glass, her breasts like slippery round fish splashing in the spill, all of her, there, was more than my Catholic conscience could withstand. I became an unrepentant sinner. I decided I would go gladly to hell.

There was nothing of Malcolm's obscenity in my fall from grace. I lived for Evelyn's nakedness and longed to touch her but my longing was pure. I loved her.

One afternoon, in the second week of my anxious vigil, while I watched Evelyn offer her body, and perhaps her soul as well, to the sun and water, while I watched her with love and grief, I heard, all-of-a-sudden, downstream, a splash. I turned with fright, pushed aside a curtain of leaves, and saw Malcolm making his way up stream toward the falls. In one hand he held a bamboo pole, in the other a skivver of trout.

Before I could begin to think what to do, he had reached the edge of the falls pool. He lay his catch of trout in a small run inside the main stream and weighed it down with a rock. He stood, poised to cast his line into the pool, and saw Evelyn under the falls. For an instant he stopped, frozen, his pole suspended in the air over his shoulder. Then, when he realized that she had not yet seen him, he put down his pole and crept, like a thief, into the alders across the brook. There he concealed himself with unobstructed view and there he remained until Evelyn had put her dress on over her wet, and suddenly ugly body, and gone up the path toward the road and home.

Malcolm came out of hiding, picked up his pole and his skivver of trout and went lazily up the path behind her.

I remained hidden in the alders. I felt grotesquely betrayed as though I had been tricked into eternal damnation for the sake of something I'd foolishly thought precious and entirely mine. I might have wept, but all I could think was how much I hated Malcolm for violating my secret with his lust.

In the afternoons that followed, I did not pursue Evelyn to the falls until one day I saw Malcolm go down the path after her, stalking a cautious way behind.

In a fury, I scrambled from the house. Down the road I ran and went from yard to yard until I had gathered Gerald and Roland and Tooty and Freck and Doris and Margo and Eugene and everyone I could find. Evelyn, I told them, was down at the falls with no clothes on.

A long column of whooping warriors, we went down the path and descended on her like a hoard of wild savages. Tooty threw her dress in the brook. Gerald waded into the spray and drove her out with an alder switch. She came out, stumbling among us, a look of absolute terror in her eyes. We slashed at her with switches, we shouted the foulest words we knew, we grabbed at her wet hair. For a confused minute, she tried to shield herself from our abuse, then she let out such an animal scream, we stopped and stepped away, our wooden whips arrested in the air. Evelyn ran up the path, still screaming. For safety's sake, we let her have a head start. Then we chased after her.

Malcolm had, all the while, kept himself hidden in his hideout across the brook and I had to bite my tongue to keep from telling the others he was there.

The road talked a long time about the day Evelyn went running naked down the road past the houses, the gaping men at the gates, the incredulous wives and toddling youngsters.

That was the day they came to take her away. From the sanctuary of our front porch, I saw her vain struggle and heard her cries as they packaged her into the back seat of a car, a hefty neighbour on either side.

That was the last time anyone ever saw Evelyn on Buckingham Road.

That was the night I knelt by my bed and begged God to forgive me. So that He could see the profound depth of my contrition, I promised Him that, as soon as I was old enough, I'd become a priest.

Evelyn
Al Pittman

Evelyn the adopted girl
went daily to the falls
below Mountbatten Road

went naked to the falls
stood there in her nakedness
let the falls tumble over her
let the water splash away from her shoulders
let it slide down her white stomach
let it bubble about her feet

it was the sort of thing
you expect to encounter
only in dreams
or in pictures of paradise

on Mountbatten Road though
they said she was touched
said the devil had a hold on her

her scream
like the sound of a thousand devils
brought everyone
to their doorsteps
when they came to take her away

(untitled)
Michael Cook

Once upon a time—
I remember it was a long time ago,
there was nobody here. Nobody.
There were silences inland
where the salmon and trout
kept the pools from falling asleep.
Sometimes, in winter
came the crack of a tree falling;
it would echo, like change.
And when the lightning struck
the fires ran.

Ancestors
Tom Moore

Each in his own way,
They just came. That's all.
Each in his own world of cousins,
Sisters, loves, and friends,
One day home in Europe,
And the next
With the movement already in his veins,
Threw down the reins of home
Said good-bye to homely paths
Left behind a native sod
Left behind a nation growing
Left behind a doubtful god
And came, perhaps to fish for cod.

The Foure Elements in Newfound-land
Robert Hayman

To the Worshipfull Captaine John Mason *who did wisely and worthily governe there divers yeeres*

The Aire in *Newfound-land* is wholesome, good;
The Fire, as sweet as any made of wood;
The Waters, very rich, both salt and fresh;
The Earth more rich, you know it is no lesse.
Where all are good, *Fire*, *Water*, *Earth*, and *Aire*,
What man made of these foure would not live there?

(1628)

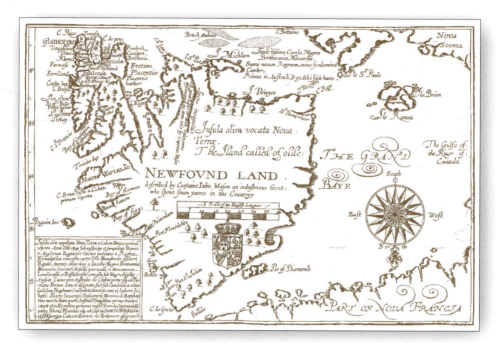

Map of Newfoundland by Captain John Mason, 1616

Excerpt from a Letter

Written by Warrick Smith to J. R. Smallwood
St. John's, March 17th, 1943

Quodlibets…contained a map of Newfoundland made about 1616 by John Mason who made a rough survey of this island…. The map was a good one. It follows what was the universal practice up to the year 1500 namely it had the south at the top of the map. This practice was started by the Greeks and the Romans….

This map with the north at the bottom and the south at the top was the frontispiece of Hayman's book. The late Mr. W. A. Munn informed me that it was impossible to get the book with the map in it…. He said that every shipmaster sailing to this country wanted a map of Newfoundland. They bought or stole the map or if they owned both book and map they tore out the map and pinned it up in their cabins and used it for navigation of our coasts. Hence, they got into the habit of saying "up to St. John's" and "down to Labrador," "up south" and "down north." The map was in use from about 1630 to 1780 (when James Cook's map became common). Thus it was that the expressions "down north" and "down to Labrador" became common. When folk talked thus for about one hundred and fifty years, it is not to be wondered at that the phrases have lasted for another century and a half and more.

Finos Mapas / Fine Maps

Jorge Luis Camacho

Mis amigos van a Europa o a América
y nunca más regresan.
Yo hojeo las paginas de un mapa donde imagino
ellos caminan,
calles ganadas ahora por la nostalgia
y la soledad.

Camino a su lado, compro su felicidad
en el mercado más cercano, y ellos me sonrien,
se emborrachan y lloran,
con la misma brevedad con que paso el dinero
sobre el mostrador,
y el vendedor mueve la cabeza satisfecho.

Todo ocurre en un instante,
bajo las lámparas grises, en los finos mapas
que nos dan en la clase
para aprender de política y geografía.

My friends go to Europe or America
and never come back.
I turn the pages of the maps
where I imagine they wander,
streets now gained by homesickness
and solitude.

I walk beside them,
I buy their happiness in the nearest market
and they smile, get drunk and cry,
while I pass the money over the counter,
and the salesman nods at me, satisfied.

Everything happens in an instant,
under the grey lamps, in the fine maps we are given
in the classroom to learn about politics
and geography.

Introduction to
The Winds Softly Sigh
R. F. Sparkes

"What men or gods are these?"

Keats

Some years ago I took a friend by boat into one of the most isolated settlements in Newfoundland. It was on the Great Northern Peninsula. We sailed a couple of miles up a narrow fjord until we came to a tiny land-locked harbour where cliffs rose almost sheer a thousand feet into the air. Houses and fishing stages seemed to be clinging to the cliffs with both hands with their feet in the water. There was barely enough land to provide a narrow footpath round the little haven, but here and there between the rocks where some soil had collected, grew little patches of potatoes, cabbage and a few other vegetables.

My friend had never seen anything like it before. With a look of consternation he said, "Dear God! I can understand a man coming in here to die; but to live? I just don't believe it."

There are, of course, many places like that in Newfoundland, settled by men who intended to win an easy living from the sea. They lived as close to the fishing grounds as they could get and as long as there was a safe harbour for their boats and a good supply of wood and water, they were content. Perhaps the original settlers never intended to live there permanently, but the temporary too often becomes the permanent and when children are born there and grow up it is then too late to move, for to those children the place is home.

Fortunately for most of us Newfoundlanders, the great majority of pioneers in this island wanted something better than that which so astonished my friend. Thus the man who was to become my mother's great, great grandfather, when he sought a home in the north, sailed until he found a harbour sheltered from prevailing winds by hills clad with pine and fir, where there was plenty of birch and forests of spruce to supply their timber and fuel needs. There was a salmon river, brooks, springs of sweet water and enough good soil to provide rich gardens for all who came with him and for all who would come after him.

My ancestors, as did all the pioneer settlers, brought with them in their ships, not only the tools necessary for building, but sheep, cattle and poultry, seeds, plants and herbs. In most of those older settlements you may still find caraway seed, and chives, tansy, hops and wormwood gone wild from the plantings of the first settlers.

Here they found game in abundance on the hills, rivers teeming with trout and salmon, the bays, harbours and coves literally swarming with cod, herring and mackerel, edible berries growing in prodigal profusion on the marshes, hills and meadows and seabirds in their season in the tens of thousands.

To such a northern "wilderness" came my great, great, great grandfather and his companions and amidst that "dreadful isolation" they built their houses, laid out their gardens and created homes. Later on came other settlers, some from other parts of Newfoundland and a few from England. There was plenty of room and the village grew and prospered.

The last Englishman to arrive in our village came in 1869. He was a young Londoner of twenty-four years named Joseph Raisin. He soon found a wife and they settled down in one of the few remaining uninhabited coves. They had no children so they adopted an orphan boy and were always kind to other people's children. Uncle Joseph Raisin was never too busy to make or mend a boat for a boy, and Aunt Mary's needle prepared many a little girl's doll for Easter.

I was ten years old when he was seventy-two or thereabout so I knew him well. Everybody called him "Uncle Joseph Raisin," not Skipper nor Mister, nor Uncle Joe, but always Uncle Joseph Raisin.

One day when the coastal steamer brought the mail, my father found in the missing persons column of his newspaper an enquiry from a woman in London about one Joseph Raisin, her brother, last seen in London in 1868 and believed to have emigrated to Canada or Newfoundland. There could be no doubt about such an unusual name, so the old man was sent for and the news imparted to him.

He was wildly excited and right away began to make preparation for the journey "Home." "I must go see my poor old sister and visit the Old Country before I die," he said. He could talk of nothing else for the four days of waiting, but the "Old Country" and "Home."

He joined the *S. S. Prospero* for St. John's and England. Twelve days later, when the *Prospero* came again from St. John's, there at the gangplank, suitcase in hand, was Uncle Joseph Raisin.

Beaming with delight, he shook hands with everybody as if he had been away for years. He told my father, "When I landed in St. John's and saw how it had grown in fifty years, the lights, the traffic and the crowds of people, I asked myself what London would be like. 'No place for you, Joseph Raisin,' I said. So I wrote my sister a nice letter and took the first boat home again."

Who were those people who came and set themselves down in the coves, bays and islands of this then scarcely known land? What sort of men and women were they to cut themselves adrift from the life they knew and leave their motherland, the land which for the rest of their lives they would refer to as "back Home," and which they trained their children to call "The Old Country," and sail into the sunset in search of a new life in a western land? Was it a faint vision of El-Dorado, a Shangri La they sought, or did they dream of a mystic Eden in the North? Perhaps it was a little of all those things, but I dare say most of them came because of the inquisitiveness of young blood, the lure of adventure and perhaps a faint echo of Drake's drum summoning them to plant another bit of England beyond the seas.

It pains and angers me to hear unthinking and uninformed people talk in hard tones of the "dire poverty" and the "misery of isolation" suffered by our ancestors in this island. Tommyrot!

The independent settlers suffered far less than many of the authorized colonists. The men who sailed their own ships to that "haven where they would be" were well equipped to meet Nature on a fair field, and as for the curse of isolation, they had things to do far more rewarding and interesting than to sit and pity themselves. I dare say most of us today would be better off if we had some of that isolation and hardship; we might regain a little of the courage of our fathers and perhaps some of their spirit of independence.

Of course there was some poverty, and plenty of hard knocks, but real poverty came much later on, when men began to barter their independence for the goods in the merchant's shop. Hard work there was in plenty, but hard work need not be hardship. Did the colonists of our remote bays suffer more hardship than their brothers in the towns? Was life in the Old Country entirely free of it?

It should be remembered that nowhere at any time have all men been equal. Given equal opportunity and equal equipment, there will always be men who will be in need in the midst of plenty. They are the people, so well described by my old friend, Skipper Harry Hawkins, "who begin a piece of work in the middle and try to knock off at both ends."

Good Times, Danielle Loranger, oil on canvas

Independence

Richard Greene

The edge of all the world,
An island, huge and empty,
Swimming in fog, worn away
By currents warm and cold,
And the memory of glaciers
Stripping soil from stone,
Oppression which preceded history.
Torn from North Africa,
Floating through its million years
Of independence, always at sea,
And the mystery of its inhabitants
Before the Beothucks, Brendan,
Or the Vikings,
Before empire or dominion,
The republic of its solitude.
To study politics in the stone,
Those hills which were volcanic,
The wrinkling and subsidence
Of an ageing land,
The palm tree becoming pine,
And still the wandering.

Tickle Cove Pond

Mark Walker

In cutting and hauling in frost and in snow,
We're up against troubles that few people know;
And only by patience, with courage and grit,
And eating plain food can we keep ourselves fit.
The hard and the easy we take as it comes,
And when ponds freeze over we shorten our runs;
To hurry my hauling, the spring coming on,
Near lost me my mare on Tickle Cove Pond.

I knew that the ice became weaker each day,
But still took the risk and kept hauling away;
One evening in April, bound home with a load,
The mare showed some halting against the ice road.
And knew more than I did as matters turned out,
And lucky for me had I joined in her doubt.
She turned 'round her head and with tears in her eyes,
As if she was saying: "You're risking our lives."

All this I ignored with a whip handle blow,
For man is too stupid dumb creatures to know.
The very next minute the pond gave a sigh,
And down to our necks went poor Kitty and I.
For if I had taken wise Kitty's advice,
I never would take the short cut on the ice.
Poor creature she's dead and poor creature she's gone;
I'll never get my wood off Tickle Cove Pond.

I raised an alarm you could hear for a mile,
And neighbours turned out in a very short while.
You can always rely on the Oldfords and Whites,
To render assistance in all your bad plights.
To help a poor neighbour is part of their lives;
The same I can say for their children and wives.
When the bowline was fastened around the mare's breast
William White for a shanty song made a request.
There was no time for thinking no time for delay,
So straight from his head came this song right away:

Chorus
Oh lay hold William Oldford lay hold William White,
Lay hold of the hawser and pull all your might;
Lay hold of the bowline and pull all you can,
And with that we brought Kit out of Tickle Cove Pond.

Newfoundland

Robert Lowell

O rugged land!
Land of the rock and moss!
Land whose drear barrens it is woe to cross!
Thou rough thing from God's hand!
O stormy land!
Land where the tempests roar!
Land where the unbroken waves rave mad upon the shore:
Thine outwalls scarce withstand!

O wintry realm,
Where the cold north winds blow;
Where drifting, bitter sleet, and blinding snow
All man's poor work o'erwhelm!
O bleak, bleak realm,
Whose homeward-hastening bark
Is crisped with ice: sails, cordage, stiff and stark,
And iced the unruly helm!

What hast thou in thy gift?
The kindly sun has shone,
These thousand years, the stubborn cliffs upon
Which thou on high dost lift:
What hast thou in thy gift?
A stinted growth appears:
Grass, shrub, and tree, slow-growing in long years,
Where gapes the rocky rift.

Yet thou art good:
Thy barrens feed the deer;
And birds of other lands do summer here.
In thy lone humble wood.
Ay, thou art good;
The poor man at his door
Gathers his fuel; and year-long thy shore
Yields, in free gift, his food.

And better, still:
Beneath a guardian-crown
The poor man freely walks and lays him down,
Free in all things but ill:
And better, still:
Here Holy Faith hath come,
Teaching that God will give a glorious home
To those that do His will.

[1847]

The Founding of The Newfoundland and Labrador Genealogical Society

Janet Miller Pitt

Genealogy, the practice of tracing family descent, is concerned with families, sets of parents and children, or of relations, living in the genesis, origin and mode of the formation of the family. In Newfoundland, consciousness—and curiosity—of family origins is high, and arguably it appeals to all present Newfoundlanders and expatriates and their descendants. It is usually the first thing enquired after the weather, and forms the basis for much of the ensuing conversation between Newfoundlanders anywhere.

Anthropologists, who study the origin of man, have traced the formation of the family group to the need for mutual support. In Newfoundland and Labrador for the past half century, anthropologists and sociologists have studied people of this island, and the basic unit, the "extended family" which has been the nucleus way of life. Family reunions in Newfoundland are held officially on an island-wide scale. In 1904 a local committee of The Cabot Club of Boston, a group of expatriate Newfoundlanders (estimated to be four times the province's population) decided to "bring together the exiled sons and daughters of Terra Nova so that they might meet again." An old Home Week saw "thousands come back to Newfoundland for a full week of festivities." In 1966 then-premier Joseph R. Smallwood called all Newfoundlanders home for Come Home Year, and thousands came.

In Newfoundland and Labrador the need for mutual support and desire to know one's family is a public and private condition of being. Genealogists, who study the origins of families, naturally band together the world over to form associations of persons, united by the common interest in families, who can lead assistance, bear out, substantiate and confirm the derivation of common groups of people. On October 9th, 1984, approximately twenty-five people met at Memorial University of Newfoundland through the efforts of Elsa Hochwald to discuss forming a society devoted to the inquiry of origins, of Newfoundlanders and others.

A committee composed of Elsa Hochwald, Cliff Andrews, Keith Davis, Judy Foote, Ed Chafe and Janet Miller Pitt was selected by those present to meet and discuss the formal organization of a genealogical society.

Motif for genealogy from a tombstone in a Heart's Content churchyard

Beyond the Obvious

John F. O'Mara

Genealogy is the personification of history. It is the purest form of history as it concerns individuals. It is about life. It is a tapestry of all those who ever lived and to whom we owe our very existence. All our ancestors are interesting because all were necessary in handing down life to us. Every single one of our ancestors since mankind began is part of the chain. We cannot ignore any one link.

It is a natural extension of our search to want to know more. Some genealogists only focus on the bare essentials. They develop various forms of Family Trees, pedigree charts, and so on. These provide basic information on ancestry, relationships and vital personal information. There are others who produce detailed family histories, fleshing out the lives and times of their ancestors. In fact, there is an extraordinary variety to genealogy beyond what we normally think of:

Iconography: the search for portraits of our ancestors, photos of the town or community from which they came, pictures of their houses or belongings;

Graphology: the study of personality from handwriting, from which we can inherit common characteristics;

Heraldry: coats of arms, crests, armorial bearings, mottos, their origins and significance;

Historical Geography: the study of where people came from and their migration patterns; and,

Genetics: heredity, personality, inherited talents, family resemblance, inherited diseases, longevity. Medical history is an area of study receiving more and more attention as the relationship between heredity and illness becomes clearer.

Genealogy can also lead us to study and better understand demographics, cartography, sociology, politics, economics and more.

No matter what area or areas of study we pursue, we should always remember that genealogy is a science. As such, it must be based on objectivity using rational methods and mature criteria of proof. Unless the truth is precisely sought and revealed, genealogies are no better than myths or fairy tales.

Researching Your Family History in Newfoundland

Dianne C. Jackman

The basic process of tracing your family history is the same whether you live in Newfoundland or any other part of the world. You should begin by questioning senior members of your family and constructing a small family tree. Soon you will find you are collecting family records. You will go through bibles, old letters, scrapbooks, diaries, photo albums, newspaper clippings and legal documents.

Before you begin collecting these records you should get yourself a loose-leaf binder or index cards so you can keep a record of everything you find. Always write down where you obtained the information before you record it. You will be using so many sources it will be impossible to remember where you got them in the future. If you have to go back to check something it can be very frustrating if you do not know exactly where to look. Next, get some pedigree charts and family group sheets. These will help you keep each family organized. Make up a family history question sheet; this will be helpful when interviewing family members and others while you are gathering information. It will remind you which questions you want to ask.

Then, you should sit down and record all the information you know yourself. Check the family bible, school yearbooks, diaries, letters, photo albums and scrapbooks. Next visit or write to your oldest family members. Call first to let them know what you are doing and to give them a chance to collect past memories. It may take several visits before you see results. If you cannot visit in person then you can make up an informal fill in the blank questionnaire and send it to your relative. Be sure to include a stamped, self-addressed envelope for the reply within Canada. International reply coupons are required outside. Coupons can be purchased at any postal outlet.

A lot of our ancestors came to Newfoundland in the eighteenth and nineteenth centuries. During this time the government did not require the recording of vital statistics. Civil registration was not required in Newfoundland until 1891. Therefore, church records and headstone inscriptions are of great importance.

Other sources of information include: land deeds, probate records, census records, wills and crew lists and log books of British Empire vessels.

Most of this information can be located in St. John's. Sometimes, however, it is necessary to travel to individual communities or write to parishes or historical societies.

Epitaphs or Tombstone Inscriptions

From Winterton:

Oakley — Sacred to the memory of Robert Oakley who departed this life 5 November 1817, Age 48 years, A native of Wimbourne in Dorsetshire. No unjust action in his whole life.

Hannum — Sacred to the Memory of Catherine, wife of Robert Hannum, Departed this life 20 July, 1869, Aged 89 years. A virtuous woman is a crown to her husband.

French — In Memory of John French, Departed this life August 7, 1880, Aged 85 years. Also his Beloved wife Grace, Departed this life June 26, 1876. Aged 72 years. Remember all Ye that pass by that you like us must droop and die. As you are now so once we were, Prepare for Heaven and meet us there.

Clerk — Martha, Wife of Joseph Clerk, March 27, 1794, 18 years. (This tombstone was carved out of a sedimentary rock.)

From Middle Brook, Gambo:

Pritchett — Sacred to the Memory of James Pritchett, Departed this life December 19, A.D. 1858, Aged 57 years. Weep not for me but for yourselves, Here lies my body born but to decay. Yet no eye wheresoever my soul shall stay, but shall unite at the judgement. (Ingraver J. Hays)

– collected by Otto Tucker

Epitaph of a blacksmith on the monument in the Anglican Cemetery in Greenspond, Bonavista Bay:

> My sledge and anvil I'll decline
> My bellows too have lost their wind;
> My fire extinct, my forge decayed,
> And in the dust my vice is laid;
> My coals consumed, my iron is gone,
> My nails are driven, my work is done.

The following epitaph appears on the beautiful granite cross erected in 1964 to the memory of the famous Newfoundland opera singer Georgina Stirling who was born in Twillingate in 1867 and died there in 1935 aged 68. Her professional name was Mademoiselle Toulinguet (the original French name spelling of the Notre Dame Bay town). The epitaph reads:

> Georgina Stirling (Mlle Marie Toulinguet)
> Prima Donna, died April 21, 1935. The
> Nightingale of the North.
> Sang fairer than the Larks of Italy,
> She Entertained Royalty by the Sweetness
> of her Voice, and the Poor
> by the Kindness of her Heart.
>
> – collected by Leo Moakler

In Belvedere Cemetery, St. John's, this epitaph is recorded by Paul O'Neill in his *Seaport Legacy*:

> Peter Brennan, born County Kilkenny (Ireland),
> A centenarian and a celibate April 15, 1887,
> An expert in bone-setting and generous
> benefactor to his country and his church.

This epitaph is reported to come from the St. John's area as reported in O'Leary's Homemaker Radio News, February 13, 1961:

> Here lies the body of John Power,
> Who played with the gun at Cabot Tower;
> The gun went off and shook the nation,
> And they found John Power at the
> Railway Station.

Genealogy One-Liners
Compiled from several issues of The Newfoundland Ancestor

Genealogists—the ancestrally challenged.

Genealogy is not fatal, but it is a grave disease.

Genealogists do it generation after generation!

My ancestors must be in a witness protection program.

My family tree is lost in the forest.

When you marry, your family tree can become a forest.

A family tree can wither if nobody tends its roots.

An ancestor is a person who plays *hide* and you go *seek*.

The fastest way to trace your family tree—run for public office.

Genealogy is relative.

Genealogists never lose their jobs, they just go to another branch.

Diet for a genealogist—fiche and chips.

When I searched for ancestors, I found friends.

Add to your genealogy the fun, easy way. Have grandchildren.

Can a cousin, once removed, return?

Don't bother me now, I'm digging up my roots.

My Grandmother and Knowlton Nash

Carl Leggo

my grandmother's world
was framed by her bedroom window

with eyes almost blind she saw
a twilight world of shapes and shadows

the harbour and the paper cargo ships
on which her husband once sailed as cook

the world's largest pulp and paper mill
where her brother worked for a day

the Blow-Me-Down Mountains
where her father had been a guide

Meadows across the harbour and at night,
lights where a daughter's house had been

with eyes grey-sad my grandmother saw
a haphazard world, helter-skelter, no shelter

and like an air traffic controller
she tried to organize and direct her world

every night flitted back and forth
between her room and the telephone, calling,

checking on the children and grand-children,
everyone home? everyone safe?

always flying with the northeast trade winds,
said Skipper, I wish she'd get stuck in calms

but she was forever sailing on the waves
of her fears, unending tempests

the world like the underside of a tapestry
woven by Knowlton Nash in the multicolored

threads of disaster, danger, disease, death,
destruction, depravity, debacle, damnation

when I told her from grade eight geography
Newfoundland was in the Tropic of Cancer

she was convinced we would all get cancer
and when Knowlton Nash reported the mystery

of Legionnaire's disease, my grandmother
heard engineer's disease and feared

her son and grandson, both engineers,
would get the dread unknown disease

nothing to worry about, Missus, said Skipper;
no, nothing, she replied, but I'm still

worried, and Skipper nodded, knowing
nothing cannot be fixed

and nights Skipper often drove downtown
and to the west side to confirm all was well

and nights my grandmother phoned the neighbours
of her children to confirm all was well

while death for me was almost always a fiction
on television, my grandmother knew death,

had not so much stared death in the face
as been smothered by death like heavy blankets

her father drowned on a hunting trip
a brother crushed by a hill of pulp logs

her husband lost in a truck-train collision
a daughter and three grandsons in a housefire

like my grandmother who framed her world
in a window, a resistant, uncontrollable world,

I stare through a window and try to control
my world in words like erecting cairns

to guide navigation in treacherous country
but my grandmother and Knowlton Nash

remind me constantly that the world
cannot be framed by any window

Advertisement from *Devine's Folk Lore of Newfoundland* (1937)

foremother

Lillian Bouzane

my great-grandmother watched her husband
wash overboard
in a Labrador gale
just one more fishing skipper lost
in the Strait of Belle Isle
nobody noticed

she was a grieving woman
until the merchant at Quirpon
moved to short-change her by fifty quintal
on the fish from their last voyage
with a scorn she bothered to show
she ordered the catch reloaded
took the wheel herself
and set her course for the next harbour
where she sold it at a neat profit

steeling her nerve
she raised her flag to full staff
and sailed into her home port
the priest came to see her
to admonish and comfort
she gave him good whiskey
with a glint in her eye
that said "don't meddle with me"
he didn't

each year thereafter
she made two voyages to the Labrador Coast
spring and summer
hired for hands only bedlamer boys
kept her name clear
took one trip to Boston each year
left the children behind
with orders to say to the neighbours
"don't meddle with my mother's good name"
they obeyed her

when she was fifty
and had fourteen schooners in her name
she married again
a man half her age
she made him her bookkeeper/bartender
he was good at both
she got ten winters out of him
she said so herself

once she sailed her flagship
to Montreal to buy a dress
her only purchase
when the Duke's son came
to plant a tree
and settle other matters of State
she danced the night through with him
at the government ball
he walked her down to the harbour
they sat on her quarter-deck 'til dawn
drinking port and singing bawdy songs
it was said he asked her to marry him
it was said she turned him down
she already had more ships than he

before the bank crash of 1894
she liquidated her assets
bought gold
lived another ten years to be ninety
to the consternation of her sons
and the delight of her daughters
who loved her
and got her money
they passed it on to my mother
who educated my five sisters and me
with what was left of it

I, her offspring, thrice removed
write this poem in praise of her
and tell only half I know

Grandmother Figure I
Scott Fillier

                                        Child,
                              Summer visitor,
          I would sit in Grandmother's parlour
                    and play her harmonium.
    Grandmother would stop
her kitchen work, ease her heavy form
into her rocker…and cry!
    She cried without quakes,
without sobs, looking out past orange-lichened rocks
and trap-skiffs restless as boys in chafing hemp collars
on a blue sea of Sunday pews. I was her lens
to a new perspective on the fixed past
which now scanned ever closer, ever nearer
—perhaps a harvest moon rising red.
She looked inwardly and her love for a long dead
child who had also played this tune
mapped the round, regal contours of her face.

                              Grandfather liked
                    to touch folk with humour,
              but after each sally at dinner,
            Grandmother would say to him,
        smiling through plaintive oboe tones
          "Don't make me laugh, Pop, it hurts."
And she pressed palms against her sides,
kneading, eyes furrowed at some unexplained pain.

    I played, oh so simply, her request
    "You are my sunshine," and Grandmother,
    without ever telling me to stop because it hurt wept
    for her once happy child
    , or for herself
    , or for us all.

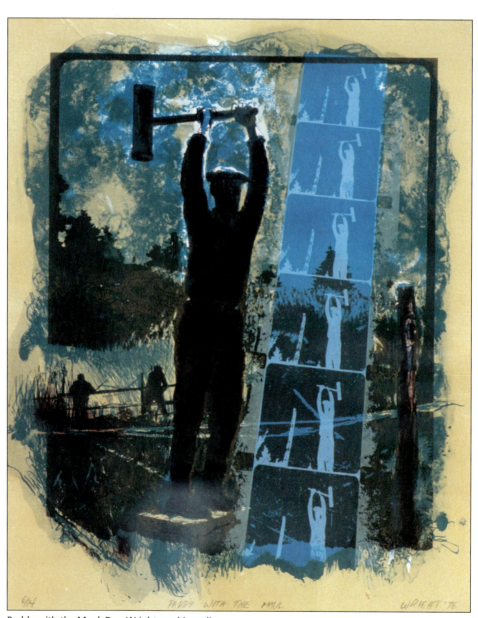
Paddy with the Maul, Don Wright, multi-media

A Profile
Don Wright 1931–1988

Don Wright was a prominent artist as is borne out by the fact that he was chosen as one of the most significant artists in *The Telegram*'s millennium survey. He was also a teacher and co-founder of Newfoundland's first printshop originally located in St. Michael's but now in St. John's.

Wright produced a large body of work expressing his talent in many different forms and media, including sculpture. The picture portrayed here called *Paddy with the Maul* combines two artistic processes—photography and lithography of which the artist was very fond. Note the hand applied washes on the somewhat realistic photo. Quite often the artist used prints like this one to show people at work in Port Kirwin the small Southern Shore community on the Avalon Peninsula where he lived. Wright focused on commonplace objects, places and things (such as salt fish) in many of his works but he could also be complex and controversial in artistic works that used mixed media, were multi-layered and created on a large scale.

Wright was a maker of art for 40 years. His last body of work shows his concern for his impending death. He died at the age of 57.

Walking

Helen Porter

She steps through the doorway, turns to lock the door, tries the knob once. Then she walks down the steps and toward the sidewalk. Her loose black coat hangs well below her knees; the grey slacks showing beneath the coat are turned up around the ankles. Her shoes are black, with laces and low heels.

She walks in the middle of the sidewalk, a grey purse hanging from her left shoulder. Her dark hair, with its few strands of grey at the front, falls loose to her coat collar. She wears a bright red beret, pulled slightly to the right side of her head. In her right hand she carries grey gloves that look too shiny to be real leather.

She looks neither to the right nor to the left. A young man, almost running, passes her on the outside of the sidewalk. He glances at her; she does not look at him. A man and a woman, arms linked, nearly collide with her before they move to one side.

With her index finger she rubs the skin behind her ear. She looks at the finger, then lets her hand drop to her side. A black cat, white at the throat, rubs itself against her legs. She pays no attention.

Her eyes are brown, with flecks of grey around the irises. They look larger than they are because she seldom blinks. Without pausing or looking in either direction she crosses the first intersection. A red Toyota, crowded with young people, swerves and almost hits the edge of the sidewalk. The driver sticks his head through the open window, yells and shakes his fist at her.

Still looking straight ahead, she steps onto the opposite sidewalk. The street begins to slope here. Her feet in their plain black shoes adjust to the change, her steps becoming a little shorter. There are holes and bumps in this part of the pavement; she avoids them without looking down. When she passes the green house with the peeling paint she stops, turns her head and stares at the closed front door. Almost immediately she lowers her eyes, her shoulders twitch, and then she is again looking directly ahead.

At the bottom of the street she turns right. A man standing in a doorway on the opposite side of the street looks at her and opens his mouth. He does not speak. An old woman with long grey hair leans through the open window above him and calls, "Here, Ringo, here, Ringo." A brown and white beagle barks and bounds toward the front door of the house. The man pats the dog's head and lets him in. The woman in the black coat is still looking straight ahead as she walks. Her body jerks when she hears the dog barking. The strap of her purse slips down her arm; she pushes it back to her shoulder again.

She crosses the street, turns left and walks down the hill without altering her pace. She passes a crowded parking lot. When she reaches the wrought-iron fence surrounding the large cream-coloured house she stops. The house has brown trim and a coloured brick front. It's much larger than the other houses nearby. The lawn is thickly sodded and smooth. There are two flower beds near the house; the flowers, red and yellow and purple and pink, are all the same height.

The woman stands near the open gate. She wraps her hand around one of the iron fence-palings. She grips it so tightly that all the colour leaves her hand and it turns a chalky white. As she stands there two women look at her and then at each other before they pass in through the gateway.

She takes her hand away from the fence, moves it to her head and pulls off the red beret. She steps through the gateway, stops, and steps back. Two teenagers standing on the verandah laugh nervously. She passes the beret through her fingers a few times, then walks slowly toward the corner of the street. Her steps quicken as she walks back along the sidewalk. She does not look back toward the big house. The red beret dangles from her hand.

A New Name

Jim Wellman

It was a tough decision. "Scary" is perhaps a better word. Changing the name of the "Fishermen's" Broadcast took a lot of thought and it took a lot of guts.

Kathy Porter was the driving force behind the idea. After working as co-host on the Broadcast for a couple of years, Kathy wondered if it was time to change the name. But it was Kathy the "listener" who became convinced it was the right thing to do. Kathy was on maternity leave in late 1989 and early 1990 and during her time listening to the "Fishermen's" Broadcast at home, she decided to lobby for a name change when she returned to work.

Kathy said there were several reasons for the decision. Women had taken on much higher profiles in the fishery by 1990. "Hundreds of women had started fishing full-time and the majority of plant workers were women, so I thought the name was not representative anymore," Kathy recalled. "There were lots of female voices on the air; we had female co-hosts since 1980 and we were making a conscious effort to include more women on the Broadcast as guests, so it occurred to me that the title excluded a large section of those people."

The FFAW* and the Department of Fisheries and Oceans were also making an effort to be more gender-inclusive as well. Press releases referred to fish harvesters as fisherpersons or fisherpeople. Obviously word had been passed down through the union to the rank and file because a lot of fisher "men" started referring to themselves as fisherpeople or fisherpersons. A few years later, DFO decided on "fishers" as the appropriate designation; others preferred "fish harvesters."

As Kathy's co-host in 1990, I supported her lobby for the name change. While I agreed with her rationale, I also felt the Broadcast had significantly broadened its scope to include coverage of the entire fisheries spectrum and was no longer centred mainly on the harvesting people of the industry.

---

* Union of Fishery, Food and Allied Workers. [Eds.]

Although she was convinced it was the right thing to do, Kathy said it was still a tough decision: "I loved the tradition of the name Fishermen's Broadcast, which created the image of the lone fisherman in the boat; but it was no longer the reality and I felt strongly it was the right thing to do."

Later that year CBC management agreed with Kathy and the Fishermen's Broadcast became the "Fisheries" Broadcast.

Despite grave concerns about a backlash to the name change, we never received a single negative call. CBC Television News decided to do a story about the new name, but when they took their cameras out to a fishing community for reaction, not one person objected. It became what they call in the business a non-story.

But a gender-inclusive or politically correct title is still somewhat an academic issue, as the program is still known to the vast majority of its listeners as "The Broadcast."

Names and Souls

F. W. Peacock

Most Inuit believe that individuals have three souls. One is the immortal spirit who leaves the body at death and goes to live in the future world. The second is the vital breath and warmth of the body that ceases to exist at death. The last is the name soul and is not really a soul, but that which embodies the traits of the person who is named for the deceased. In Labrador, it was the custom to give a child several names of deceased relatives; later, it was decided which of these names would normally be used by the child.

Often one would hear a small child being addressed as *itok* (the old man) or *ningiok* (the old woman), because it had been named for the grandfather or grandmother.

The namesake (*atitsiak*) was held in honour and respect by his, or her, opposite member. Gifts are exchanged by those who are *atitsiat* (plural) on different occasions…

Among Inuit, the name was something specially precious and was to be guarded lest it be used by a spirit, or enemy, in order to obtain power over one. Until modern times, an Inuk meeting another person after dark would be reluctant to mention his name to the other, and upon being asked "*Kinauvet?*" (Who are you?), would reply: "*Uvangauvunga*" ("It is I.")…not from fear of the questioner, but from the danger of unfriendly spirits that wander in the darkness of night.

Fumigating the Map

Harold Horwood

The island of Newfoundland is justly famous for placenames with a punch. Famished Gut is an example. And Rogue's Harbour. There are also Horse Chops and Hole-in-the-Wall, not to mention Sally's Leg and Virgin Arm, all named in the distant past by sailors and fishermen with a sense of humour.

But the Post Office Department is doing its best to abolish these salty place names and to substitute such masterpieces as Port Elizabeth and Fairhaven. The improvement will be obvious, I am sure, to any fair-minded reader. We Newfoundlanders are all in favour of these improvements. We do not want to live in Hole-in-the-Wall. We want to live in Parkdale. It sounds so nice and sanitary.

We feel that if the Canada Post Office succeeds in getting rid of all the old place names we will be much the better for it. We are even prepared to help them out by supplying them with a list of old names that they've never heard of yet. At least, we are pretty certain that they have never heard of them, since they have never managed to deliver any mail there. Devil's Thumb, for instance. I'll bet they've never delivered a letter to Devil's Thumb in all their born days.

And then there's Fom. That isn't really the way you spell it. On the map it is spelled "Femme," but everyone who lives there calls it Fom, so Fom it must be. There's a story about Fom:

An American yacht with a fishing party was plying along the northern inlets of Fortune Bay one evening, and tied up to a stage head in a small cove. The island offshore was known as Petticoat Island, but the Americans didn't know that. The yachting skipper accosted the first baccy-chewing character he met on the stage.

"Hello," he greeted. "Where are we? What do you call this settlement?"

"Fom," said the baccy-chewer, casting a speculative eye at the weather.

"OK," said the American. "We want to send a message home. Where's the telegraph office?"

"Fifteen miles out the bay," said the native, adding that they usually rowed there in a dory.

"Post office?" said the American hopefully.

"One over in English Harbour East," the fisherman explained. "Ye must've passed it comin' along shore."

"No telegraph, no post office, no roads!" the American exclaimed. "Do you have radios here?"

"Well," the fisherman drawled, "they's a couple. But we don't turn 'em on much. Can't get the stations up in St. John's, and them Canadian fellers never seems to have any news worth while."

"Well!" exclaimed the American. "You people in Fom are really cut off from the world, aren't you?"

"S'pose so," said the fisherman.

"Why," continued the yacht skipper, "if New York burned down tonight you wouldn't know anything about it!"

"That's true, I s'pose," the fisherman admitted, "but then,"—and he paused to squirt a philosophic stream of baccy juice over the stage head—"if Fom burned down you fellers up in New York wouldn't know anything about it either!"

You will agree that we can't have places like Fom in this day and age. The sooner they are changed to Fairhaven the better.

Our greatest misgivings are on the subject of the speed with which the Post Office is forging ahead. As a prominent politician once remarked, officialdom should never move faster than the public, but we are afraid the Post Office may be a step or two ahead of common usage here and there.

In fact, public confusion has reached the point described in an old folk tale from one of the recently renamed harbours of Fogo Island.

The tale concerns George Coles, one-time "king" of the little settlement of Hare Bay, just as his friend Henry Nipper was the unofficial "king" of neighbouring Shoal Bay.

One night after an evening of old-fashioned square dancing during which the moonshine can went round many times and everybody got very jolly, George fell asleep in his boat, tied to his own stage, in his own harbour. Some of the younger element, with a taste for practical jokes, towed the boat, George and all, to Shoal Bay, and tied it up to the stage owned by Henry Nipper.

Imagine George Coles' consternation when he awoke in the cold and chilly light of dawn, a little shaky perhaps, in the wrong harbour, tied to the wrong stage! His reported remarks have become a classic of Newfoundland folklore:

> *Who be I and where be I?*
> *Be I Jarge Coles or bain't I?*
> *Or be I Henry Nipper?*
> *Be I in Hare Bay or be I in Shoal Bay?*
> *Or have the devil got I?*

The Canada Post Office will see my point, I'm sure. If things continue at their present pace we shall all, before long, be as badly off as George Coles. We won't know whether we are in Hare Bay, Shoal Bay, Ice Tickle or Happydale Acres.

I have sometimes regretted the fact that the men who originally named the Newfoundland coves cannot be present today to see how we are improving on their work. The men who built the villages of Heart's Content and Seldom-Come-By, the sailors who named Pushthrough and Run-By-Guess, the old castaway who, with a grim laugh in the teeth of fate, named Black Joke Cove—I regret that they cannot come back to see the job which the Canada Post Office is doing on those places now. They would if they could, I'm sure.

We have one other little word of censure:

Among the host of lovely new names with which the Post Office is redecorating the map there are a few—just a few—which strike some of us as being a doubtful improvement. We do not refer to such names as Sunnydale and Pleasantview (nobody with a pint of good red Canadian blood in his veins could object to such strikingly original names as those). No, rather we refer to such names as Pickersgillville, a settlement in Bonavista Bay named after that eminent Canadian John Whitney Pickersgill.

Usually we allow statesmen to pass on to their just reward before enshrining them on the map, and since Mr. Pickersgill is still in robust middle life I feel that this haste to embalm him is rather indecent—like giving a man a coffin for Christmas.*

Besides, I don't think Pickersgillville will last. It is too long and hard to say. People are bound to start calling it Pickersville instead. Once this process of corruption begins there is no telling where it will end. But in this case we can guess. It will be elided to Piggersville, which is still easier to say, and from that it is but a step to Pigsville or even Pigville. It is bound to happen, and what will the Post Office do then, poor thing? It will be faced with just another ugly name, fully as bad as Famished Gut, and it will have to go through the painful process of changing it to Silverdale or something of the kind.

---

* John W. Pickersgill, politician, statesman and Companion to the Order of Canada, died in November 1997, aged 92. [Eds.]

Avery's Mill, Walt Pinsent

Newfoundland Name Frequency List in *Gazetteer of Canada*

Editors' Note:
The introductory comments and the list of place names below are from "Appendix E – Newfoundland Name Frequency List" in *Gazetteer of Canada* found in a pamphlet entitled *Where Once They Stood: A Gazetteer of Abandonment* by Mobilewords Ltd., 1998.

The eleventh principle of nomenclature, in the *Gazetteer of Canada*, says new names should be euphonious and in good taste. This list has birds, beasts, fish (all of them tasty), colours, place, size, shape, geography, condition and trees.

Greens, reds, and whites are more or less even but blacks preponderate. There are more littles than bigs; more lowers than uppers and a tremendous number of longs.

Animals in order of frequency are: seal, fox, deer-caribou-stag, beaver, horse-cow-goat, bear, otter, whale, cat, muskrat, moose, lynx; perhaps reflective of their (both wild and domestic) order of economic importance to outport life.

Name	#	Name	#	Name	#	Name	#
Aspen	15	Deer	49	Island	139	Saddle	27
Back	73	Dog	63	Juniper	15	Sandy	107
Baker	32	Duck	101	Lance	31	Salmon	112
Bear	75	Eagle	11	Little	495	Sculpin	28
Beaver	103	East	180	Long	351	Seal	135
Big	330	Flat	99	Lower	115	Shag	81
Birch	62	Fox	117	Lynx	5	Ship	69
Black	315	Freshwater	53	Man-o-War	29	Shoal	149
Blowmedown	33	Goat	20	Middle	158	South	381
Bull	35	Goose	106	Moose	17	Spruce	25
Burnt (ed)	147	Grass	65	Muskrat	23	St	193
Caplin	35	Great	80	North	400	Stag	40
Caribou	18	Green	208	Otter	68	Sugar	35
Cat	29	Gull	220	Pigeon	81	Trout(y)	62
Clam	18	Hare	51	Port	21	Upper	85
Cow	26	Hawk(e)	19	Rabbit	15	West	265
Cross	25	Herring	42	Red	200	Whale	57
Crow	57	Horse	43	Rocky	125	White	220
Deep	66	Indian	104	Round	108	Wild	85
						Wolf	29

Relocating from Silver Fox Island to Dover, Bonavista Bay, August 1961

Places That Were

Geraldine Rubia

These were outports
when we came this way before
but now are merely
landmarks on the shoreline:
Richard's Harbour
Cape la Hune
Dog Cove
Cul de Sac.

It seems as if the boat
must slacken speed
but no, we go on by,
the Captain trying to make us see
(academic question now)
the only point
at which a boat
could safely venture in.

Yet there are places
still for us to go
where children run to wharf or hill
to wave a welcoming:
Grand Bruit, Piccaire,
La Poile, Rencontre West,
Francois, McCallum; but in all
we know that now

already is past tense
nostalgic history
a fast receding backdrop
for newer ways of life
in road-connected towns,
the chance to work
or fight
or plead for better days.

Here, we will say,
were things that really mattered:
the stubbornness of fishermen
who built another boat
as soon as one was battered
on the rocks;

the faith of women
coaxing scanty soil
to nourish rhubarb roots
and bleeding hearts
and flowers whose names
they never knew;
the still childlike children
climbing barefaced cliffs
and painting stars
to prove that they'd been there.

Here a thunderous waterfall
forever drowned

the sound of the sea
and the moaning wind
that tried to wrench
the cabled church from the rock
while black sheep
calmly chewed;
here you could see the sun set twice
if you walked away
from the shade of a hill
to where the light was golden
still striking into henhouse doors
along the yard-wide road;
cemeteries, of course,
but one you could not see
behind a hill where there was earth
enough to bury the dead;
and another carpeted
from end to end
with wild blue irises.

All, we will say,
seemed either right or human:
one man thought it hard
to go and seek the Dole
when his summer's catch was small;
another never did a tap

and thought that all
the government might give
was scarcely half his due;

no neighbour went unhelped
whose luck turned bad
and the child who said
"I got no father, sir"
seemed not to carry
mortifying scars.

Though no way out is seen
from certain sheltered coves,
the way is there
between the lines of land
and over it will pass
the last livyers
on the last boat
abandoning wharves
to the unchecked waves;
the good luck mat
will fade on the back porch floor,
wicks dry out
in rejected lamps
and holy pictures blankly gaze
from the walls of empty rooms.

I wonder
will anyone try
to find the passage back.

West Moon

Pat Byrne

Oh, tonight the west moon hangs over the harbour,
Shines down 'cross the headland and out 'cross the bay,
Shines down through the trees and rests on the graveyard,
The only reminder of a long ago day.

But my mind takes me back to a time in that harbour,
When stout boats at anchor dozed on the sway,
When the laughter of children sent glad cries to heaven,
And women looked seaward from meadows of hay.

But no longer I see those fish-covered flakes now,
No green rows of garden stretched over the hill,
No punt in the beach gleaming red with fresh copper,
No fine sturdy stick freshly cut for a keel.

For the government men came bribing and preaching,
They convinced all the livyers to just move away,
Now they're scattered like dry leaves from hell to high water,
But the wind and the west moon elected to stay.

So tonight the west moon hangs over the harbour,
Shines down 'cross the headland and out 'cross the bay,
Shines down through the trees and rests on the graveyard,
As if looking for the souls of the ones moved away.

Looking Back

Enos D. Watts

Even when he knew
they had all decided to leave the island
the old man
sat, with his face to the sea,
and was not heard to make a sound.
For days now
he had been silent auditor
to the sounds people made
in preparation for moving away.
He heard many sounds
but the one that grieved him most
was the ring of the hammer
boarding up the church;
and with each irrevokable stroke
one could see his hands
tighten into a claw,
but the agony that lined his face
spoke poignantly
of something that pained him more
than the mere ripping of nails
into rotted pine.

On the final day
in the yard behind the church
he moved like an outcast
among the half-sunken, tilting stones
until his sensitive fingers read
the time-shallowed symbols
shrieking out at him
their cruel, eloquent truth;
he was certain now
that the gulf between them
would always be widest
at this rock.
And as the boat took him away
from his home
he, for the first time, was glad
that he was blind
knowing there'd be no purpose served
in looking back.

St. Leonard's Revisited

Al Pittman

We came ashore
where wildflower hills
tilted to the tide
and walked
sad and gay
among the turnip cellars
tripping over the cremated
foundations
of long-ago homes
half buried
in the long years' grass

almost reverently
we walked among the rocks
of the holy church
and worshipped roses
in the dead yard
and came again to the cove
as they did after rosary
in the green and salty days

and men offshore
hauling traps
wondered what ghosts
we were
walking with the forgotten sheep
over the foothigh grass paths
that led
like trap doors
to a past
they could hardly recall

An Off-Shore Wind

Tom Dawe

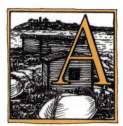

A caustic March wind blew down from the shale cliffs that seemed to hang over the few remaining houses in the Cove. It was a little after nine in the morning and a crew from the local mainland was busy down by the old community wharf. Out over a dull, purple sea blew the sounds of their labours: the sharp precise taps of steel hammers, the excited laughter and shouts of instruction, the wind-chopped whirr of a power saw, the withdrawal cries of long rusty nails being ripped from tough wood. Another house would be floated across the tickle today.

Against the smeared, green-tinted window of the Cove's remaining shop, the wind continued a steady assault, lashing showers of sand down from the southwest, bending the grimy panes, and tapping billions of grains along their surfaces. High in the vapour of the off-shore breeze the gulls were soaring, sometimes poising for seconds above the box-like dwellings of the Cove, and dropping to swoop by the spin-drift margin of the beach, and up, up into the heights above the Cove again.

Inside the tiny shop, a pale young girl in her middle teens shivered as she stood behind a low, drab counter. She wore her hair in curlers and seemed to be thinking of rain as she yawned and gazed through the window. Over in a coal-stained corner, the newly-lit, driftwood splits cracked and sputtered in the grate of a small, pot-bellied stove that sent a bent shaft of tin funnel-pipe up through the smoke-stained ceiling into the blast of the breeze.

She cracked gum and, absently humming to herself, stared up the dusty, outport lane. She did not notice the panes bending in front of her face as she blew a bubble, bit it and smiled to herself. Moving to the door of the stove, she dropped in a small knob of coal, and buttoning her sweater, went back to the window again. Two boys, sometimes half-figures in the swirling dust, were sauntering down the road towards the shop.

The door squeaked sharply and banged shut behind the boys as they entered the shop. They seemed to be well-built and in their late teens. They strolled over to some empty boxes near the stove.

"Freeze the Devil himself, this cussed wind would. You hot this mornin, Mary?" teased the taller one, a dark, greasy, handsome fellow in blue jeans and a worn, rust-stained leather jacket. He stooped near the stove and made some obscene gestures with an empty coke bottle. The girl seemed to blush a little, and pretended to survey the empty shelves at the rear of the room.

"Are you fellows workin today?"

"Hell, Mary," drawled the other, a stocky, moody-looking brute, "dey went and hired all mainland fellers to move dat bloody house today. I hope to God the whole works sinks under dem jest as dey are somewhere in da middle of the tickle. Hell, we figgered a year's work off and on, at least, with dis racket."

He plopped himself down on the nearest wooden box. He stretched, yawned briefly and began to grin at the girl. He winked at her. She smiled back at him and fingered at the top of her sweater.

Soon the three young people were drinking cokes together, sitting around the sputtering stove, teasing, joking and just talking against a background of wind howling in the stove-pipes. The sands from the cliffs continued to pound the window. The hammering down by the wharf occasionally punctuated the breeze.

"Tis one bitch of a place here in the Cove now," mused the taller boy, throwing a dime across the counter-top, and whipping the cap off another soft-drink. He half-emptied its contents and burped before he spoke again: "Our government provides some money and the big shots and the outsiders lap it all up. They lap it up, just like that." He snapped his fingers and swallowed from his bottle again. "It isn't fair."

"Figgered fer sure we'd get work helpin people move, once dis government made up its bloody mind," snarled the stocky boy, and he continued to repeat himself. "Dis old shop will blow off its stilts today I can tell ya."

The morning slowly waned. The dwarf-spruce hummed on the low drumlin across the lane. The winds continued wearing away the cliffs and sending grains in billions to tap on the panes. The crew worked on busily near the barge by the wharf, and nobody watched the clusters of gulls screaming high in the shredded clouds adrift on the wind.

Nobody else came to the store and the three young people by the stove continued to catalogue their woes that morning: the juke-box store out on the point, closed down now…good buddies gone off to live on the mainland…the poor stock of candy-bars and drinks…the dwindling supplies…the smart "brat of a teacher," aged seventeen…the nagging of the folks…but worst of all, the "strangers," the fellows who were "puffed up in themselves," the fellows who talked of government grants, re-settlement, indoor toilets, and things like that; these fellows seemed to be "looked up to" by most and especially those "sissies up in the school."…And the wind carried their voices out over the open sea, as they talked.

Sometime after eleven that morning, Roy Pinter, the oldest student in the Cove's only school, entered the shop and bought a chocolate bar. Fat and red-faced, Roy gave the appearance of labouring with the four books he carried under his arm. Since they were writing "spring tests" in the school that day, and Roy was the only grade eleven student in the school, he was given the afternoon off "to review."

The two boys slouched by the stove and watched Roy. They were winking to each other and making gestures behind his back as he paid the girl for the bar. She giggled and tried to avoid Roy's face as she rejoined the others near the stove. The wind ripped at the plank in the ceiling; a gull screamed somewhere near the roof. Roy gathered his books, buttoned the neck of his sweater and prepared to leave.

Roy seemed to notice the stocky boy preparing some taunt for him, but he munched his bar and continued to arrange his books. The girl giggled again and cracked her bubble-gum.

The tall boy sought Roy's attention: "Tell us somethin we don't know already, schoolboy," he challenged. Somewhere outside, the wind banged an old tar-bucket

over the rocks. The stocky boy began to make rude, hooting sounds in the neck of his empty bottle. The girl smiled and put more coal in the stove.

"I could tell you lots of things, boys," retorted Roy, trying hard to control himself.

"Yeah…but I bet you couldn't teach Mary much," bawled the stocky boy, slapping his knees and laughing with his friend. The girl seemed to enjoy this too. "Why Roy, you're blushing," she cried with a giggle.

"Are you going to tell us what 'economics' are today, Roy?" teased the tall one. "Remember you swallowed the dictionary the other day?" The three laughed again. Down by the wharf there was a long, deep grinding sound. The voice of a child called somewhere up the Cove.

"Can you tell us any better than you did the other day what a poem is good for?" asked the tall boy.

"Hell, any learnin is of precious little use in a hole like this," snarled his stout friend. "Have you read any good comics lately?"

Roy was on his way through the door. He headed into the face of the gale and up the dusty lane. As he fought his way along, he nodded to old Walter Blake on his way to the shop.

The voice of the stocky boy droned on: "He'll git some big lazy job outside somewhere with them big shots; in some warm office where he'll never do a tap of work for the rest of his fat little life. He'll move fer the softer life. They kind always does."

"Everything comes easy for the likes of people like Roy," mused the tall boy. He grinned and winked at the others when he saw old Walter move slowly in through the door.

"Morning Walter, any big ships get in your nets last night?" he shouted at the old man who was a little deaf. The others laughed and the girl tried to conceal her grin from the old man; she fought hard to keep a straight face. Old Walter seemed in a hurry and determined not to notice them anyway. He remained silent. He was intent on buying his stick of beaver and leaving. His big, clumsy, line-sawn hands fumbled for small coins in a tiny lady's coin purse with a delicate metal clasp. He spread his payment on the counter, took his tobacco and headed for the door. As he did, the tall boy called: "Watch out for the big ships again tonight." The others laughed in the background.

The old man banged the door behind him and plodded down the lane towards the wharf. A gust of wind carried more of the cliffs across the valley of the Cove. Somewhere down by the beach, the playful cries of children mingled with the screams of gulls in flight…and the wind carried all sounds out to sea.

"Poor silly old Walter," mused the girl, "he'll never leave the Cove. Can you picture him alone here next year screaming his stories to the gulls and the winds in the cliffs? Nobody to prate his troubles to." She slid over to gaze through the window again. She saw the bending panes and stepped back.

"Da old bugger!" The stocky boy was speaking again: "All his talk about big boats in da nite. Gives me da creeps, it does. Rippin up his nets in the dark. To tink, he frightened me so when I was young. I never did much listenin to him though. Always wanted the government to pay fer his losses. Always singin out fer aid. Some says he got someting out of it too. When big icebergs come down the coast on nights when there was a offshore breeze, they was always big ships in the night to old Walt."

"I'll never forget his ghost stories," chuckled the other boy. "What a liar though. Something to leave behind in this windy hole. Him and his ghosts, his phantom ships, his deep-sea devils, his haunted lofts, and his so-called 'omens.' We'll be leaving something, I can grant you that." The others laughed; they snickered, joked, poked and yawned the morning on towards another noon. And the winds did not abate….

A few minutes before lunch, the foreman from the bargecrew came up to the shop. He smoked a cigarette and gazed through the window, chewing his match and looking philosophically at the dust swirling in the winding lane. The other three young people seemed to lose their identities against the background of empty shelves, salt-caked barrels, stove-pipe and boxes. And a shaft of pinched sunlight showed a streak of quivering dust in front of the dying fire. The foreman stepped through the sun-shaft and spoke: "Nice scenic spot you people will soon be leaving behind." The girl smiled at him and fastened a clip in a stray wisp of her hair. Overhead the wind seemed to be tearing shreds of felt from the roof. A couple of minutes blew away before anybody spoke.

"Wit a bit of work, we would stay here," growled the stocky boy. "We don't have to go away to be educated either. We've had our share of educated men in dis Cove too. We can take our places anywhere though. Never slow to pick tings up. Why, Roy

Pinter will finish his schoolin soon. Got it here in the Cove. Will be able to amount to anyting soon." He wiped his nose with his sleeve and stared at the stranger.

The girl tried to add to the discussion: "Some poets have even come from this region, or, in any case, regions like this. Why, our teacher used to read to us about that fellow, a poet living up in Toronto now...."

"We'll leave a lot behind," cut in the tall boy, "lots that books could never tell too; our stories and histories that have been kept here. Why I know some people in this Cove, the older ones that is, who could...." He stopped.

The stranger did not even seem to be listening. He continued to chew on his match and stare out over the Cove. All of a sudden, he looked up. "Say, do you fellows want a couple of hours work?" he snapped as he buttoned his coat, "We got a big house to float across this afternoon."

The boys got up and followed him through the door. The girl watched the three head down towards the barge. A gust of wind sprayed sand on the pane close to her face. The cliffs seemed smaller to her as she peered across the Cove. She yawned and scratched her elbow. Faintly she heard the teeth of a power saw, the cries of a few children on the beach, the shrieking of nails pulled from tough wood, the screaming of distant gulls...and the wind from the hinterland was carrying all out to sea.

NEW KIND of TONIC in FOOD FORM

Cocomalt

Contains Vitamin D

—helps build up strength, energy. Marvelous for many run-down men and women. Wonderfully delicious.

Medical authorities agree that to-day's tense high-pressure living calls for special attention to diet. If you feel worn-out, "on edge"—here's a suggestion! Try Cocomalt—the delicious tonic in food form.

Helps Renew and Maintain Strength

For years Cocomalt has been the favorite food-drink in millions of homes. It not only furnishes Iron for red blood and strength; it is rich in Carbohydrates for furnishing the food energy needed for the strenuous activities of our high-pressure living. It contains proteins for building solid flesh and muscle, Vitamin D, Calcium and Phosphorus for strong bones and sound teeth.

Advertisement from *Devine's Folk Lore of Newfoundland* (1937)

It's a Glacial Sound That Quiets the House

Boyd Chubbs

It's a glacial sound that quiets the house
that locks the doors, boards the windows
And the chimney's an empty yawn
No more will the small feet scatter the stones,
trip the water on spring roads and go
with dream and windflow

This is the land of the eternal caravan
and phantom ox and wagon
fording rivers and straits, hands fierce around
Bibles and other maps. From here to there
is a long-treated road where the whips crack
and the 'huddled masses' stare back

Save a piece of home for our treasure-box
for the worn cedar to breathe. And throw
a prayer to the weather for our long turn of wagons
We are dead many times but twist again
to suck the air in starts and stops
where kettles attempt a song on stranger counter-tops

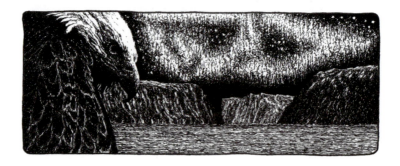

Birthday Voyage (for B. W.)
Pat Byrne

You were right
to slip the moorings
and ease the old *Evette*
away from the wharf
before the rest of us were awake

That way the dream was held intact

Smooth as a dab
the mists clinging to the island tops
creating bottomless reflections
while the school of porpoise
cut the tinfoil surface of the unusual April sea
skimming the sheen in benediction
letting us know it was all right
for us to be there too

The boat seemed
to share our indecision
and came around reluctantly off Buffett Head
as if she sensed
it was not the "essentials"
left on the wharf in Arnold's Cove
but the small failing
in her mechanical heart
that put (for today) Merasheen out of our reach

But the brief return was fortunate
because Skipper Nat added so much
hovering behind you
a guiding hand
from a long-ago time
on the test run through Batt's Gut

I know now
why we tired so early
and sought the bunks
that evening in Spencer's Cove

Recreating a mythology
(even for a day)
refusing to let old fires die
demanding more than a birthday
refusing to accept anything less
than a rebirth
a reaffirmation
takes a lot out of three brothers
and a friend

Cover of Al Pittman's *West Moon* featuring "No Longer May Sea Gulls Cry At Their Ears" by Gerald Squires (1995)

Excerpts from
West Moon
Al Pittman

Author's Note

The characters in this play are dead and in various states of decay. Their bodies are buried. They recline in coffins beneath the ground. On All Souls' Night their voices, their memories, their mental faculties, their personalities, their emotions are returned to them. So for a while they are, to some degree, resurrected. The play itself does not suggest any kind of bodily resurrection and, in fact, denies such in its references to eyeless skulls, etc. How to portray them on stage? Certainly not as skeletons and rotted flesh. Certainly not entirely as they were in real life. Somewhere in between these two extremes. Perhaps as they were in death at the time of burial, but with the ability to move. Clothed perhaps in their burial clothes. Not, God-forbid, in sou'westers and rubber boots, not with pipes and chewing tobacco, not with knitting needles and kidney pills. Funeral clothes. The fact that these people are dead and confined to the grave cannot be forgotten, must always be emphasized. Their movements must be punctuated by their confinement. Nowhere in their recollections can they have access to the accoutrements of their former lives. As they move they are limited to movement within the perimeters of their own grave space. Nowhere can they touch one another. They can stand, sit, lie, slouch, jump, and so on in their own territory but they are forever frustrated in any inclination they have to move outside the boundaries of their death. The props they may use are the props at hand. The bushes, the gravel, the grass, the gravestones and so on. Nothing that isn't present naturally in the graveyard and within reach of the resurrected corpses can be placed within their reach. Always they are dead and remain dead, always they are confined to the grave and remain so for the duration of the play. Within these limitations all liberties of movement, gesture, posture, and all else may and should be explored. An ingenious set combined with an ingenious approach to animation could be conducive to the intention of the play without in any way rendering it static or boring in its immobility. Then again, someone more creatively courageous or more courageously creative might see it differently. And that might make all the difference.

> Dead men, naked, they shall be one
> with the man in the wind and the west moon.
>
> – Dylan Thomas

Cast of Characters

	Born	Died	Age
A Voice			
Jack Leonard	April 11, 1900	September 2, 1955	55
Raymond Dwyer	June 6, 1908	October 13, 1960	52
William Sullivan	May 2, 1880	August 9, 1953	73
Rose Anne Hepditch	June 23, 1872	December 10, 1962	90
Margaret Greene	November 9, 1925	November 21, 1961	36
Sheila Connors	July 19, 1940	April 15, 1951	10
Edward S. Shea	September 19, 1905	April 5, 1965	59
Bridget Sullivan	May 25, 1885	May 30, 1965	80
Aaron Leonard	August 6, 1936	November 22, 1964	28
Ignatious Rogers	January 12, 1914	September 8, 1965	51

The Scene

The time is November 2nd, 1965. The place is a graveyard in a small isolated coastal community in Placentia Bay, Newfoundland.

Part I
This Side of Heaven

> I shall say you were young, and your arms straight,
> and your mouth scarlet:
> I shall say you will die and none will remember you.
>
> – Archibald MacLeish

A Voice: In all the dark world there is no darkness like the dark of an outport night. Here on the coast of Newfoundland, darkness comes in all seasons as sudden as sudden death, comes coasting unannounced from its hideaway over the hills, sweeps silently down upon the seaside settlement of St. Kevin's, and covers the quick-silver, looking-glass sea like a shroud thrown from the sky to fall on the face of the funereal earth.

No human eyes can pierce the eternal darkness as it lies like death upon the dead village. And in St. Kevin's now, this November All Souls' Night, there are no human eyes alive and shining where once, not too dark a time ago, fishermen returning from their dreams upon the sea could see with blazing eyes the firebrands waving the way for livyers moving from house to house upon the hills, their bright kitchen visits over for the night, as they blinked their way, with caution, curses and prayers, home to their wide-awake beds.

Tonight, with no human eyes to see them, the only fires alive are the fires in the eyes of the animals as they go about their animal business in the dead dark, in a wilderness of ruins.

The sleek otter gliding over the cold stones of Middle Brook, a quiet gurgle splitting the village in two as it runs unseen down from the warm wooded hills, leaps at a quick spark of silver somewhere in the sound of the brook, and comes up with tiny otter-appetizer of sparkling brook trout.

The rabbit, running erratically down the grass-grown road to or away from God-knows-what, stops suddenly at the grey decayed gate on the edge of Jack Leonard's hayfield, perceives some rabbit threat in the black breeze, and leaps-a silent flash of fur swallowed by the meadow in one grassy gulp.

A forlorn fox laps at the chill water of the spring at the foot of the scrape behind the cathedral ruins of Bill Sullivan's house and, by the light of his eyes, sees his amazed self in the gun-metal gleam of the pool. One look is enough, and away he races to the shelter of the woods pursued by his own vicious image of himself.

In Chapel Pond the arrogant frogs croak their solemn sermons to the night as the trout doze irreverently, a faithless congregation heeding only the dreams they inhabit as they lie suspended in sleep among the lily pads.

On the beach below the old beach road (below the grey-green skeletons of stages and stores standing like the amphibian invaders from worlds beneath the sea, their crooked strouter legs wading in the shallow, their grotesque headless torsos thrust lumbering in the air) a million crabs crawl lopsided over the rocks rolled round and smooth by a million years of wave break, swish and roll.

In the graveyard below the waterfall of Ladore the mice run hunting or playing hide-n-seek among the headstones which announce mutely to the living night all that matters concerning the dead decayed lives of those buried in the sinking soil below.

(Thunder)

(Silence)

(Thunder)

(Silence)

(Thunder)

Jack: Hello!

(Silence)

(Thunder)

    Hey!

(Silence)

    Hello!

(Thunder)

Ray! Skipper Bill! Anyone!

(*Silence*)

(*Thunder*)

Ray: Hello!

Jack: Hello!

Ray: You, Jack?

Jack: Yeah! That you, Ray?

Ray: I s'pose it is.

Jack: We're still here then!

Ray: Looks like it.

Jack: Is it only us?

Ray: Don't know.

Jack: No sound of the women and them?

(*Thunder*)

Ray: Can't hear 'em. Can't hear nothin' 'cept you and the thunder.

(*Thunder*)

(*Silence*)

Ray: P'rhaps they're all gone.

Jack: All at once?

Ray: P'rhaps they didn't all go at once. It's a year now since the last time.

Jack: I guess they could be gone by now. Some of 'em anyway.

(*Thunder*)

Ray: Listen.

Jack: Just thunder.

Ray: No! Listen.

Jack: What then?

Ray: Listen.

(*Thunder*)

Bill: Hello there!

Ray: See, they're not gone.

Jack: Hello!

Bill: Hello Jack!

Ray: Bill?

Bill: That you, Raymond?

Ray: Yeah! Me and Jack. We're still here.

Bill: Me too. And Rose is still here. I heard her groanin'.

Rose: That's a terrible thing to say, Bill Sullivan. I certainly was not groanin'. Ninety years alive and at least twelve dead, and in all that time I haven't been heard to utter a single groan. It wouldn't hurt you to have a little respect for the dead, you know.

Bill: Sorry, Rose. I thought I heard you groanin', that's all.

Rose: I was sayin' my prayers. Like the rest of ye ought to be instead of goin' on with your chatter.

Bill: Sounded like groanin' to me.

Jack: Just tryin' to find out which of us is still here, Aunt Rose.

Ray: We're wonderin' if there's any of us gone.

Rose: So who is it haven't spoke up yet?

Jack: I guess it's just Maggie and Sheila now. There was ever only the six of us put down here. Up 'til this time last year, anyway.

Rose: Well, I don't know about Sheila, poor child. Could be she's gone to Heaven. But I doubt very much if Maggie is. So if she's not gone to Hell, she must be hangin' around here someplace.

Maggie: I heard that, Rose Hepditch, you old bitch! Always holier than thou.

Bill: That's Maggie! That's Maggie for sure.

Rose: A year deader and no better than ever.

Jack: Ah, Aunt Rose, that's just Maggie. You know what she's like.

Maggie: And what difference do it make? You're the saintly one, Rose, or so you think, and you're still here. I'm one of the devil's own, accordin' to you, and I'm still here. And the men, they're a fine lot aren't they? And they're still here. And if you ever thought we'd ever get out of here, I doubt if the grubs got either bit fat eatin' your brains, maid.

Ray: Now, knock it off, Maggie. Besides, there's Sheila yet. She could be gone by now.

Sheila: No, I'm not. I'm still here, still wishin' I wasn't.

Jack: Ah Sheila! It's good to hear your voice again.

Maggie: Misery likes company, I s'pose.

Jack: I don't mean it like that, child. It's just that I'd miss you if you was gone.

Ray: That's it then. Anyone who was ever here is still here.

Rose: I hoped some of us, one of us at least, would be gone by now. What was it we did so wrong to keep us here like this?

Jack: That's not for us to say, Aunt Rose. We're here, that's all.

Maggie: Shouldn't we find out if anyone else's come? They can't live forever, that crowd up there. They got to perish sometime.

Bill: Yeah, there might be someone. It'd be good to get a bit of news.

Jack: It's a sin to think it, but I almost hope someone's come.

Rose: They all got to come sometime, sooner or later.

Ray: It's three years now, since anyone was buried here.

Sheila: It'd be nice to hear something from Mom and them.

Rose: If they was buried here this year, wouldn't they have spoke up by now?

Jack: Maybe not. Mind the year Maggie came? When we got our voices back, she didn't speak for the best part of the whole time. Scared to death, remember, afraid that the devil might get her.

Rose: It's a wonder to me that he haven't got her yet.

Maggie: Oh, shut yer trap, Rose. Besides, who wouldn't be spooked out of their mind in a place like this, with corpses goin' on all around you.

Jack: That's what I mean. It isn't a easy thing to get used to. Whoever might be here might be a bit nervous about it. (Loudly) If there's anyone besides us lyin' here in this graveyard, anyone who was buried here since this time last year, could you let us know?

Ray: All you got to do is talk. You got your voice now, for a little while at least.

Jack: And there's certainly no need to be afraid. I'll tell you who's here. All people you know, most likely. Sheila's here. Little Sheila Connors.

Sheila: I drowned under the ice.

Jack: And Aunt Rose. Rose-in-the-bed, she's here.

Rose: It's a fine bed I'm in now. Lovely linen, no mistake!

Jack: Ray Dwyer, he's here. Used to make up the songs, remember. Always makin' up songs and singin' all the time.

Ray: I sung all the way from the cradle to the grave. Got to the grave too quick.

Jack: And Maggie Greene is here.

Maggie: Maggie Greene, the old bag. Remember? What would they call me, if they could see me now? A old bag of bones I am now, the same as me betters.

Jack: And Skipper Bill Sullivan.

Bill: I should of drowned in The August Gale. A watery grav'd be a damn sight better than this.

Jack: And me, Jack Leonard. Died in fifty-five, in the best of health. Been here ever since.

Rose: We're all here ever since.

Ray: And we only get this time of year with voices. All Souls' Night, that's all we got. Whatever we're allowed of it. So, if there's anyone else here, and you can hear us, then speak up for Godsake.

(Silence)

Rose: If there was any of them that did die these past three years, they mightn't be here anyway, because they could of gone straightaway to Heaven. Or to Hell.

Maggie: Even if they went to Hell, they'd be better off. Hell can't be no worse than this.

Jack: We got this spell at least.

Bill: Then back to nothin'.

Rose: I'm beginnin' to think all my prayers is gone to waste. All the thousands of rosaries I said, and the novenas I made, and the advents and the lents, and all the fastin', and the penances, and all The Acts of Contrition. All gone to waste.

Jack: Maybe not, Aunt Rose. Time is different here. It seems so long in passin', seems like centuries. But it's only a few years we been here. That's all.

Ray: Sure we was always told that even a venial sin, the tiniest kind, could keep you in purgat'ry for a hundred years or more. God knows we all committed a scattered one. And who knows, but this might be purgat'ry. It could be.

Jack: It don't seem to be nowhere near the same purgat'ry I learned about in school.

Ray: Still, it wasn't more than fifteen years ago and there wasn't nobody buried here at all.

Rose: We used the old graveyard before that. The one up by the church. A nicer place it was too. I bet the ones buried up there isn't in such a state as this.

Jack: Sheila was the first one put down here. I can mind the day we buried her. The first grave ever dug in the new cemet'ry. That was fourteen years ago. If time adds up at all.

Sheila: I should of done what I was told. Mom told me not to go playin' out on the ice. But I went anyway, not thinkin' nothin' would happen outside of gettin' wet and gettin' bawled out for it. And then the pan went over, and I was under the water, and I couldn't breathe, and there was ice in my mouth chokin' me, and I got a awful pain in the head, and I tried to screech out, and the salt water came in and made me sick, and I vomited. And then it was like I was into a dream and all I could see was rainbows everywhere, and they was all broken into pieces, and the colours hurt my eyes, and I didn't remember to think of nothin'. Not even to say the Act of Contrition.

Rose: Your poor mother nearly went out of her mind.

Ray: The cove was full of slob and we was out there tryin' to hook you up from the bottom. The whole crowd of us was out there, and I kept waitin' for someone to shout out that they got you. I kept hopin' it wouldn't be me, but if it was me, that the jigger would be caught in your coat or something. But when I hauled you up and saw where the jigger was hooked, I passed out in the punt, and the line slipped out of me grip, and you went to the bottom again. The rest came over then and took hold, and hauled you in. But it was me that jigged you in the eye.

Sheila: I got no eyes now, Mr. Dwyer. So it don't make no difference. (Weeping) I got no eyes at all now.

(Thunder)

Jack: Listen!

Bill: More weather, that's all.

Jack: No listen. It was a voice I heard.

Ned: It's me you heard. Tryin' to get used to the sound of myself.

Jack: Who is it? Who are you?

Maggie: It's Ned Shea. I'd know him anywhere.

Ned: It's me, Ned. You remember me, Jack.

Jack: Ned Shea! I dare say I do.

Bill: Well, I'll be damned!

Ned: Skipper Bill?

Bill: Yeah!

Ray: And me, Ray Dwyer. Sorry to see you here, Ned.

Ned: Me too Ray. Me too.

Maggie: Robbed from the poor 'til the day you died, I s'pose.

Ned: That got to be Maggie.

Rose: Don't pay no mind to her, Ned.

Ned: And that must be Rose Hepditch.

Rose: Rose-in-the-bed is what they called me. Remember?

Ned: Sure I remember you, Rose.

Sheila: Hello, Mr. Shea. I used to be Sheila.

Ned: Ah, freckle-faced Sheila!

Bill: And yourself, Ned. How are ya, b'y? How ya doin'?

Ned: It's dead is how I am, Bill. And not lookin' very good, I can tell you. Mostly bones is what I am now. Mostly bones.

Maggie: You'll be all bones, like the rest of us soon. The worms'll see to that. How's my one and only? How's my Tom, Ned? How's he gettin' on?

Ned: Damned if I ever thought I'd be talkin' to you again, Maggie. Contrariest customer I ever had.

Maggie: Well, you was the crookedest shopkeeper I ever dealt with.

Jack: Now, don't go gettin' on with that stuff. That's all over with, all past, that stuff.

Maggie: How's my Tom, Ned? How's my handsome one, he's self. Is he still mournin' over me?

Ned: If he is, he's doin' it in fine company.

Maggie: What company?

Ned: Tom got he'self a new woman, maid.

Maggie: No! That's a damn lie, that is.

Ned: No, Maggie. No lie at all. Tom is all tied up now. Goin' on three years I'd say.

Maggie: Tied up? To who? Who got my Tom now?

Ned: Edna Leonard.

Maggie: That can't be. It couldn't be.

Ned: It is Maggie, maid. It's the God's truth.

Maggie: *(Wailing)* Oh no! No. No. No.

Jack: Now, now girl. No use gettin' yourself all upset about it.

Maggie: Edna Leonard! Tom and she? My Tom and the likes of that! I don't believe it. He couldn't stand her. Nobody could. She was always so stuck up. And all she was was a streel, really.

Ned: Well, whatever she might of been, she is proper enough now, since the wedding.

Maggie: Wedding? They went and had a wedding? In church and everything?

Ned: The most beer I sold in six months.

Maggie: They celebrated it?

Ned: The whole place was hung over for a week.

Maggie: White wedding dress and all?

Ned: Yes. And a pretty penny it cost too.

Maggie: And she about as much of a virgin as Tim Slade's cow.

Rose: No cow I knows could hold a candle to you.

Ned: She still owes onto it too. Like they all owes me on one thing or another. Now I s'pose they'll just tear up their slips and be done of 'em. If I hadn't of died, I'd be in the poor-house.

Rose: Yes, I allow now. So far as I could tell, you was every bit as crooked inside as you was out.

Ned: I never dealt crooked with no one. And besides, I'm not crooked no more neither.

Bill: You mean you got no more hump-back?

Ned: I'm as straight as a whip now.

Jack: How come, Ned? How'd you get cured of that?

Maggie: You was bent near to the ground all your life.

Ned: I guess they had to straighten me out to fit me into a coffin.

Jack: Christ! Couldn't they have built you one to fit?

Ned: Oh, I'm sure they would've. But I bought me coffin off me ownself, out of me own stock. That way I got to keep the mark-up on it, see.

Rose: What did you think? That you could take your ill-gotten gains to the grave with you?

Ned: No gains I ever got was ill-gotten, Rose. And they wasn't what you'd call a wealth of money neither. But for what they was worth, I did take 'em with me.

Jack: Go on!

Bill: How?

Ned: I got it sewed into the lining of my coffin. Every cent I had is buried right here with me.

Maggie: A lot of good it'll do to you here.

Rose: Once a merchant, always a merchant.

Ned: A man got to get along the best he can.

Jack: Is there others, Ned?

Ned: Other what?

Jack: People. Ones that died that year. Any more besides yourself?

Ned: I don't know. Aunt Bride was ailin' the same time I was. But I think it was just the flu she had. It was the damn cancer got me, so I was done anyway. But you know Aunt Bride. She's liable to outlast the works, no matter what she got.

Bill: Eighty she'd be now. Time for Bride to give up on it. Time she took her place here alongside of her old man. I gets lonely for she betimes.

Bride: That's very nice now Mr. Bill, wantin' me to come to a place like this.

Bill: Bride! You is here. Thank God! I was beginning to think you was never goin' to die.

Bride: Well, I certainly didn't try to, you know, even though there was times I missed you bad enough.

Jack: It's too bad Bride, that we got to meet again in such a place as this.

Bride: It's not what I hoped for, Jack.

Ray: Not what any of us hoped for.

Maggie: We hoped to be out of here before you or anyone else ever come.

Bride: This seems to me to be a good place to get a chill. I hope you got your long underwear on, Bill.

Bill: Ah, no need for that here, girl. The cold can't do us no harm now. No more need for pills and hot-water bottles and beef-iron wine. No need for none of that stuff now. The only thing can harm you here, love, is time. Thinkin' it might go on forever. Still, I finds it nice to hear your voice, Bride.

Bride: All the prayers I prayed to you, Bill, thinkin' you'd be up in Heaven among the saints. Thinkin' you could do us poor mortals some good. Isn't no one at all gone to Heaven?

Jack: We're all here, Bride. All of us that got put down here in this place.

Jack: She'd be goin' on sixty-two now, Maud would. I dare say she's beginnin' to show it, all she's went through. Fifty-two she was when I died, and didn't look a day more than forty. Always looked younger than her years, your mother did. But I allow it's all catchin' up on her by this time.

Aaron: It never came to me about you missin' her. It was always how much we missed you our ownselves. Do you miss her more than anything else in the world? The way I misses Donna?

Jack: Now, that's no easy question to answer, Aaron. What do a dead man miss most out of the life he had? For myself, I can say I miss the whole of it, the works. I miss your mother, and everyone around, miss being with 'em. And I miss a bit of music now and then, and a game of cards, and a nap on the day-bed come evening. I miss it all, the good and the bad. But what do I miss most of all, out of my whole life? Well, my son, let me put it this way. If I had one day back at it, just one day give back to do what I pleased, what would I want to do on that day? Just one day given back, mind, and I could pick the day. I'd pick a day in July month, or maybe the first week of August. I'd be at the wheel of the *Alice-Eileen*. That was the first real boat I ever owned, outside of punts and skiffs. A nice littlejack she was, the *Alice-Eileen*. And she'd be under sail, all fresh paint and good canvas. And I'd be at the wheel of 'er with a nice sou'west breeze blowin'. Just a nice enough breeze around fifteen knots, a nice easy breeze. And we'd be takin' her down past the Grey Gull in lee of the Ragged Islands. And the sun would be lovely on the water. And we'd be loaded down with fish. The best kind of salt fish from off of my own flakes in St. Kevin's. We'd be takin' 'em down to Spencer's Cove, to A. Wareham and Sons. Nothin' but madeira on board and she loaded down to the gunwales. With the sun on the water, a nice sou'west wind, and me at the wheel of my own boat. Well, I guess if that's the way I'd want to spend one day with body and soul together again, one day if I had it, then I guess I got to say, that is what I miss most of all.

Sheila: I misses my mom tuckin' me in, sayin' "goodnight, God bless," kissin' me on the cheek where I got none now.

Rose: The wallpaper in my room, the little purple flowers climbin' to the ceiling. Always there, always growin', always in full bloom, summer or winter.

Ray: Snow. Snow clung to the eaves like upside-down waves, white like…like snow.

Maggie: I misses my lookin' glass most. It was the nicest thing I ever laid eyes on.

Bill: It'd be the sound of the sea for me. The sound of the sea with a sea on.

Ned: The smell of cinnamon, and cloves, and new leather. The smell of fresh dustbane. The smell of new things.

Bride: The sound of Bill's snorin'. You could always tell when Bill was in off the water. The house'd be shakin' with the snores comin' out of him. Oh, what a lovely racket!

Aaron: The touch of her underneath her blouse. Soft like soft glass.

Bill: How about one [a song] now, Ray?
Rose: What!
Ned: Why not?

Rose: Because we don't have forever. Any minute now, just you watch, we'll be back to silence. Back to nothing. We might have enough time with voices to say the Rosary. And that's what we should be at, too. No wonder we're kept here the way we are. Every year comes and goes and we only get a little while each one being able to talk and all, to say a few prayers, to ask God's mercy and forgiveness. And what do we end up doin'? Gabbin' the whole time away with no purpose to it. No wonder we're kept here like this lyin' in our own rot. No wonder at all, when we should be at the Rosary, and not carryin' on like it was a garden party or something.

Jack: I don't think there'd be any harm in a song.

Ned: No harm at all.

Bill: Come on Ray, give us one, b'y.

Ray: I don't want my songs to get in the way of anything.

Maggie: So, who apart from Rose, got any objection?

Bill: What about "The August Gale"?

Ray: Oh, that'd be too long Skipper. That's a long song, that one.

Bride: Bill always wants to hear "The August Gale" just because he's into it.

Bill: I'm not the only one likes it.

Bride: What's the one you used to sing about Cradle Hill? That was a lovely song!

Aaron: That's where me and Donna done it for the first time. The first time for the both of us. Up there in the meadow on the side of Cradle Hill.

Ray: It's a long time since I sung that one.

Rose: Well, ye might as well get on with it. As far as I can see, some people are no better dead than alive. But I'll have nothin' to do with any of it. Either your songs or your sins. So, if you'll excuse me, I'll be at my prayers.

Ray: *(Singing)*

When the sun goes down on Cradle Hill
And darkness then fills up the sky
And memories fill up your mind
I hope you do not cry

I hope you do not weep for me
For I am always with you still
As on evenings long ago
We strolled up Cradle Hill

Oh do not weep my darling one
Oh no don't ever weep for me
For I'm far beyond the reach
Of the wild and the raging sea
For I'm far beyond the raging sea

Remember what it all meant then

The fragrant flowers were blooming there
And birds whose summer song
Did fill the evening air

These are the things I keep with me
These are the constant joys of love
And they were ours and still will be
While stars shine up above

Oh do not weep my darling one
Oh no don't ever weep for me
For I'm far beyond the reach
Of the wild and the raging sea
For I'm far beyond the raging sea

Aaron: Damn it! I wish I was still alive.

A Voice: So it goes! While death lies buried deep beneath the foot-steps and voices of visitors who come loving and longing to the long remembered, the worms can go about their slow, busy feast, and it won't matter. While death decays no distance at all from the smells of fish frying, and outhouses freshly used, and savoury hanging upside-down in brown paper bags behind the stoves, the rivulets, running like tiny subterranean rivers to the sea, can carry their residue of flesh with them all their flowing lives, and it won't matter. While death sleeps deep in the soundless ground beneath the sighs and cries of babies buried in cribs full of blankets, and the sing-song sound of women weeping in beds full of husbands, and the tiny talk of big men rolling home from the fields of fish on the zillion acre ocean, the silent sleep can last forever, and it won't matter. Nothing of death's desolation will matter as long as dead lovers are loved still in the wishes of lovers left alive and longing. Nothing of it will matter as long as the honoured dead are honoured still in the heart-felt toasts of drunk and drinking men, or as long as cursing men still curse their dead enemies, glad to be rid of them and their interventions. It won't matter how long the dead lie dying of hunger, as long as children remember the taste of their dead mom's milk and the feel of breasty flesh upon their cheeks. It won't matter as long as the living live and remember. Whether they thrive or endure, as long as the living live and remember, the dear deceased cannot be diminished by the fearful fact of death.

All this, and more, the ever-remembered of St. Kevin's have learned. However brief, however uncertain their time alive, they learned, before they died, that there is no survival this side of immortality, no final gladness this side of Heaven.

Part II
The Coming Of Winter

None know if our deaths are now or forever: —
We lie down and the snow covers our garments.

– Archibald MacLeish

Bill: I allow you are tired my dear, after all this. It's enough to make anyone wore out, this is.

Ray: Just like me not being able to think of any songs. That's the way it's went before. The kind of tiredness that comes on just before this spell comes to a end.

Jack: Do anyone else feel like that? Like a sleepiness overtakin' 'em?

Nish: I do. And…all-of-a-sudden it…it's gettin' hard…harder to talk. It's like I was…was goin' back to the way…the way I was when…when I was a…alive.

Ray: Don't worry about that, Nish b'y It got nothin' to do with that. We'll all be deaf and dumb soon. Like we were since this time last year.

Maggie: Maybe now it'll be all over and done with. None of this no more. And it'd be better, really. What's the use of being able to talk and think when there's nothin' more to be thought about or said?

Nish: I wish now that…that they buried me…outside…outside of the fence. Or didn't bury me…at all. I'm not…not sorry for what I done…to myself. But I do feel bad for…for what I went and said. I'm sorry for that. It would of been…better…if I hadn't of told ye…told ye what went on. It'd be better…better if ye never knew.

Jack: No need to feel like that, Nish. The truth do hurt. But we got to put up with that. What went on up there is no fault of yours.

Bill: And besides, it's no worse for us than it is for yourself. You're here too, isn't you?

(*Silence*)

Jack: Nish!

(*Silence*)

    You still there, Nish?

(*Silence*)

Is he gone?

Ray: Nish!

(*Silence*)

Bill: I allow he's gone.

Jack: Looks like it, don't it?

Ray: Poor bugger!

Ned: Is he the first?

Jack: I suppose he is.

Ray: What about Aaron?

Jack: Aaron! You still here? Aaron?

Aaron: Still here. Tryin' to remember something. Something to do with a girl and a…a….

Jack: Hard to remember, hey!

Aaron: Like a dream I might of had. There's bits and pieces out of it. There's a cradle into it. A baby's cradle and a ring…and a girl. And there is a awful explosion, like thunder, and a bird, a bird goin' to wing, a bird with a woman's face flyin' out to sea. And I callin' out to 'er, callin' 'er to come back. But I can't remember her name.

(Silence)

Jack: Aaron!

(Silence)

Ray: Gone?

Jack: Gone!

Ned: Gone and better off.

Jack: Aaron!

(Silence)

He was a fine young fellow, you know. Him and Peter, the finest kind of fellows. I was always proud of 'em. Proud of the both of 'em.

Rose: I'm sure you had cause to be, Jack Leonard. What father isn't proud of he's own sons? But what father don't turn a blind eye to their faults, too?

Bride: *(Weakly)* Mr. Bill! I feels like I'm gettin' weak. Like I'm fadin' away from ye. All that talk is all cloudy to me, like a fog. Words comin' and goin' all around with no sense to 'em at all. Too tired to keep up with it anymore. It's like I was dyin' all over again.

Bill: Don't go frettin', Bride. We'll all be goin' that way now. Into nothin'. It's the most we can hope for now, girl. And there's no harm in it. No harm at all.

Bride: *(Fading)* I wish…I could…come over and…and tuck you in.

Bill: I'm tucked in tight enough, Bride. It's nice to know you're here though, not gone off on your own with the crowd up there. We lived a long spell together, me and you, and it's only fittin' that we're together here, wherever we is. I hope you has a good sleep now, Bride, a good rest with nothin' or no one to bother you.

Ray: I think she's gone, Skipper Bill.

Bill: Is you, Bride? Is you gone, girl?

(Silence)

Rest in peace, my dear. Rest in peace.

Ned: You might as well wish me…the same…Skipper…if you got a mind to…because I'm on the way out too. Everything is closin' in on me.

Jack: There's nothin' to be done for it, Ned, b'y. Just let go easy is all.

Ned: I wouldn't mind so much if…if I could keep a good picture of the shop…in my mind. I spent over half of my life in…in that shop and…I can't even picture it…the way…the way it used to be. Can't picture where things was…where I kept things…the biscuits…or the kerosene…or the cheese. I wish I could have…one more look at 'er…the way she used to be…with the shelfs full of provisions…right up to the ceiling…and people comin' in and goin' out…on their way up and down the road. It'd be a good memory…like a snap…to take with me. But mostly…in my mind…now…it's a picture of 'er all beat up…smashed to pieces. Everything beat to…beat to…pieces.

Ray: It's hard to keep anything good in mind anymore. It's a hard old racket we're into now, Ned, b'y.

Ned: Well, it'll be…goodnight to you now. Time…time to close 'er up…for the night. Time…to close…'er up for good.

Ray: Goodnight to you, too, Ned.

Jack: Goodnight, Ned.

Bill: Goodnight, Ned.

Maggie: *(Mimicking)* Goodnight, Ned! What a lot of foolishness. Like that's all it was, just another night, with another mornin' comin' on.

Jack: Now, Maggie, don't go makin' it any worse than it is. It's just as well to be civil about it.

Maggie: Yes, I suppose it it. Seein' as how we're into such a civilized place.

(Thunder)

Bill: Ah, there it is, b'ys. Time for all of us to say goodnight.

Jack: just like all the times before. The thunder on the first of it and the thunder at the end.

Ray: I wonder is it real thunder. Up above, I mean. Is it the night up there we're hearin', or is it just a thunder in the ground?

(Thunder)

Sheila: (*Screaming*) Mom! Mommy!

Jack: It's only thunder, child. Just a bit of weather. Nothin' to be frightened about.

Sheila: (*Shivering*) It ain't that, Mr. Leonard, it ain't the thunder.

Jack: What then?

Sheila: I'm frightened I won't get to sleep. Scared I'll be here wide awake all by me ownself, after ye're all gone.

Jack: No. No. I'll stay here with you, here by your side, until you falls sound asleep. I won't leave you here alone. I promise.

Sheila: I don't want to be left all alone in Hell.

Jack: Now, see, that's just people puttin' things in your mind. Don't you pay any attention to stuff like that. It's only talk, that's all, and no truth to it at all. You're nowhere near Hell here, believe me. And you're not goin' to go to Hell either. It's Heaven you're goin' to. And soon too. Sooner than you think. The best thing is to go to sleep now.

Sheila: I don't feel sleepy.

Ray: Remember when I used to sing you to sleep? You was just a infant then. I'd come to have a spell with your father in the evenings after supper, and your mother would put you in my arms where I'd be sittin' on the daybed by the stove, and I'd sing you a little song I made just for you.

Sheila: (*Singing*)
   Sleepy-time child the sandman is

Ray: here.

Sheila: He's sprinkling sand in your eyes.

(Pause)

Ray: Your Guardian Angel will stay very near

Sheila: (*joining in*)
   'til you wake with the morning sunrise

Ray: Sleepy-time child it's time to let go
   Let go of your wide awake day
   It's time to close your sleepy blue eyes
   And let your dreams drift you away

   Sleepy-time child the stars are aglow

Jack: *(joining in)*
   The moon is a silvery bright
   Your Mommy and Daddy want you to know
   They love you and wish you Good-night.

Ray: (*Alone*) They love you and wish you Good-night.

Sheila: (*Slowly*)

   Now I lay me down to sleep
   I pray the Lord my soul to keep.
   If I should die before I wake
      I pray the Lord…my soul…to take.

(*Thunder*)

(*Silence*)

Jack: Is she gone?

Ray: I think she is. And none too soon either.

Jack: It's a shame youngsters got to die.

Bill: It's a shame anyone got to die, if this is what it's all about.

(*Thunder*)

Jack: Not much time left now.

Bill: None at all left for me, b'ys. Time for me to pass on.

Jack: Well, Skipper, havin' Bride here alongside must be a bit of comfort to you.

Bill: Yeah! No more I'll be leavin' she to go to Golden Bay. No more her havin' to wait and wonder, with the wind enough to knock the house down, and us out on the water with nothin' but a bit of canvas to get us home. No more of that misery for Bride, now. No more cryin' out of relief to see me comin' in with neither spar left upright, and every man-jack of the crew still aboard of 'er. No sir, no more August Gales for Bride to ride out.

Ray: One in a lifetime is enough, old man.

Bill: Still, I could stand one more, myself Ray, b'y. One more storm to be out in. One more load o' salt to carry back from Spain. One more trip to the West Indies. One more summer on the Labrador. Or just one more day out in a dory with a little gaff sail. That'd be enough. As long as it was on the water, it'd be enough. But them times is gone. No more of that for me. So it's just as well I knocked off rememberin' it. just as well I knocked off everything all together. So I'll see ya b'ys. See ya.

Jack: Be seein' ya, Skipper.

Ray: So long, Bill. So long, old man.

Bill: So long, b'ys. See ya…come…come summer…in Golden Bay.

(*Thunder*)

(*Silence*)

Ray: I guess we're all that's left then, Jack. You and me.

Jack: Looks like it, Ray, b'y

Ray: Our turn now then.

Jack: Yeah, our turn now.

Ray: I wish I knew what to say to ya, Jack. But there's nothin' to say now that'd make any difference, is there?

Jack: You can tell me one thing, Ray, before the both of us is gone. I hadn't the nerve to ask you while the child and the women was still here. But you're a sensible fellow, always had a good head on your shoulders and I know I'll get a honest answer out of you. I been thinkin' more all the time that we might very well be cast off in Hell. Know what I mean? I'm not altogether certain about it. But I must say, it looks that way to me. What do you think, Ray? Makin' no bones about it, do you think we're all stuck in Hell?

(*Silence*)

Or do you think there's either shred of hope left yet? What do you say, Ray? Are we stuck in Hell or what?

(*Thunder*)

Ray!

(*Silence*)

You gone too, Ray? So quick as that?

(*Silence*)

I guess you are then. And that means it's time for me to turn in too. It's a long night ahead, and no one to say goodnight to. (Louder) Except you Maud, maid. (Shouting) I don't hold it against you for goin', Maud. I want you to know that. I know you had no choice in it. And even if you did, I know it couldn't of been a easy thing to do. I hope you're not down-hearted on account of it. What with me and Aaron passed away and Peter gone off, there wasn't much left to stay on for even if you could of. So I don't blame you none, Maud. The main thing is for you to be content. No sense grievin' over what's gone past. Just be glad you're alive, girl. (Quietly) Wherever you are now, wherever you're gone to, just be glad that you're still alive.

(*Thunder*)

A Voice: The sleeping dead lie silent now in the soil of their discontent, their souls embalmed with their bones. The insects resume their remedy for rot and the echoless earth again fills up the mouths of the dear departed.

The darkness the dead inhabit inhabits the world above them, and even the animals move from minute to minute with unfamiliar fear. The pitch-black oval of water that is Chapel Pond slips slowly into Middle Brook and whispers its way down the dark land to its eternal communion with the darker sea.

The debris in the landwash flows in and out with the rise and fall of the ocean's endless edge. Here the relics of lives once lived glow in the phosphorescent dark. White plastic bleach bottles, red plastic motor oil bottles, tin cans, bits and pieces of nylon rope (red, yellow, white, and blue), an enameled oven door, an iron damper, a rocking chair rocker, a broken cradle, a picture frame framing what might have been a picture of The Scared Heart, the keel and stern-post of an old skiff, pieces of longers and ochre-coloured boards, a rusty awl, a tobacco tin, a baby's bottle with nipple erect, pleading for a mouth. These are the artifacts, the left-overs of human lives, seeking their consumation in the sea or the sand.

In the graveyard below the waterfall of Ladore, where once the meagre rituals of the living sustained them in their fervent hope of everlasting life, the dead, lying alone in desolate death, their eyeless eyes blind to the geography of the sky, are unaware that the first snow of winter is just now beginning to fall on the vacant village of St. Kevin's.

The Road Home

Michael Crummey

The highway takes you only so far,
roadsigns and pavement right to the coast of
the mainland and the island somewhere out
there beyond it, a rock cradled in fog,
a gloved fist

The ferry shoulders its way into the north Atlantic,
into rain and an easterly wind, making for
Newfoundland which is no longer my home
but the place I come from still
the place that made me
and being a stranger there now I am
more or less a stranger wherever I find myself

From the terminal in Port Aux Basques
the Trans Canada works north up the coast,
picking its way through the Long Range Mountains
before turning east to the interior of
spruce forests and marsh, clouds of black flies,
acres of rolling barrens
where only wind and rain and winter have
ever been completely at home;
driving through, I recognize the landscape
but not my place in it, a stiff wind
rocks the car like a small boat,
and I don't have the words to say
the countryside properly though I feel it
moving inside me, its dark strength

Coming home teaches me that I own nothing
that there is nothing in the world
I have a claim to
though this one place has a claim to me—
turning south onto the Buchans highway
I follow the Exploits River further into bush,
through Buchans Jct. buried in waves of spruce
and past the cold length of Red Indian Lake which has
forgotten me completely since I left
here years ago…

Quoth the Raven

Angela Mercer

Nick would never admit it to most of his friends, but he actually liked hanging out at the library. It was better than being stuck at his grandparents' house while his mother went to night school.

The library held happy memories of Saturday-morning story hours when he was little. It was the place he'd go when his parents fought. Now he always felt a thrill of anticipation when new arrivals showed up on the paperback rack. He liked the building too. With its high ceilings, dark wood panelling, and cushioned window seats, it reminded him of a mansion from an old horror movie. The library was his favourite place in the world—until the bird came and ruined it all.

The bird was the first thing Nick noticed when he entered the library one night. It sat perched on a tall pedestal at one side of the arched entrance to the fiction section.

"What's this?" he wondered when he spotted it. "A new security guard waiting to swoop down on book snatchers?" When he inched closer, though, he realized that the bird's swooping days had ended long ago.

It was big and looked even bigger sitting on the branch that served as a stand. Its ruffled black feathers had lost their sheen and its dull slate-grey toes, ending in long curved claws, looked dry and brittle. One of its stiff wing feathers was bent near the tip and poked out at an awkward angle. But the fine feathers that covered the head were sleek and smooth, and the slightly parted beak seemed poised to emit a screeching cry.

It was the beady yellow eyes that bothered Nick the most. They seemed to glow with an eerie light all their own. He stared at them as he sidled past and they stared back, cold and menacing.

"Creepy," he thought, as he slipped into a chair and dropped his writing folder onto the table in front of him. He had to come up with a third verse for a poem that was due the next day.

"How about: 'Crow, crow go away. Stand in front of a Chevrolet,'" he mused, stealing a peek at the sinister sentinel. He felt as if its eyes were following his every move. "Why don't you go read a book or something?" he asked silently and turned back to his work.

He sensed Miss Kelly, the librarian, behind him before she spoke. "So, it's poetry tonight, is it?" she asked. Then she smiled and pointed at the bird. "I'm sure you'll get some inspiration with him here." Nick frowned. What on earth was she talking about?

"He helped a writer before you know," Miss Kelly added, "or at least we think he did. The research isn't complete yet, so we're not absolutely sure, but it looks like this is the same stuffed bird that once shared a room with Edgar Allen Poe. Mr. Ross—he runs the antique store around the corner on Duckworth Street—discovered it. When he suggested displaying it here we were delighted."

"I'd rather not get any inspiration from that bird. Poe's poem was pretty freaky," Nick responded indifferently.

With its wings folded against its body and its head to one side, the bird seemed to be listening to the conversation. For a moment Nick was transfixed. He felt trapped in the evil glare glowing from the creature's cold yellow eyes. Miss Kelly's voice broke the spell.

"Mr. Ross says that all the evidence that he's collected so far shows that this is the same stuffed bird that came with the furnished room that Poe was renting when he wrote the poem about Lenore. Looking at it all the time inspired him to write it. Isn't that exciting?"

Luckily, Nick didn't need to answer. A man had come over to the reference desk to ask Miss Kelly for help.

That night, the bird's menacing presence distracted Nick so much that he changed seats three times. No matter where he moved, it seemed to be watching him.

At one point, he deliberately sat with his back turned to it, but that just made it even worse. Even when he couldn't see them, he could feel the spying, prying yellow eyes boring into the back of his neck. No matter what he did, he couldn't shake off the eerie feeling that there was something unnatural about the bird, something that made his hair stand on end.

When Nick arrived at the library the next Tuesday, he headed straight for the cushions across from the aquarium. As he passed the bird, he kept his head turned away so he didn't have to look at it. He leaned back into the cushions and relaxed, watching the tropical fish play follow-the-leader through the elodea.

"Can't get to me here," he whispered triumphantly. He opened his book and started reading.

But he spoke too soon. When he looked up, a black reflection was shimmering on the glass of the aquarium. The beady eyes and parted beak were unmistakable.

"Impossible," Nick thought. "It's too far away and the angle's all wrong." He closed his eyes and looked again. The image of the bird was still there.

He scrambled off the cushions and made for the empty window seat on the other side of the room. Miss Kelly raised a warning eyebrow when he banged into a chair on the way.

"Oops," he whispered. Out of the corner of his eye he caught a glance at the bird and was relieved to see that its head was turned in the opposite direction. But his relief was short-lived.

Like someone who keeps bending a sprained finger hoping to find that it has stopped hurting, Nick kept checking the raven. The next time he looked, he noticed that he could see part of its right eye. Moments later, the whole eye was visible. When he looked again, he could see both eyes. Slowly, but surely, the bird had turned its head. Its stare carried an unspoken threat that made his blood run cold.

He turned away and blinked several times. When he looked back the bird's wing tips were quivering and rising ever so slightly. "It's trying to fly," he told himself. "But it can't. It's dead."

The piercing shriek that followed was more than Nick could handle. He clapped his hands over his ears and crouched in the window seat, waiting to feel the talons he was sure were about to sink into his neck.

Instead, he felt a tugging at his arm and heard Miss Kelly saying, "Don't be afraid. It's only the fire alarm. Stay calm and walk over to the door with me."

Nick struggled to his feet, feeling ridiculous. Then he smelled the smoke. He snatched up his book bag and followed the librarian and the other kids she was herding towards the front door.

As he passed under the stairway, he couldn't resist taking a last peek at the bird. What he saw stopped him in his tracks.

It was no longer staring at him. Its eyes were shifting from side to side, its wings were quivering, and its beak was opening and closing, as if it were trying to speak.

"Miss Kelly," Nick croaked, pointing at the raven.

"What? Is someone else back there? Where?"

"There," Nick pointed.

"Oh, Nick, this is no time to worry about the bird. Come on, let's go."

As Miss Kelly nudged him towards the exit, he heard it—a low squawking sound. Again and again, all the way to the door, it echoed faintly above the din. It was the bird's voice, of that he was certain, and it kept squawking what sounded like one word—"Nevermore."

A month later the library reopened. The fire had been a small one, confined to the area between the main desk and the arch. Although Nick was wary of returning, he'd had his fill of his grandfather's stories about the one that got away. So, two days after the library opened its doors again, Nick was back.

When he walked in, the first thing he noticed was the new carpeting. The old oak counter, the one that had served as a front desk, was gone too. A sleek white one, that angled off on each side to form a U-shape, had replaced it. And over near the archway to the right, where the pedestal had stood was a large new revolving stand bulging with paperbacks. Nick scanned the rest of the main floor. The bird was nowhere to be seen.

He breathed a sigh of relief and headed for the big table. He sat down and dug out his history notebook, ready to study for the test later on that week.

But try as he might, he couldn't concentrate. He found himself looking up every now and then to make sure that the bird was really gone. "Good riddance," he thought.

Miss Kelly slipped into the chair beside him. "The bird was lost in the fire," she said, as if reading his mind. "I felt terrible leaving it behind…and I felt even worse explaining what had happened to Mr. Ross. Luckily, he wasn't nearly as upset as I thought he would have been."

"How come?" Nick asked.

"Well, it seems that the bird wasn't Poe's raven after all. Mr. Ross was terribly disappointed. When all the evidence was added up, he realized he was wrong. Apparently, our bird was just somebody's worthless old stuffed crow."

Nick frowned. He wasn't so sure. "What if Mr. Ross was right?" he began cautiously. "What if the evidence is wrong?"

Miss Kelly smiled indulgently. "No, Nick, I'm afraid that's just wishful thinking."

As she stood up to leave, Nick suddenly knew what he had to do. He stopped her with a question. "Wait. Can you show me where to find that poem about the raven?"

"Of course. Come with me."

Nick followed her as she wound her way through the many aisles in the main stacks.

"It should be in here," she said as she pulled out a fat book. "Yes, here it is. 'The Raven.'"

Nick took the book to his table, spread it out, and read. The raven finally showed up in the seventh verse.

"Ghastly and grim," it read.

"Poe's got that right," he thought. Then his heart skipped a beat. The word leapt out at him from the end of the next verse. The word the raven kept repeating— "Nevermore."

Nick stared as the words blurred and a vision swam before his eyes. His head was spinning, he saw a man sitting in a cold, dark room. The only light came from the flickering embers of a dying flame. The man was scribbling furiously, his eyes blazing with fear. A huge black bird, mounted on a stand behind him, was screeching one word—"Nevermore."

"Nick?"

Nick jumped.

"Sorry," said Miss Kelly. "I didn't mean to startle you. I was just wondering if you found what you were looking for."

"Uh, yes, thanks," Nick mumbled, handing her back the book. "I don't need this anymore."

"Anymore. Nevermore. Poor Lenore." The words bounced around in his head. "Poor Poe," he thought, "stuck in a room with that…thing!"

"And poor Mr. Ross. But it's just as well that he doesn't know he had Poe's raven all along. He'd be so disappointed that it's gone. But I'm not," he thought as he stood up to leave. "I never want to see that bird again. Nevermore."

The Monologue in Newfoundland
Wilfred W. Wareham

Whether the traditional "time" in Newfoundland occurred in the informal contexts of the kitchen, the fish store or the forecastle of a fishing vessel, or more formally in the community hall, the occasions were generally characterized by music, dancing, drinking, singing, storytelling and what is referred to in most areas of the province as "recitations"—recitations such as the widely known "The Face on the Barroom Floor," "The Shooting of Dan McGrew," and numerous local compositions. Just as there were people in every community who specialized in singing, or storytelling, or some other activity, there were people like Francis Colbert of Job's Cove, Conception Bay, and Tom Linehan of Colinet, whose specialty was "saying recitations."

Various local terms such as "poem" or "recitation" exist with various meanings from one area to another. For instance, "The Lobster Salad" and "The Yankee Privateer" are both thought of as "recitations" by Baxter Wareham from Placentia Bay, while Francis Colbert of Conception Bay would label the former a "recitation" because it is in a poetic form and the latter a "monologue" because it is in prose form.

Whatever the folk name, I follow Kenneth S. Goldstein's suggestion in using monologue as the academic term for this neglected folklore genre. The points presented here are based on my own fieldwork in Newfoundland and on discussions with Dr. Goldstein.

The monologue, as presented here, may be defined as a solo, stylized, theatrically mannered, oral performance from memory of a self-contained dramatic narrative, in either poetic or prose form. In form, content and performance, it appears, in many ways, to bridge prose storytelling and verse singing. For example, the poetic monologue is related to the ballad in that they are both rhymed narratives. They differ in that the monologue is recited rather than sung. The relationship is important because some people, who perhaps feel they are unable to sing, will recite rather than sing a ballad. The reverse is also true with singers sometimes putting a melody to a rhymed monologue.

The main feature distinguishing the monologue from other folklore genres lies in the manner of performance. Ballad singing in Newfoundland, as in the Western European tradition in general, is noted for lack of interpretation of the narrative by the singer who usually sits and stares at one spot while performing. There is little dramatization and projection of self. The monologist, on the other hand, usually stands back from the group and performs in a theatrically mannered way. This is done in a number of styles. For example, if the content is serious, the message is generally not communicated literally. The performer may use a wide range of vocal characterization, grimaces and gestures to undercut the seriousness. When the lines are humorous, the performer pretends seriousness. The more ridiculous the lines the more serious the performer. The same applies to prose monologues such as "The Yankee Privateer." The humor lies not so much in what is said but how it is said. The audience recognizes this as a stylistic convention for the performance of the genre and the performer depends upon the identity of his audience with the material performed. Even when a monologue such as "The Soul of Jean Despré" is performed in a literal style, the speech used is usually more assertive than that used in ordinary conversation or in regular storytelling.

Newfoundland is rich in monologues. Themes appear to be few, dealing generally with such topics as history, local disaster, politics, religion and bawdy scenes. Many were learned from older performers, some were learned from books and newspapers, and many are local compositions.

The Lobster Salad

Traditional monologue

Last Saturday night I was invited by an old-time friend of mine
To eat his lobster salad and drink his beer and wine.
We drank a toast unto each other until the hour of two
Me head felt kind of shaky and me legs was shaky too.
But, anyhow, I staggered home and I think my prayers I said.
But, anyway, I was paralyzed when I got in the bed.
I dreamt I died and went to heaven and met St. Peter at the gate,
And I found repentance for me was just a bit too late.
"You go out," St. Peter said, "you know you can't come in.
You know you have to pay for your awful gluttonous sin."
Slowly then I turned away tied be grief and shame,
And I saw St. Peter's clerk close by, he wrote 'lost' above me name
Next there come was a Hebrew, a friend that I knew well
And I listened to the story that he had to tell.
"Oh, goodly Father Peter, I come to you at last
And one request I ask of you if you would let me pass.
On Earth I had a clothin' store and me clothes was good and strong,
And to show you this nice little overcoat I'll fetch it along."
"You go out," St. Peter said, "for very well you know
That you'll have no place for overcoats in the place where you got to go."
Next there come was an Italian, one on earth that I knew well,
So I stepped aside and I listened to the story he did tell.

This monologue is also known as Kelly's Dream, Burke's Dream and Kelly and the Wren Beer. [Eds.]

He said, "Oh, goodly Father Peter, I come to you at last
My peanut days over, my banana days are past,
While on earth I treated my neighbour like myself—no beg, no rob, no steal.
And never on the side walk did I throw banana peel."
"You go out," St. Peter said, "your gains are all ill gotten,
Your peanut shells were empty, your bananas oftimes rotten."
Next there come was an old maid and she was bound to have her say,
And she addressed St. Peter in a pure sort of way.
"Oh, goodly Father Peter, I come to you at last,
And one request I ask of you if you would let me pass,
Oh, holy Father Peter, oh won't you let me in?
And give me a nice little place to meself away from those naughty men?"
"You go out," St. Peter said, "no angels have grey hairs,
You have no sons or daughters, so you cannot come in here."
Slowly the old maid turned away forever to repine,
Like me and all the rest of us she entered in the line.
Next there come was a German and he was paralyzed with fear,
And while on earth he often paralyzed his customers with beer.
He said, "Oh, goodly Father Peter, I come to you at last,
And one request I ask of you if you would let me pass."
He said, "The wife she ran away from me and to hide me shame I tried.
So I went down by the river and committed suicide."
"You go out," St. Peter said, "and suffer your disgrace.
You come before we sent for you, now we can't find your place."
Slowly the German turned away forever to repine,
He came and stood beside us with a teardrop in his eye.
Now, next there come was Paddy, yes, a son of old Erin's Isle,
And he addressed St. Peter with a loving, gracious smile.
"Ah, 'tis yerself, St. Peter, you're lookin' so nice and sweet,
Open the door, boy, and let me in and show me to me seat."
"You go out," St. Peter said, "your case like the rest must be tried.
You have to show a pass for it before you get inside."
"Ah, hurry up, St. Peter, or for supper I'll be late."
He then took off his old slouch hat and hove it inside the gate.
"Go get that hat," St. Peter said, "you sacrilegious slouch."
Pat ran in, closed the door and he barred St. Peter out.
Then through the keyhole Paddy cried, "I'm skipper now you see,
And I'll give up me crown and the keys to heaven if you'll set old Ireland free."
Now when I awoke me head was jammed between the bedpost and the wall.
Me legs was tangled in the sheets.
'Twas them lobsters done it all.

The Prince of Wales

Traditional

"Come tell me a story, Grandad, your hair is turning grey,
You must have heaps of good ones when you get to your time of day.
You told me about the fairies and the good the little folks do,
But please for this time, Grandad, tell me one that's really true."

"Come sit on my knee then, laddie, and I'll do the best I can,
I'll tell you one that will please you some day you might meet the man.
And if ever you have the luck, boy, with cheer to make welcome ring,
For the hero of Grandad's story will one day be England's king.

"In a dear old home in London a dying soldier lay,
And o'er him stood the padre who came to watch and pray,
And the God that orders all things and orders them for the best,
Will comfort that dear old soldier that the Lord is taking west.

"They'd fought in the trenches together did the priest and the dying man,
And nothing fosters friendship like the field of battle can.
They talked of the nights in the trenches of the awful sights they'd seen.
God boys, those glorious victories were dearly bought to win.

"The most talked of all the adventures, the most cherished of all the tales,
Was the time they fought in the trenches side-by-side with the Prince of Wales.
The old soldier's strength was waning, and the padre said, 'Brother dear,
You've reached your great objective and the end is drawing near.

"'Before you go, dear brother, will you not tell us plain,
Is there no friend in the wide, wide world that you're longing to see again?'
'Yes there is one, dear padre, but I know my wish is in vain,
But I would die so happy could I see the prince again.'

"The padre smoothed out his pillow just as white as the driven snow,
And he asked the dear old soldier if he'd be allowed to go
To call on a friend who lived hard by only a short distance from here.
'I'll be back before you miss me and the nurse will stay quite near.'

"But not home were the footsteps headed, but straight to the banquet hall
Where he knew that the prince as usual would be answering duty's call.
But he learned that His Royal Highness had left half-an-hour ago,
So straight to the royal palace did the faithful padre go.

"Quickly he told the story but hopeless was his request,
For he learned that His Royal Highness had retired and he was undressed.
'Sorry for the intrusion,'—he was about to withdraw,
When walking along the hallway who do you think he saw?

"The Prince of Wales, God bless him, was there ever such as he
He wanted to hear the story, could he of service be?
'Of course I'll go with you, padre, one moment till I get dressed,
And we'll comfort that dear old soldier that the Lord is taking west.'

"Straight to the house they hurried right up to the soldier's side,
The prince bent gently o'er him and softly spoke his name.
But the spark of life burned dimly and they could see by the vacant eye,
That an angel stood in the offing and the end was drawing nigh.

"So, with heavy heart, the padre committed him to the care
Of the giver of every blessing and they left their comrade there.
Now the end came shortly after but, awakening as if from sleep,
Said the soldier in broken accents, 'Dear sister you must not weep.

"'For I dreamt that the Prince of Wales was here in answer to my prayer.
I could see his face quite clearly as if he was standing there.'
'It was no dream, dear brother, the Prince was here all right.'
'Then I'm happy little sister, God bless the prince, goodnight.'

"Now I've come to the end of my story, but before I go let me say
That the hero of Grandad's story will be your king some day.
And whenever you speak of the flag, boy, of England and her guns,
Thank God that the House of Windsor has produced such loyal sons."

Smokeroom on the *Kyle*

Ted Russell

Tall are the tales that fishermen tell when summer's work is done,
Of fish they've caught and birds they've shot, and crazy risks they've run.
But never did fishermen tell a tale so tall by half-a-mile,
As Grampa Walcott told last night, in the smokeroom on the *Kyle*.

With 'baccy smoke from twenty pipes, the atmosphere was blue,
There was many a "Have another boy," and "Don't mind if I do."
When somebody suggested that each in turn should spin
A yarn about some circumstances he'd personally been in.

Then tales were told of gun barrels bent to shoot around the cliff,
Of men thawed out and brought to life, who had been frozen stiff,
Of barkpots carried off by flies, of pathways chopped through fog,
Of Uncle Bill, who barefoot, kicked the knots out of a twelve-inch log.

The loud applause grew louder when Uncle Mickey Shea,
Told of the big potatie he'd grown in Gander Bay,
Too big to go through the cellar door, it lay at rest near by,
Until one rainy night that fall, the pig drowned in its eye.

But meanwhile in the corner, his grey head slightly bowed,
Sat Grandpa Walcott, eighty-four, the oldest of the crowd.
Upon his weather beaten face there beamed a quiet grin,
When someone shouted "Grandpa…'tis your turn to chip in."

"Boys leave me out," said Grandpa. "Thanks, don't mind if I do.
Well, alright boys, if you insist, I'll tell you one that's true.
It's a story about jiggin' squids I'm going to relate,
It happened in Pigeon Inlet in eighteen eighty-eight.

"Me, I was just a bedlamer, a-fishin' with me Dad,
And prospects for the summer were lookin' awful bad.
The capelin scull was over…it hadn't been too bright
And here was August come and gone, and nar' a squid in sight.

"Day after day we searched for squids till dark from crack o' dawn.
We dug up clams and cocks and hens till even these were gone.
But still no squids, so in despair we give it up for good
And took our gear ashore, and went a-cuttin' firewood.

Like other recitations there are many variations of this one. We have presented here the version found in Ted Russell's *Tales From Pigeon Inlet*, Breakwater, 1977. [Eds.]

"One mornin' we were in the woods with all the other men,
And wonderin' if we'd ever see another squid again.
Father broke his axe that day, so we were first ones out,
And as we neared the landwash, we heard the women shout.

"'Come hurry, boys, the squids is in.' We jumped aboard our boat,
And started out the harbour, the only crew afloat,
But soon our keel begun to scrunch like scrapin' over skids.
'Father,' says I, 'we've run aground.' 'No, son,' says he, 'that's squid.'

"Said he, 'The jigger—heave it out,' and quick as a flash I did,
And soon's it struck the water 'twas grabbed up by a squid.
I hauled it in, and what do you think…just as it crossed the rail
Blest if there wasn't another squid, clung to the first one's tail.

"And another clung to that one…and so on in a string,
I tried to shake 'em loose, but father said, 'You foolish thing.
You've got something was never afore in Newfoundland,
So, drop the jigger, grab the string, and pull hand over hand.'

"I hauled that string of squids aboard till we could hold no more
Then hitched it in the risin's and rowed the boat ashore.
The crews were comin' from the woods, they'd heard the women bawl,
But father said, 'Don't hurry boys, there's squid enough for all.'

"So Uncle Jimmy took the string until he had enough,
Then, neighbour like, he handed it to Skipper Levi Duff,
From stage to stage that string was passed throughout the whole night long,
Till daylight found it on Eastern Point with Uncle Billy Strong.

"Now Uncle Bill, quite thoughtfully, before he went to bed,
Took two half hitches of the string round the grump on his stagehead.
Next mornin' Hartley's Harbour heard the news and up they come,
In trap-skiff with three pair of oars to tow the string down home.

"When Hartley's Harbour had enough the followin' afternoon,
The string went on from place to place until it reached Quirpon.
What happened to it after that I don't exactly know,
But people say it crossed the Straits, and ended in Forteau."

Tall are the tales that fishermen tell when summer's work is done,
Of fish they've caught, of birds they've shot and crazy risks they've run.
But never did fishermen tell a tale, so tall by half a mile,
As Grampa Walcott told that night, in the smokeroom on the *Kyle*.

A Tall Tale: My Adventure with a Giant Squid

T. E. Tuck

The tallest tale I ever heard
I heard the other day;
Related by a fisherman
From out around the Bay;
And if he sees these lines in print,
Don't feel one trace of shame,
For, do not worry, Buddy,
I'll never tell your name.

In telling this adventure
While lying on his bed,
I listened like a little child,
And this is what he said:
I've done all kinds of fishin'
'Round the shores of Newfoundland,
There's no job I like better
Than a deep sea fisherman.

For there's all kinds of excitement
You are always gay and free,
And Oh! What ugly looking fish
You pull out of the sea.
I remember one fine morning
As I on the waves did float,
Seeing an ugly looking monster
Down underneath my boat.

I gently lowered the grapnel down
Towards its mighty jaws,
And all at once some lengthy arms
Were wrapped around the claws.
I pulled away with all my might—
To discover was my wish
What had devoured my grapnel
Such a monster looking fish!

I called for help with all my might,
Until my throat was sore;
I played my catch, for I was no match,
And headed for the shore.
Full speed ahead, my engine raced
My voice was but a screech!
When fifty fishermen, or more,
Assembled on the beach.

They thought, for sure, that I was mad,
By the way I heard them cry;
But I kept my engine on full speed,
And ran her high and dry.
I threw a line, they strung along
To pull with no retreat,
And when on shore, it measured
Just twenty-seven feet!

Some called it this, some called it that,
As it lay there on shore
But the oldest man that was on the strand
Never saw the like before.
"I've seen all kinds of funny fish,
All kinds of shapes and forms—
I'd call this one the Devil
But he has too many horns."

You may think that I am joking,
Or telling you a fib.
But what I really captured
Was a monster, a giant squid.
Now the men all got excited
Some came with axe and saws
To try and get my grapnel,
Embedded in the claws.

And when the arms asunder came,
And stretched out all their length,
My grapnel looked an awful sight,
For every claw was bent.
From tip to tip we measured
Those horns—Oh, what a sight!
One hundred and fifty feet, correct
If I remember right.

The people came from far and near
To see the giant squid,
Saying, you can make your fortune
If only you use your head,
So I then put up a poster
So as everyone would know
If they want to see a devil-fish,
It would cost ten-cents a show.

I collected fifteen dollars
From those who came around,
And later sold the whole darn works
To a business man in town.
He paid me fifteen dollars more;
Thirty dollars was the sum
I didn't make my fortune,
But I had a barrel of fun.

The people said they could not think,
Or at least believe their eyes;
That a little squid could grow so big
To such tremendous size.
But after we had the earthquake,
The squids got on the bum,
And I believe to God, with all my heart,
They were all knocked into one.

Advertisement from the Biology Department, Memorial University of Newfoundland, looking for specimens of the kraken or giant squid (1988)

The Terror of Quidi Vidi Lake

Otto Kelland

Now every pompous merchant,
And every Lew and Jake,
All jeered there is no terror,
In Quidi Vidi Lake.
Abe Bellman was a schooner man,
He saw the monster first,
When he visited his sister
To quench a little thirst.
He left her house at midnight,
And was walking up the road,
When something blocked his pathway,
That looked like a giant toad.

The night was calm and beautiful,
A full moon, brilliant shone,
You could count the leaves on every tree,
Both large and small, every one,
But an ordinary toad is tiny,
This thing stood fourteen feet,
Its head was easily two yards long,
With eyes as red as meat.
With long clawed toes so rapier-like,
And fiery, fetid breath,
That bayman was no coward,
But he shrank from certain death.

Now as the thing with scaly arms,
Reached out to grab the man,
He did, no doubt, what I would do,
Just turned about and ran.
And after record running,
He safely reached his craft,
But when he told his story,
His shipmates cried, you're daft.
Yet every little capelin,
Each salmon, trout and hake,
All knew there was a monster,
In Quidi Vidi Lake.

Laughed the mate, that 'shine your sister brews,
It sure must be mighty strong,
To make you see night monsters
That's more than twelve feet long.
Next day the story got about,
While Abe still suffered shock,
And he learned that on the waterfront,
He was the laughing stock.
A girl of sixteen saw it next,
But she would never tell,
For they found her torn body
At the bottom of a well.

And with the doctor's verdict,
There were none who could find flaws,
That the poor girl had been torn apart
By long and mighty claws.
Now every pompous merchant,
Each labourer and fake,
Thought, maybe, there's a monster
In Quidi Vidi Lake.
Then Inspector General Carty,
Sent two constables to guard,
The folks of Quidi Vidi
And patrol each lane and yard.

But at daylight next morning,
A man stepped through his door,
And found two dead policemen,
Each lying in his gore.
Both men's skulls were fractured,
And their flesh was ripped and torn,
Though gruesome as this is to tell
Some limbs from them were shorn.
That, the brave policemen fought the brute,
He had not the slightest doubt.
For chewed splinters from their batons
Lay scattered all about.
And those who'd heard Abe's story,
And who by much mirth were rent,
Now rose the bayman's stock up to
One hundred-plus percent.

Then the folks in every mansion,
And on every street and flake,
Were frightened of the terror
Of Quidi Vidi Lake.
So, promptly was a meeting held
And 'twas decided sure, that
One hundred men all armed with guns,
Backed up by a dozen more,
Would surround old Quidi Vidi
And sound the dying knell,
And for all time the village free
Of this monster up from hell.

Then the people got lightheaded,
And the whole place rang with cheers,
As from other places on the coast
Came ready volunteers.
For as the sun was setting,
O'er cliff and meadow green,
Twelve men from Flatrock hove in sight,
With twelve more from Bauline.
And Torbay sent three dozen,
Who were armed with guns and sticks,
From Bay Bulls and Petty Habour
There showed up twenty-six.

And from the city of St. John's,
There came a hundred more,
Determined that for those three deaths
They'd even up the score.
Now in those times long past and gone,
If disaster vile would feed,
Each neighbour travelled swiftly,
To aid in his neighbour's need.
Then three sarcastic braggarts
Appeared to view the throng,
Sneered they why this brave army
A full two hundred strong?

To slay one little monster,
Ye ought to be ashamed,
But if you're short on courage,
We s'pose you can't be blamed.
Go home me noble hearties
And sup your old maid's tea,
If this monster need a killin',
It can be done by we.
If yon straight gut a terror,
Might well be slain by three,
My friends will stand on either hand,
And slay the fiend with me.

Two hundred men, indeed, with guns,
Ye must be in your cups,
Then said a Petty Harbour man,
The monster might bring pups.
And if she brings her young along,
The Lord knows how many she's got,
It'll take every gun we got here now
And all the powder and shot.
To put an end to that creature,
If she's as big as they say,
Yer braggin' and boastin' is a lot of bluff,
So why don't you fade away.

Thus spoke the Petty Harbour man,
And scarcely had he spake,
When from the inky caverns
Of Quidi Vidi Lake,
There rose a slimy monster,
Whose eyes were flashing fire,
So overcome by dread, were some
They grovelled in the mire,
Now our three bogus heros,
Took just one fearful glance,
Then left old Quidi Vidi's shores
So swift, they shed their pants.

They ran so far and fast that night,
And covered so much ground,
No trace of those bold sneersters
Has ever since been found.
And now two hundred muskets,
Were trained upon the fright,
Then acrid smoke and orange flame
Were belched across the night.
And while the grand old village,
Lay buried 'neath that screen,
The blast from all the muzzles,
Was heard in Merasheen.

An asthma-plagued old-timer gasped,
And prayed there'd come a breeze,
For faith, quoth he, this gunshot cure,
Plays hell with my disease.
Now when the smoke had cleared away,
From every lane and house,
All saw the monster still alive,
And playful as a mouse.
And now it turned toward them,
Then straightaway climbed the bank,
While the stoutest heart among them
Just fluttered and then sank.

And with all hope near vanquished,
They saw the crowd divide,
Then through the ranks two clergymen,
Came on with fearless stride.
Now, the terror, paused right in midstep,
As she eyed the firm approach
Of the Reverend Mr. Hawkins
And the Reverend Father Roach.
While each a cross on high now held,
Toward this monster dank,
It screamed but once, yes screamed and died,
Then toppled down the bank.

And the waters of Quidi Vidi,
Were seen to boil and yaw,
Then the terror quickly vanished
Into their avid maw.
While men and guns against the foe,
Had been of no avail,
It had been demonstrated
That the Holy Cross can't fail.
Some lines ago you may have seen
I thrust all jokes aside,
This tale contains a moral
Whose strength I will not hide.
Perhaps I'm not a Christian man
But this advice I give,
When evil dark enslaves you
Look to the Cross and live.

The All 'Round Newfoundlander

P. C. Mars

Come! Listen to me, whilst I relate a tale that's never been told
About the Viking of the north—the Newfoundlander bold;
And search ye all this world around from Zanzibar to Flanders,
Ye ne'er can find the equal to the all 'round Newfoundlanders.

I'm told our Navy's famous for its hardy, handy men
Who are ready, aye! and willing to perform the work of ten;
But the man who hails from 'way up North, ah! who can tell his worth?
He's a natural Empire builder from the first year of his birth.

He tills the ground, erects his home, and fells the mighty tree
From which he builds his sturdy boat that rides the raging sea;
He's a miner, sailor, farmer and mechanic all in one,
And although his deeds are legion, to him they're merely fun.

As a logger, he's a princeling; he can drive a stream as well,
And often when he "Blasts the Jamb," he takes a chance on hell;
He's the devil in white water, when the logs go racing by,
He revels in the danger for he's not afraid to die.

He'll build a road, construct a dam, or drill down deep for ore;
He'll sail a schooner thro' dense fogs, e'en though the growlers roar;
God gave to him a wondrous skill, a fearless heart and brave,
And many a Northland sailor now fills a hero's grave.

He's trapper and a hunter and a sportsman all combined;
He's a marvel with sly foxes and furred game of any kind,
With dog and gun he'll trail for miles, and his bag he'll always fill,
Whilst he'll coax out "speckled beauties" with an angler's deadly skill.

He's a tireless packer through the woods, and on unbroken trails
He makes the stars his compass and his judgement never fails,
And if perchance a storm arise, he never shows alarm
For his trusty axe is all he needs to shelter him from harm.

He smells the storm signs in the wind, e'en like the "canny moose,"
With sweeping strokes he'll quickly lop large branches from the spruce,
Then blow ye torrents from the clouds and let the tempest roar,
He's safe beneath his shelter, and his camp fire's by the door.

He'll mush a dog team through the snow with the best Alaskan breeds;
As a sealer and a whaler, they must follow where he leads;
He's a genius in a motor boat, his engine always pulls,
And a piece of rusty wire does the work of twenty tools.

He's a sailor of the old school and a soldier of the new,
The Navy pays him tribute for his work upon the blue;
From sunny Egypt to the Somme he nobly played the game,
His deeds of reckless daring brought to him undying fame.

When Sir Douglas, his Commander, came to bid the last farewell
To the gallant Newfoundlander who had been with him through hell,
The great tribute that he uttered bore no idle thought or jest:
"Newfoundlanders! I salute you, you are 'Better than the Best.'"

When Banking Schooners put to sea and nose out through the fog,
You'll find he knows his business e'en to writing up the Log;
And with hand upon the tiller he will watch the billowing sails,
As he drives through the smother of the snorting Western gales.

When the International Contest was sailed to test the pace
Of the pride of Nova Scotia and the famous Yankee race;
Lo, the skipper of the Yankee hailed from North of Baccalieu
While the "Bluenose" beat to win'ard with a Terra Novian crew.

He's a serious politician, and when 'lection time comes 'round
As a thinker and a speaker, he can cover lots of ground;
And as for his religion, it's the essence of his life,
So he prays that God will guard against turmoil, care and strife.

I've known him now for many years—he's a white man thro' and thro';
He's a specialist in forty ways, and he'll always stick by you;
No duplicate of him exists; he's a specimen "most rare,"
As an all 'round man and worker none can with him compare.

And here's a toast I'll gladly drink to him, my trusty friend,
God grant that he may never change e'en to his journey's end;
And I'll raise my old Scotch Bonnet and proudly grip the hand
Of the best all 'round man on the earth, the man from Newfoundland.

(1924)

The Cliffs of Baccalieu

Jack Withers

We were bound home in October from the shores of Labrador
Tryin' to race a strong Nor-easter and snow too;
But the wind came down upon us making day as dark as night,
Just before we made the land at Baccalieu

We thought we'd make the island as we hauled her farther south,
As the gale from out the nor'east harder blew,
But the lookout quickly shouted, and there right dead ahead
Through the snow-squall loomed the land of Baccalieu.

It was hard down with the tiller and we struggled with the sheets,
Doin' our best to haul 'em in a foot or two,
And her deck soon sharply tilted 'till t'was hard to keep your feet,
As we hauled her from the rocks of Baccalieu.

Oh to leeward were the breakers and to win'ard was the gale,
The sleet and snow would cut you through and through;
With our lee-rail two feet under and two hands at the wheel,
We hauled her from the cliffs of Baccalieu.

The combers beat her under 'till we thought she'd never rise
Our main-boom was bucking nigh in two,
And all hands clung to win'ard and stared with straining eyes
Down to leeward at the cliffs of Baccalieu.

Oh, we hauled her to the south'ard and our canvas stood the strain,
As the whistling snow-squalls from the nor'east blew,
But our hearts were beating gladly, for no longer could we gaze
Down to leeward at the cliffs of Baccalieu.

My Political Career

Art Scammell

About 35 years ago I was teaching in a small outport in Newfoundland when I was suddenly catapulted into politics. There was an Orange Lodge in the place and thinking that by joining I could enter more fully into the social life of the community I sent in my name to become a member. I joined.

One winter night after we had finished our business we were all racking our brains for something to enliven the proceedings. In an unguarded moment I suggested that we hold a mock parliament. At that time political interest was very keen and everybody from the Master of the Lodge to the Tyler instantly showed great enthusiasm for the idea. We had a good crowd there that night and prospects of a ready-made political career without the bugbear of elections seized us. None of us knew the first thing about it, but being Newfoundlanders we were used to improvising. Never in the political annals of our country, or of any other country, was there a government formed in such a hurry, or with more disregard for parliamentary protocol.

The Tories were in power at that time so I was elected Tory Prime Minister by everybody, including the potential opposition, and given ten minutes to form a cabinet. The customs officer, a man of lion courage, boldly risked his job by agreeing to be Leader of the Opposition. In the fever of the moment we even forgot to enquire if he had been successful in the last elections. For all we knew or cared he might not have saved his nomination fee.

On my mettle, with the fate of the country trembling in my inexperienced hands, I hurriedly looked over my political material and made some split-second decisions.

"Uncle Bill Glover," I yelled, singling out the only man in the harbour who owned a codtrap, "you take Marine and Fisheries."

"Right you are, your honour," growled Uncle Bill, loosening his muffler and hooking a small squid jigger bottom up in his turtleneck sweater as a badge of office.

Henry Knight, the mailman, was a natural for Minister of Posts and Telegraphs.

Bill Searle was on the local school board so I made sure of our school grant by giving him the Education portfolio. For an amateur I was learning fast. I might want the school again the following year. After all, this political job mightn't last out the night. I noticed Bill combing his hair on the sly and putting up a hand to straighten a tie that he'd left home.

I asked the local merchant, Jim Squires, to be my Minister of Finance. Jim was pretty hard-headed about handing out favours, as he had to be to keep his business afloat in those days. At first I had been seriously considering Skipper John Parsons for the job. John was a Justice of the Peace and had some little means. But he was a bit too free for watchdog of the Treasury, I figured. He had a delightful habit of turning up at the annual Sunday School picnic with a huge bag of peppermint knobs and scattering them with lavish hand all over the 'green' to be pounced on by cheering youngsters. I saw in my mind's eye John's big, generous hand dipping, not into a bag of candy but into the government chest. I shuddered and Skipper John, J. P. became my new Minister of Justice. He would, I knew, temper it with mercy.

By this time my ten minutes were just about up according to the dollar watch given to me by the school youngsters at Christmas. I quickly completed my Cabinet and we lined up the chairs on opposite sides of the House. We had some difficulty in getting the members seated. Two members of the Opposition had already bummed a pipeful of Edgeworth tobacco each from my Minister of Finance, and my own Posts and Telegraphs was badgering him for money to buy a new leader for his dog team. Trying to live up to his new important role in the national economy, Jim had temporarily thrown off his strict business habits. He was promising loans, squaring accounts and generally heading straight for bankruptcy when the Speaker of the House, tall, slim Peter Courtney, the tidewaiter, called the House to order. And high time too. He just saved Posts and Telegraphs from giving away his job as mailman to Opposition member Joe Bursey who had been doggedly, but unsuccessfully, sending in tenders for it to the government for the past ten years.

I rescued my Cabinet and we squared away for debate. The Leader of the Opposition started off with a blistering attack on my government's agricultural policy, especially taking us to task for the bad seed potatoes we had distributed the previous spring. The pent-up resentment of months was in his speech and we had to sit and take it. Imagine my horror and consternation when I heard my Minister of Agriculture and Mines joining loudly in the "hear, hears" of approval. Big Jake Carroll had forgotten that that was his responsibility. He was remembering only the poor potato crop and the canker in the government-imported spuds that had caused it. I hurriedly scribbled a note and passed it along the line to him. He opened it and read, "Jim, shut your big mouth. In a few minutes you have to get up and answer that rat satisfactorily or your job is gone and you'll be back with an old black punt and a killick, trawling tomcods." That fixed the "hear, hears" from him. He got up in his turn and did a masterly job of justification for himself and us in his maiden speech, making up in vehemence what he lacked in logic. The Speaker had quite a job getting him to speak of his attacker as "my honourable opponent." Jim had some more colourful adjectives thought up and his cabinet colleagues were contributing others to him freely in loud whispers. But I was agreeably surprised by his political astuteness. He succeeded in shifting all the blame for the poor seed across the Gulf onto the Prince Edward Islanders.

"How was I to know," thundered Agriculture and Mines, "that our order for seed potatoes was going to turn out like that? I put in four barrels myself and you all know what I got out in the fall. Just enough to feed one small pig till Old Christmas Day. When I killed en he was so lean I had to go to the Minister of Finance there and buy good salt pork to fry en in. Didn't I, Jim?" This dire reversal of fortune enlisted the heartfelt sympathy of both sides of the House and Jake sat down, a martyr to Newfoundland agriculture, with his skin-booted feet fixed firmly on the first rung of the political ladder.

Foiled in their first dastardly attempt on us, the Opposition rallied their forces and attacked next our most vulnerable ministry, Fisheries. Uncle Bill Glover's face was getting redder and redder, I noticed, as he winced under the barrage of sarcasm and invective hurled against his department. His bonus scheme on vessel-building, the cull on fish, the bad drying weather—it was all blamed on poor old Uncle Bill, and my heart bled for the honest old sea dog who was getting hotter under the collar all the time. Two of my non-cabinet men were so overcome by the eloquence of the Opposition that they tried to cross the House. We yanked them back to the Tory bench after a miniature tug-of-war with our gleeful opponents and the debate went on. I tried to catch Uncle Bill's eye to give him a heartening wink but couldn't, as he was trying to shed his big home-knit turtleneck sweater with his pipe still in his mouth. Justice was helping him, but some hot ashes had fallen into the sweater and it was beginning to smoulder. All political differences were forgotten and the Speaker hurriedly called a recess until we could put out the fire in our Fisheries Department.

My Finance Minister took advantage of the diversion to confer with his Prime Minister, meaning me.

"Suppose they ask me to bring down the budget?" he queried nervously.

"Bring it down," I said. "It has to come down sometime. Might as well be tonight. Here, wait a minute. I'll scratch down a few figures on the back of this old school bill."

I hurriedly concocted some figures, giving Education a princely sum and earmarking it plainly for teachers' salaries.

"Better let the other ministers see this before the House resumes sittings," I continued. After all it would never do to have my own Ministers arguing about the budget after it was read and saying they'd never seen it before. I wanted to limit the argument if possible to what would come from the other side. Next I had a few words with Uncle Bill Glover and gave him a few points on answering the attack on Fisheries. Uncle Bill's sterling qualities were not what was needed in this game of mental gymnastics, and I knew his defence would not be a strong one. Suddenly, I heard my Agriculture Minister arguing hotly with Jim Squires, the merchant.

"Look here, Mr. Squires, I want another $100,000 to try out better breeds in sheep and cows. It's nothing out of your pocket."

Jim grinned. He was beginning to enjoy this. He had had to turn down Jake's request for $25 credit in his store the day before and it tickled him to hear Jake talking in the hundred thousands. He rubbed his chin reflectively.

"Well, Jake, I don't know. I might let you have $50,000 or so but I'll have to take it off somewhere else. Guess it'll have to come off Education. You know you didn't have that much to spend last year."

It was Jake's turn to laugh. "You should know. When I squared my account you didn't leave me much to spend."

After the House reopened, Uncle Bill handled the debate on Fisheries rather lamely and then we brought down the budget. Sniping from the Opposition couldn't have been more intense if the figures had been real.

Criticizing the Fishery estimates, one of our opponents wanted to know if there was anything in them provided for a 'groaner' on Jerry's Rock just around the point of the harbour.

"That sunker is dangerous," he emphasized, "I've struck my boat's skig there more than once."

Public Works came in for a flood of requests and Jim Squires had to keep revising his figures for that department to take care of wells, bridges, and wharves. He had to get the loan of another stub of pencil from Posts and Telegraphs, and the original budget made out on my used school bill had spread to cover a page torn from the Lodge minute book (the last one), the backs of four fish receipts (contributed by Finance) and an old Custom entry form (donated by the Opposition Leader).

It was 12 o'clock by the time we had all our paper used up and that was too late to start on the Dog Act, although the Minister of Agriculture, who had three sheep killed by Posts and Telegraph's mail-dogs, threatened to resign unless something was done. He was mollified by the promise of a job as messenger boy for his son as soon as the post became vacant and everybody heaved a sigh of relief. We were all exhausted physically and mentally. In my closing speech I struck a serious note for education, pointing out that every Newfoundland child should have the chance to be thoroughly equipped to discuss public matters intelligently and that I was sure the night's experience had proven this to be no easy accomplishment. ("Hear, hears" from exhausted statesmen on all sides of the House.) We closed by singing "God Save the King" and I crossed the House to shake hands with the Leader of the Opposition.

Lighthouse—Cabot Island c. 1917, 1978
acrylic on canvas, 18" x 24"

E. & S. Barbour Store, Newtown, Bonavista Bay, 1987
acrylic on canvas, 15 1/2" x 19 1/2"

Captain Carl Barbour (1908-1990)

David Blackwood

When Captain Carl Barbour passed away in 1990, those of us who knew him well and counted him a friend felt a great loss. He represented a vital link with Newfoundland's maritime tradition.

The Barbours of Newtown rank as the pre-eminent seafaring family of Newfoundland, producing ten of the province's leading sealing captains and numerous skippermen in the Labrador cod fishery. Captain Carl spent much of his life as a captain on various ships. His working knowledge of ships was phenomenal, reaching back to the great days of sail.

Between Carl Barbour's first painting, done in 1925, and his second, done during the 1970s while recovering from a shipboard accident, there is a gap of over 40 years.

The true naive painter often is interfered with by well-meaning individuals. Fortunately, Carl was never given a book explaining "how to paint waves" or "how to paint clouds." But like most primitives, he was sensitive to judgmental remarks about his work and told me that a friend didn't like his clouds. This might account for the blank blue skies which appear in some of his later paintings instead of his wonderful early cloud shapes.

Carl was quite taken aback by the term "primitive" used to describe his kind of painting. For him, primitive meant one thing—primitive. For every Bonavista North man, the word means something awful and Carl himself would have used it in a remark such as, "He made a wonderful primitive job, repairing that boat."

The highly respected Toronto art dealer, Doris Pascal, became very excited when she first encountered Carl's work in 1975. She immediately had visions of a very successful exhibition. But Captain Barbour was doubtful. He did not consider his work "professional" and was alarmed at the prospect of it going on public display in Toronto. Reluctant to sell his works, he had great difficulty attaching monetary value to them. A wedding present, a birthday gift, yes, but not an item for sale in the marketplace.

He had great curiosity about traditional materials and techniques of painting but preferred his own flat acrylic method, direct and free from complications. Carl Barbour's paintings are like the songs of the great blues singer, "the Immortal" Mississippi John Hurt, clear, simple, strong and beautiful. They represent a valuable addition to our total view of ourselves as Newfoundlanders.

Inuit in Labrador: The Old Way of Life

Brenda Clark

The Labrador Eskimos, or Inuit as they call themselves, are the direct descendants of the Thule Inuit, an Alaskan people who migrated into Canada and Greenland about 1,000 years ago. Archaeologists believe that the Thule people first arrived on the Labrador coast around 1400 A.D., coming southward from Baffin Island.

Upon their arrival in Labrador, the Inuit may have encountered the Dorset Eskimos who had been living on the Labrador coast for over 2,000 years. The Dorset people, called Tunnit in the traditional stories of the Inuit, were not related to the newcomers. The two groups had very different tools and house structures although they hunted the same animals. Archaeologists are not sure what happened to the Dorset people in Labrador or elsewhere in the Canadian Arctic. They may have disappeared before the Inuit arrived or the Inuit may have killed them or driven them out. Whatever the case, the Inuit have lived in Labrador for about 600 years.

During the early period in Labrador, 1400 to 1700 A.D., the Inuit population expanded as far south as Hamilton Inlet. Although they had no permanent settlements south of Hamilton Inlet, we know that the Inuit sometimes journeyed to the Strait of Belle Isle to trade, hunt and even to raid the camps of European fishermen, including the 16th century Basque whaling stations. At this time the Inuit had some contact with European explorers and whaling ships along the northern coast but this contact did not affect their way of life to the extent that it did in later times.

The Inuit travelled a great deal during the year seeking animals which were their sources of food, clothing, light, warmth and tools. Summer travel was either overland, on foot, or on the water using skin boats. The *kayak* was an enclosed, skin-covered boat which carried only one person. The larger umiak, an open skin-covered boat, could carry about 20 people. For winter transportation, a *komatik*, a large sled pulled by a dog team, was used. Dogs were an extremely important part of the economy. The Inuit depended on them not only for transportation, but also for help in the hunt and as an emergency food supply.

The sea provided many animals for the Inuit hunter. Seals, walrus, whales, cod, char and salmon were taken at different times of the year. Caribou, the only important land animals, were mainly hunted late in the summer. Birds, lake trout and berries were other sources of food.

A harpoon was used to hunt the sea mammals—whales, seals and walrus. This weapon consists of a blade of bone, stone, or in later times, iron, a harpoon head and foreshaft of ivory or antler, a long shaft and a sturdy line. Men hunted these animals by *kayak* during open-water weather and on foot in the winter and spring. When hunting larger seals and walrus in open water, an inflated seal bladder float was used to help drag the harpoon line as the animal attempted to escape. Large whaling harpoons were employed in the hunting of whales. Several hunters cooperated in the hunt and the *umiak* was used for their transportation in this dangerous pursuit.

Hunters also worked together on the late summer caribou hunt in the interior. Once the herd was located, several people, usually women and children drove the animals into a lake or river. The caribou were then slain from kayaks using pointed lances or with bow and arrow. A great deal of ingenuity was involved in the caribou hunt. Because of the large numbers of animals killed, it was important that the slaughter be convenient to the desired butchering and catching place. Therefore, the hunters drove the animals as near to the place as possible before killing them. In this way, the "meat" provided its own transportation!

The remains of Inuit fish weirs are often found at narrow channels in rivers and streams. The weirs are constructed of large, heavy stones piled together forming a trap for the fish, which will mill around a barrier rather than turning back. They were taken with a fish spear, constructed of a long shaft with a sharp point and two side prongs which had small barbs attached at right angles. When the spear penetrated the fish, the side prongs, held with sinew, flexed away from the point. Once the fish was firmly on the end of the spear, the side prongs closed together and the barbs helped prevent the fish from slipping off. With the aid of the weir and the fish spear, the Inuit family could take several hundred fish in a single day. These would be dried and cachéd for human and dog food the coming winter.

In addition to these and other hunting tools, the Inuit had a wide range of domestic utensils, including lamps and rectangular pots made of soapstone, the *ulu* or circular-bladed woman's knife, mattocks for digging and snow beaters for beating loose snow from clothing; these last two were often made from whale bone. One of the most ingenious devices was the bow-drill, used for boring holes in *umiak* and *kayak* frames and in such tools and weapons as harpoon heads, endblades, toggles for dog harnesses and needles.

The Labrador Inuit had three types of dwellings. During the summer they lived in conical skin tents. Large rocks weighted down the edges of skins. Hundreds of stone tent rings, left by the Inuit after the skin covering was removed, dot the northern landscape. Snow houses were used as temporary dwellings on winter hunting trips. The more substantial semipermanent winter houses of stone and sod were dug into the ground for added warmth. The entranceway was excavated approximately 20 cm lower again than the living area, forming a "cold trap."* The foundation was lined with large rock slabs and a framework was erected to support a skin lining and a sod roof. This framework was usually made of wooden poles if spruce was available; elsewhere whalebones, as shown in the [Newfoundland] Museum diorama, may have been used as rafters to support the roof. These houses were very snug and warm. Light and heat were obtained by burning seal oil in flat, crescent shaped soapstone lamps. With the addition of a rectangular soapstone pot suspended above it, the lamp was also used for thawing and heating food. The lamp was a woman's prized

---

* "Cold trap": this helped to keep the cold drafts in the entrance from drifting into the main room. When it struck the rise, or step, the cold air tended to circulate back out of the tunnel. The "cold trap" entranceway was a significant advance in arctic house design and gave the Thule and later Inuit a much greater degree of comfort than would have been known to the Dorset Eskimo.

possession, she took pride in keeping it filled and trimmed during her lifetime, and after death it was placed in her grave, with a hole neatly drilled through it, to allow its "spirit" to join her in the afterlife.

Labrador Inuit clothing consisted of a hooded coat, trousers (either knee or ankle length), knee high boots and mittens. Men's and women's styles varied slightly. Sealskin boots were worn all year round. In the summer the skins were dressed but in winter the hair was left on.* Winter clothing was usually made of caribou skin and summer clothing made of caribou or sealskin. Two layers of clothing were worn during the winter. The first was turned hair-side in to form pockets of air which provided both insulation and protection from dampness caused by perspiration. With the addition of a second layer of clothing fur side out, the Inuit winter dress was proof against the coldest weather. The beautiful designs on Inuit clothing were achieved by insetting strips in contrasting colours from various parts of the animal's body.

The life of the Inuit in Labrador during these early times reflects a strong relationship between the people and their physical environment. They depended on sea mammals and caribou for all their sustenance and worldly goods and thus required skill and suitable weather conditions on land and sea to hunt these animals successfully. Between 1700 and 1850 there were many changes in Inuit life because of their extensive contact with Europeans. Trading posts and the Moravian missions appeared along the Labrador coast making it possible for the Inuit to acquire wooden boats, firearms and iron implements as well as European foods such as tea, flour and sugar, thus reducing their dependence on their environment. Since the mid-19th century most of the old way of life has vanished. Firearms have changed the methods of hunting; harpoons were laid aside. Fur-trapping and trading with the Europeans became an important source of income and wage-earning jobs replaced their subsistence economy. Christianity, first brought to the Labrador Inuit by the Moravian missionaries, replaced the old beliefs. The tools, skin clothing and house styles common in the early period disappeared after the mid-1800s in favour of European manufactured goods and a way of life paralleling that of the European settlers. The Newfoundland Museum has created an exhibit that reflects a part of the Inuit lifestyle of the early period between 1400 A.D. and 1700 A.D. before many of these changes occurred.

---

* "Dressed skins": this refers to the practice of scraping the hair off the hide before tanning. The Inuit used dressed skins mainly for making waterproof boots and mittens, and covers for kayaks and umiaks.

Photograph of the "Kimatullivik Exhibit" at the Newfoundland Museum, 1998

The following are descriptions of some of the Inuit artifacts represented in the "Kimatullivik Exhibit" at the Newfoundland Museum:

Komatik – sled made from driftwood or other wood where available, tied together with skin thongs for flexibility. "Sled shoes," or runners, were of bones or ivory.

Harpoon shaft – the lower part was of wood, the upper, or foreshaft, was of ivory and was moveable.

Harpoon Heads – made of ivory, with a stone or iron point. When the animal was struck, the hunter pulled the line tight, causing the harpoon head to "toggle," or swing sideways inside the animal, which prevented it from sliding out.

Seal bladder – when inflated and plugged, this was attached to the harpoon line and provided both a drag to tire the wounded sea mammal and marker in case it dove or sank.

Snow beater – made of sea mammal bone, used for beating the snow off the skin clothing while in the entranceway to the house. If snow were allowed to remain on the clothing and melt, the hunter's only clothing would be too wet to wear outside, preventing him from hunting. Little housekeeping duties could mean life or death to the Inuit.

Common Threads in Inuit Culture

Enoch Obed

Culture is the sum total of learned ways of living built up by groups of people and transmitted over time from one generation to another.... I will attempt to be open with you as I reach out to you by trying to identify those goals, interests, activities and values in my Inuit culture which might be similar to those in your culture.

Inuit have a social need to control. We have a desire to influence others, to feel some sense of power over our own lives and to ensure that we have the ability to make things happen to improve our destinies.

Inuit have a social need for affection and respect which in turn gives us a sense to feel that people of other cultures will have some regard for us. We need to know that we matter to other cultures because our self-esteem is created and nourished by the respect and regard that others hold for us.

Communication in our Inuktitut language satisfies our practical needs to function every day. Our language is the key to our unique cultural and spiritual identity. Inuktitut is not merely a collection of words. It actually expresses our own cultural, spiritual, social and economic identity. It remains one of the ties that binds our Aboriginal history to our immediate present and future. Our language has withstood tremendous pressures from other cultures. The Inuit leaders have been wise enough to use the technologies of European races to preserve and advance our forms of speech, expression, and communication. We know that an inability to express ourselves clearly and concisely can prevent us from achieving our desires and goals as a self-determining people.

Inuit have physical needs for sufficient air, clean water, food, rest, decent shelter, and the ability to reproduce as a distinct human population. Inuit have always considered themselves as intelligent human beings fit to exercise their own legal rights of possession and occupancy of their lands and resources. We consider that our right of ownership comes through our historical use and from our Sovereign God—The Good Spirit of Life.

True Inuit are one with the land and its resources, and one with the sea and its resources. One of our ancient goals in life has been to become true human beings. The poet Goethe is true when he writes, "All human longing is really longing for God." The Inuit have come to believe in a loving, personal God.

The Inuit consider themselves true people who are able to enjoy their rights and liberties. Our Aboriginal right to self-determination is an inherent right which has always included the right to define who we are.

Inuit Aboriginal rights include the right to hunt, fish, trap and gather. The Inuit are skilled at hunting, fishing, trapping, gathering and making the different tools for their livelihood. These traditional means of making a living are supplemented with the wage economies of the communities.

Many Settlers have identified with and have taken on our Inuit traditions and language. The intermingling of the Inuit and Settler morals, values, beliefs and customs have enlivened and enriched the cultural dimension of Labrador. The Inuit have been clement, respectful and generous by recognizing the Settlers as having customary rights which will entitle them to share in the benefits of a negotiated land claims settlement with the Federal and Provincial governments subject to the Aboriginal rights of the Inuit.

The family is the foundation of Inuit culture, society and economy. Our social and economic structures, customary laws, traditions and actions recognize and reinforce the strength of the Inuit family unit. We need to have protection against threats to our well-being and to our family units. Only positive, constructive action by committed individuals and families can help recover our vision and zest for life. We must become willing partners in the solutions we desire to develop. We must, as one people, strengthen the fragile unity that binds and bonds us and act once more as one big family. Our very lives depend on the kinds of plans we initiate, develop and maintain in becoming whole human beings in our society.

Children are very important to the Inuit. Our Inuit blood, no matter how diluted it becomes, will ensure that our race lives on. Once our Inuit blood ceases to flow we will become a legend. The adoption of children whose parents have died or whose parents are no longer able to support or care for them has always been our practice. Those adopted children are accepted into our family unit as our own. For the most part, I believe that intercultural marriages have been good for the Inuit.

The practice of tracing family descent has always formed a strong oral tradition in Inuit life and culture. The oral history of the Inuit has been handed down from generation to generation. I'm pleased today that there is a strong resolve to write and record detailed accounts of family genealogies and to document our rich cultural history.

Our Inuit need for self-esteem gives us the desire to believe we are a worthwhile people. We have a need for self-actualization that in turn gives us the deep desire to develop our person to the maximum in order that we might become the best human beings we can be.

Migration routes and spawning, nesting, breeding, denning, calving and feeding areas of mammals, birds, and fishes, as well as species of plants, still determine where Inuit live and at what season. These influences still dictate how we as Inuit and Settlers maintain our seasonal way of life, which in turn helps to ensure the integrity of our land, resources and communal life.

Inuit music expresses emotions of love, hate, joy, sorrow, fear, pride and longing. Musical activities of our past include singing, throat singing, drum dancing, and drama with body movements. There were incantations to the spirits to have and to maintain good health, or the courage to face death toward the final end. Songs were sung to the land, air, wildlife, sea and good weather spirits to help the hunter search for food. Our spiritual leaders prayed and sang to evil or good spirits when seeking guidance and blessing. These spiritual aspects of our culture were brought into question by the early Christian missionaries. Our ceremonies and spiritual beliefs were considered not good and were discouraged and discontinued.

Our Inuit music and arts were enriched by the Europeans who taught us how to play new instruments and develop other methods of creating music and drama. Today more and more Inuit musicians are writing and recording songs in our language. Art and drama groups have done much to introduce certain aspects of our culture to other cultures.

Inuit and Settlers' arts and crafts are a functional and living expression of our cultural identity and traditions. They must be promoted and encouraged as a source of pride in our self reliance, skills, imagery and creativity, and as a focal point for our cultural history, our economy and creative activities.

Our arts, crafts and symbols are our exclusive property and must be protected from reproduction and mass production by non-Inuit. Control should be retained by the Inuit. The Inuit are beginning to maintain and promote quality arts and crafts as a means of economic activity and self-reliance. Inuit feel that the primary source of supply for our functional arts and crafts must be our natural resources and our craft producers and artisans. Part of the educational process must be to teach Inuit life skills, values, history, arts, crafts and all those things necessary for Inuit to maintain themselves their identity.

The archaeological artifacts of our lands and waters also belong to us. We want archaeological investigations to take place only after informed consent and subject to certain conditions placed by our regional Inuit organization. Archaeological artifacts should be left onsite and must not be removed without our prior, informed consent. If archaeological artifacts are removed they must be returned. We wish our dead to rest in peace. We respect their spirits.

Depiction of Inuit hunters

Inuit family in summer camp at the turn of the twentieth century

High Water, Eagle River, 1986
mezzotint, 48.25" x 35.75" paper size

The wildness and vastness of the landscape on the island of Newfoundland and in Labrador speaks to me more deeply than anywhere else I've been. This is my place. I am of this place and my work is a celebration of this understanding. I have lived and travelled in many urban centres over the last twenty-five years and, in that time, I have painted urban scenes, portraits and figure studies but it is my connection with this place that has drawn me back to the land.

The landscape has inspired and dominated my imagery since 1982. What comes through is the way I relate to the landscape. I am not a religious person in terms of man-made religions, but when I'm looking at the landscape I feel religious—totally humbled by that power.

My landscapes are devoid of humans. Newfoundland and especially Labrador are blessed for the most part by the absence of human interference; the main body of both places is untouched wilderness, untouched and unchanged from what it was millennia ago. All over the planet truly wild places like this are disappearing at an alarming rate. I feel lucky, if not privileged, to have spent the last fifteen years hiking, painting and fishing in these pristine wildernesses. With that philosophy, I do feel that my art is a quiet environmental statement.

It's hard not to make a pretty little picture of landscape. Mezzotints* help with their rich tonal qualities which have a visual pull that evoke a mood creating an elemental approach to the landscape. I'm always fascinated by the contrasts between black and white and the subtleties within shadows.

In everything I do, I try to bring to my work a real feeling—full of life—that breathes beneath the land's punished surface; not the animal life but the tangible personality of the land itself; something we understand in places like Newfoundland and Labrador.

– *Scott Goudie*

---

* Mezzotints are prints made from a copper plate which has been engraved through scraping and burnishing the roughened surface of the plate. [Eds.]

We, the Inuit, Are Changing

Martin Martin

We, the Inuit here in Labrador, right to this day still have the traditional ways of our forefathers. Right to this day we eat what our forefathers used to eat, food with no price tags on it, food created for us ever since the earth was created.

We, the younger generation, think we are hungry but we are not because there is plenty of the white man's foods available for us to obtain at any time. We only are hungry for wildlife meat because some years are plentiful and some years there is none at all. This I have found.

Our forefathers' ancestors, which we have just heard of but not seen, taught our fathers how to share any kill made amongst their people. So, my father taught me to share my kill as it was the traditional way. When I was a young man, every time I went hunting and came back successful I invited the poor, the less fortunate and the old Inuit to share my kill…. It is sad how this tradition is being forgotten. Young people now keep their kill to themselves. Some will give a little to those they wish to share with. I have said what I have seen and experienced and I am aware that this tradition is no longer practiced….

I am 100 percent pure Eskimo. I was never educated in the white society way because when I was a child this was not practiced. Our school term lasted only six months and our main subject was studying the Word of God. In this generation our children have almost a whole year to learn and study but they are learning only the white society way. No wonder they have a better knowledge than we, the elderly. I am not happy that they are only being taught the white society system. I would be happy if they were taught first the Word of God, then how to deal with life…. Our Inuit children are taught, I suppose, how to survive in white communities but not in the Inuit land. When learning the white society way was first introduced, or enforced, as a way of teaching our Inuit children, I strongly objected because I foresaw that in the future they would forget our Inuit language and also the Word of God…. I had no power to alter what was being forced on our children, my objections were not considered important. Now what I tried to bring to our attention about our children losing their traditions and culture is beginning to be realized by Inuit in different parts of Canada. All I have said is true. Our young Inuit have a completely new way of living and if it is let to continue, something will happen to show them they are leading a dangerous life. In such a short time, we, the Inuit of Labrador, have changed in many ways. We do not carry on many of our traditions. We are forced into many new ways which we do not even understand. Also in these days we have seen Inuit from other regions, those we had only heard about but we did not know if they had traditions and cultures which were similar to ours. Now, we see them in the flesh and see that our fellow Inuit share our traditions and cultures.

Last March, when I reached the age of 87, I started to think that I had lived too long. Then another thought occurred to me, why am I still living when I am no longer able to live off the land and sea? Why am I still wandering among my fellow Inuit and being observed and told that I am no longer useful to my people? I thought once more, the Lord God has been merciful to me to this day because although I am an old man I still have a mouth which can give guidance to our younger Inuit. The years have taken their toll on me, on my hearing, my sight and my ability to walk long distances. All are no longer good and I know why this is so.

I wish you peace on earth. We may never see each other on earth but through God's will we will see each other in Heaven when we are removed from the earth. So, let us look forward to meeting each other where there will be no pain or sorrow but happiness and eternal life. I am an old man now. My name is Martin Martin.*

I wish all a happy and successful life.

Martin Martin with child, Susan, and his wife Benigna, Nain 1922

---

* Martin Martin died in 1976. [Eds.]

The Northern Lights of Labrador

Don Fulford

I've tra-velled far by the Northern Star since the day that I was born; From the Car-ri-beans to New Or-leans, I've been in-clined to roam, And the beau-ty I've seen and the pla-ces I've been, I thought I'd see no more. 'Til I saw the lights that shine so bright in the skies of Lab-ra-dor.

Those northern lights that shine so bright when the night is cold and clear,
The snow is bright from the pale moon light and silence fills the air,
I cast my eyes to the sparkling skies and I can see once more,
Those northern lights that shine so bright in the skies of Labrador.

This place I've heard in every word is far away and cold,
But I have found in this beautiful town a treasure as rich as gold,
Those dancing lights with their colours so bright each night as I look through my door,
Those northern lights that shine so bright in the skies of Labrador.

Sometimes when I'm down and there's no one around to tell my troubles to,
I stroll outside and I gaze to the sky and I'm no longer blue,
The night is still as I drink up my fill as if I'd see no more,
Those northern lights that shine so bright in the skies of Labrador.

My time it will come like everyone when I must say good-bye,
I feel so sad as I look at the plane as it soars through the sky,
And I think of the time when I can say that I'll return once more,
And see those lights that shine so bright in the skies of Labrador.

Mother Boggan
Margaret Duley

Joel closed the door of his white-washed house and shambled across the meadow. As he went he plucked a taper of timothy hay, jabbing it between his teeth. It was the only way he knew of keeping his mouth shut. He was on his way to board his yellow dory and row out for a talk with Mother Boggan. The setting sun reddened her as a pillar of stone in the water with her face turned towards the horizon. More woman than rock she stood as a sentinel watching the fishermen return with the fruit of the sea. Clothed in her granite cape flowing to the water's edge, her under-skirts were of kelp, swirling like a frill. Mother Boggan's petticoats softened her Spartan figure, but Joel knew her bosom to be warm. After long sunny days he could lay his face against it and tell her about his day. The speckled hen had hatched out the gull's egg he brought from the woods, and the gull-chick was running around with the others unconscious of its difference. Annunciata Costello had sniggered at his offer of marriage, and his goat, Beaumont Hamel, bucked more every time he milked her!

Joel was the richest man in the village in actual cash, his wealth assured in the pension arriving on the second day of every month. Twelve O.H.M.S. envelopes every year, with a cheque of sixty dollars for Joel O'Toole! And he was little different at forty than he had been at nineteen when they thought he was fit to fight for his country. Except that he was lonely. Unhappiness was too definite a word for his natural state, but misery, a nag of shapeless misery, oppressed him when the sun didn't shine and warm Mother Boggan's bosom. Since his mother's death in July, 1914, she was the only person with time for his conversation.

Mother Boggan belonged to Joel. To the rest of the village, "she were a nasty bit of rock to run the skiff up agin." They were mainly concerned with getting their boats past herself and Mad Moll crouching in front. Joel hated Mad Moll. Snaky and slimy with sea-weed hair she slobbered all day with the water going over her head. The sea kept Mother Boggan clean. On violent days it leaped towards her face but Joel had never seen it go over her head. In a village where dreams and omens were all of the sea, the water mustn't go over the head. When it did the people walked dumb with foreboding, waiting for the sea to take away.

Joel walked on a road separating the beach and the sea from an arm of brackish water. The beach was built up with fish-rooms, high stage-heads with boats moored at the foot of ladders. On the stage-heads the fishermen ripped out the backbones of the cod, tossing them down to rot on the beach. There was a smell of offal blended with the clean tang of the sea. The arm penetrating the spruce-clad country, with its squares of meadow-land and potato-patches, was a glazed surface of black water. In the shade it was a deep ebony, turning iridescent where it held a sunset and an upside-down world.

Walking so far Joel turned to look. Chewing his cud of hay he yearned towards the world underwater. There was the sharp line of the hills, a green keel to keel and his own house with its bright red door joining the other in the meadow. It made him feel richer to see his two homes. Some day he would enter his house through the high polish of the black water. But now Mother Boggan's bosom would be warm with sun-fire. His round eyes goggled towards the sea, seeing a bright glow on his granite-mother. Spitting out his cud his jaw sagged in welcoming delight. He sprinted awkwardly over the beach towards his yellow dory.

Joel's mother had watched over him every day of his life until she died. Then they took her to a place where tablets were white against dark trees. Aimless and reckless, Joel wandered with as much purpose as flotsam floating on the waves. He belonged to no one, and he had belonged all his life. His mother had told him when to get up, when to go to bed, when to blow his nose, when to do simple chores, and when to sit down and rest by the fire. By some dumb routine of her nineteen years' direction he went on as she had taught him. But he had no stay: nothing to rest on. His mother was dead. If he met the slightest variation from the usual he didn't know what to do.

When his solitary state had increased his weaknesses, somebody told him there was a war on. It didn't mean anything to him. He would have been happy under any flag if his mother was with him to tell him what to do, but one day a man in a neat uniform took him by the arm and told him to come along and fight for King and country. He laughed for the first time since they had taken his mother up the hill. Somebody had told him what to do! He went gladly and submitted his body to unusual examination. They found it strong, and as his mother had taught him the difference between his right and left foot, they thought he was bright enough. He was content once more under constant direction, though it was not as kindly ordered as his mother's ways. Simple and stupid, he became the tolerated butt of his platoon. His own villagers thought he was "fair daft" to go off to the war. Several told him "he was after being a fool," and one had muttered, while heaving the fish up to the stage-head, "let de Kings and t'ings what made de wah, fight the wah." But Joel had given his guffaw of foolish laughter. He didn't know what he was going to fight for, but he was glad to do as he was told. He was sent to a barracks in the City, and across the water to another in Scotland. There he stuck closer than ever to authority, took no leave and spent no money. He was obedient to the letter, but no roistering companion could make him touch a sip of beer, or go where there were women. His mother had told him to stay clean and drink no liquor. When he got to France he was bewildered, but his first day under fire told him he would never be killed. He was doing sentry duty with his mouth sagging and his throat dry, when he heard his mother's voice, "Joel, come here; Joel, come here." Then more urgently, "Joel, come here." In responsive obedience he had stepped towards the voice and looked back to see a shell bursting where he had stood. Another time he didn't move quickly enough and a bullet went through his haversack. At Beaumont Hamel, where Newfoundlanders fell like ninepins, he couldn't be killed. His mother kept stepping between him and his falling companions. He could feel her skirts and smell the homespun of her dress. Whenever she walked through, the man next to him was always killed. The battle and carnage didn't bother him. His mother kept calling him to the places that weren't being fired over. He was the only man in France that the war didn't touch in some way, but when the Armistice was signed he went before a board of grim looking men, who found him a bad shell-shock case, and gave him a large disability. It resulted in his wealth. He went back to his house with the red door, and began to court the girls. He remembered enough from his four years' service to call his goat Beaumont Hamel.

He was twenty-four when he was demobilized, and he settled back as if he'd never been away. He ambled across the beach, went out in his yellow dory, and looked for someone to talk to. But he was lonely! Everyone was busier than he. In a village where a living was dragged from the sea, where the fish had to be split and dried, and the women worked in houses and gardens from daylight to dark, there was little time for one who didn't have to struggle for his three meals a day. Joel's wealth became well-known and its details established by the post-mistress. Prematurely aged mothers with seamed faces and backs humped from toil, told their daughters "that they could do a sight worse than marry Joel." But the daughters thought differently. As they reached marriageable age he proposed to them all, but one by one they married others who went to sea for their daily bread, and planted their bit of ground for their turnips and potatoes. There was no other man in the village with ready cash like Joel, but none of the girls could marry him for it. They went the way of their mothers and became prematurely aged. His proposals were accompanied by loud guffaws of laughter, and even a marriage of expediency was repelled by his sagging mouth. Then he began to boast and accompany his proposal with a formula, "I've got a house, a goat and a dory; sixty dollars a month; a meadow and an apple-tree." He never mentioned the hens, because they varied in number, but the rest of his possessions were always static. His formula became the joke of the village on the rare occasions when there was time for joking. Girls came to nineteen and twenty, and still more girls, but none of them would ever marry Joel. After each refusal he told it all to Mother Boggan. He began to ease his dory alongside, and talk his heart out to the woman in the granite cape. Mad Moll slobbered behind him, and seemed to remind him of his own sagging mouth. His own mother never came to him unless he was in danger. Only once since his return from France had he heard her voice, and that was during a thunder-storm in the woods. The lightning was playing about the tree-tops when he heard the unmistakable command, "Joel, come here; Joel, come here!" He had run from a place to let a tree fall without crushing him. But although he was safe, he shambled in loneliness, and many times he wished for another war to get in the sanctuary of direction.

Time passed. Season succeeded season. Fugitive summer followed bleak spring. Autumn gave itself with a fierce beauty to winter. Winter took the village and cased it in snow and ice. The sharpness of living touched everyone but Joel, and over it all thundered the angry voice of the sea. It beat against caverned cliffs and ran in foaming rage up the beach. Stage-heads were sucked back, fish-rooms disappeared, to be erected again in the spring with unquestioning patience. Nature found man puny, and reminded him of his state. While the rest of the village struggled, watching the sea destroy, Joel almost hibernated. He only left his house with the red door to go and have a talk with Mother Boggan. But many times she stood remote and inaccessible, doubly petrified in a cloak of gleaming ice. Then his mouth sagged further, and he huddled back to his kitchen and piled more spruce on the fire. He found himself forty, with new generations growing up around him. He was now proposing to the daughters of the girls he had known when he came back from the war. Somewhere in the thick spiritual sense of him, he was beginning to get very tired. Misery was a dull insensate thing with thin tentacles of pain. Every now and then he had a flash of sharp unhappiness, but it fell back to formlessness before he could shape it to his mind. He came to the day when he met Annie.

Annie was twenty: a little stout, with brown eyes and creamy skin like the underbelly of a Jersey cow. She came of respectable people who had kept the breath of life in their bodies by hard work. But her father had met three bad years, and his savings were eaten up. If this summer's fishery failed, the disgrace of the dole, and the dreaded spectre of the relieving-officer lay heavily on their minds. So far the summer had been scant in returns from the sea. There was nothing in the traps, nothing on the trawls, and little to hope from the hook and the line. Starvation or the dole stared them in the face. Their few vegetables could not maintain them.

Joel met Annie on the edge of a reedy lily pond during one of his aimless wanderings inland. It was a day of sharp beauty, clear light and bold outline of distant hills. As he parted the alders and saw the pond his jaw sagged in awe of the incredible beauty. One of his few streaks of intense living pierced the dullness of his brain. The slim reeds waved on the water in long lines of purple and green shading patches of lilies. Their white petals were flung open falling away from golden hearts. Piercingly yellow and waxen white they gleamed like solidified light burning heart shaped leaves. Annie was straining towards a lily just out of reach, and Joel tried to get it for her. He fell in to the knees with loud guffaws of laughter. Clumsily he splashed out and sat down with his legs stuck out to dry in the sun. But Annie was gentle and talked to him without a snigger. Insensibly his guffaws became less frequent and more modulated. He found he could tell her about his world of little things, and she had patience to hear of the gull's egg he had brought from the woods, and put under the speckled hen. The pond, the delicate beauty of the waving reeds, Annie, and the water lilies intensified his loneliness. His eyes grew rounder and he saw Annie wistfully.

"Marry me, Annie?" he asked without a guffaw. "I got—"

"I know what you've got, Joel. Don't tell me." But she said it without a giggle, or a 'get on with you' toss of the head.

He stared hopefully at her. "Marry me, A-annie?" he stuttered.

No fish! Nothing in the traps or on the trawls! Her father's face getting thinner and his stomach more shrunken. Her mother working her fingers to the bone, twisting and turning trying to make both ends meet. Already they knew the deprivation of vital necessities. It was the dole for her people with their simple pride in the independence they wrested from the sea! Joel whom no girl would marry! How impossible was it? Sixty dollars a month, and the amount he must have saved up! It was a fortune! She looked at the lily-pond and then she looked at Joel. His face was clean! His mother had taught him that, but his clothes were a mass of creases and some of his buttons were off. She raised her eyes hastily to his face seeing his sagging mouth and furry teeth! But Joel had never got so far before.

"Marry me, Annie?" he said with grinning hope.

"Joel, I, I—"

Joel felt like a man, he even snatched at her hand. His was clammy and cold with the nails almost bitten down to the moons. The clear health of her flesh recoiled. But her father and mother? If she could shut out the lily-pond with its pure white flowers.

"Marry me, Annie?" panted Joel. He was breathing down her neck, and she could see the awful wetness of his mouth.

"Joel, I-I-I—"

"Giv'us a kiss, Annie?"

She leaped to her feet and Joel stood loutishly up. He made a grab at her and held her arms. "Giv'us a kiss, Annie?"

That would tell. If she could kiss him without dying she could marry him! She closed her eyes on the lily-pond, and the kiss from the sagging mouth smacked from her chin to her nose leaving a wet horror. Her flesh crawled and she flung her people to the dole. Her eyes woke on the lily-pond and she knew the nature of defilement. She ran through the alders.

"Marry me, Annie?" shouted Joel.

"No, no, no!" A remnant of caution made her scream. "I'll tell you tomorrow night by the fish-room." The alders closed round her.

Joel sat back on the bank, and grinned at the lilies. He was going to be married, he was going to be married! Annie would have him, he knew Annie would have him. She hadn't sniggered and she talked to him like his mother. Tonight he would tell Mother Boggan, and her bosom would be warm with sun-fire. The formlessness of his mind blurred to a soft content. He was going to be married!

The setting sun poured a nasturtium red over Mother Boggan, and the grey of her cloak took on a glamorous richness. The sea was so calm that it didn't stir the frills of her petticoats. The edge of the shore held no line of white. All the men in the boats were squidding for bait, and the water was red with their teeming plenty.

Much bait and no fish, thought Annie, as she came down the hill. Some years it was all fish and no bait.

Annie lived on the other side of the arm away from Joel, and as she approached, she could see his house with the red door, and another upside down in the water. It looked a nice house under the water, a house any girl would be glad to live in. But it was like the lilies in the middle of the pond: something out of reach. It was a different house in the meadow with Joel as the reason for living there. She knew now what she was going to do to help her people. She had lain awake all night, and the pale dawn on the sea had brought her light for her darkness.

Joel was looking at Mother Boggan staring from an angle that hid Mad Moll. But even she wasn't slobbering that night, and her head rested quietly on the gray-green sea. In profile Joel's mouth was just as bad, and as he turned from his contemplation of Mother Boggan his eyes seemed so round that they couldn't close. She had the feeling that he slept with them open. He shambled towards her with a foolish grin, and they scrunched over the beach and stood in the shade of the fish-house. Annie stood looking at the back-bones of the cod-fish.

"Goin' to marry me, Annie?"

She raised her eyes. "No, Joel, I'm sorry." She was the first girl that had ever refused him gently. Joel's mind became sharper with misery.

"Not goin' to marry me, Annie?" he goggled.

"No, Joel. I'm going to the City in service. I can get a good place and I'll send money home."

"But Annie, I got—"

"I know, Joel."

"Y'couldn't do for me, Annie? No trouble t'you; shockin' lonesome; gettin' old. All the money for ye, Annie."

His eyes were a round emptiness of misery. Annie saw him pitifully.

"I'm sorry, Joel. Good-bye."

"Goin', Annie? Giv'us a kiss for good-bye now, Annie?"

"No, no," she said hastily. "Good-bye, Joel, good-bye." Her departing feet made hasty disturbance on the grey stone beach.

Joel stood leaning against the wall of the fish-room. He was still there when the red faded out of the sun leaving the world cold and grey. The sea kept spots of emerald where the water was shallow and opaque green where it deepened. The hills became hard lines against the dimming sky, and the black eyes of the caves peered out at the night. When Joel stirred towards his yellow dory the warmth had been drained from the village. When he reached Mother Boggan, she was grey stone; a hard woman with a cold bosom. He sagged in his boat and looked down at her skirts. Under the water they floated gently with tight sea-weed buds.

The sharp brilliance of summer changed to rain. The fishermen went to sea in yellow oil-skins and made no change in their work. The gardens had been parched for rain, and now they got it. In the strong excesses of nature it didn't know when to stop. For twelve days and nights it streamed down, and saturated the vegetation to damaging point. Growth came to the verge of mould, and green leaves were alive with snails. There were no intervals of sun. Perseveringly it rained in long straight lines, varying only to a slant when the wind changed. It filled the holes and hollows in the rocks and made puddles to dance on. The large surface of the sea, and the arm of brackish water rippled with the tread of rain, like a wild aquatic dance. Everybody was busy with the effort of keeping the scant catch of fish from mouldering in the fish-rooms. They were piled up head to tail, waiting for a break in the weather.

Joel's world was sodden around him. His fire-wood was always damp, his feet were wet, the goat's hair was dripping, and drops trickled on his hands when he milked her. The grass became soaked, and the tapers of timothy hay were beaten to a list. Mother Boggan had become a rain-woman, and no sun-fire warmed her bosom. All day he sat in his kitchen, in his house with the red door, and did nothing but the merest necessities of life. His formless misery changed to a wet wretchedness, but he didn't know what to do about it.

On the twelfth twilight the rain ceased, and if it had been dawning day the sun would have come through. A few gleams of hidden colour streaked in the western sky. The fishermen looked up and knew they could spread out their fish tomorrow.

Joel dragged himself through the meadow. His boots became sopping wet, but he shambled down to the beach. It was a washed world and the sun would have to be strong to drink the surplus moisture. Silently he unmoored his yellow dory and rowed out. The outline of everything was smudged, as if the rain had washed the hard edges away. He rowed between Mother Boggan and Mad Moll, and eased gently alongside of Mother Boggan. He shipped his oars, threw out his anchor and just sat. It grew dusk and he hadn't moved. A gull flew by and his round eyes followed it over Mother Boggan's head. He put out his hand and touched her grey cloak. Then he stood up and laid his face against her granite bosom. It was wet, wet, full of wet wretchedness, and all around him rolled the sea with a long oily swell. There was nothing but wetness everywhere. Miserably he put his arms around his granite Mother, and tried to press himself closer. He stood up on the seat of his dory to reach her granite neck. He put his face against it, and didn't know whether it felt cold, or wet, or both. Mad Moll slobbered a bit behind him: she seemed to be gulping down the rolling sea. He gave a loud laugh. Mad Moll must have a big stomach; his feet lost the seat of his dory and a screech came out of his mouth. Wildly he kicked with his arms round Mother Boggan's neck until the dory bobbed gently out of reach. He was panting, and his round eyes goggled and protruded. Then he heard his Mother's voice, "Joel, come here! Joel, come here!" It came from the hem of Mother Boggan's skirts. Then from further down. "Joel come here! Joel, come here!" His mouth changed to a happy grin and his round eyes smiled. The voice came again from below the sea-weed frills of Mother Boggan's skirts. "Joel, come here!"

The St. John's Balladeers

George Story

There are, I think, only four poets of Newfoundland who are mentioned in Klinck's *Literary History of Canada*. The first is Robert Hayman, Governor of the Plantation at Harbour Grace in the 1620s. His *Quodlibets, Lately Come Over from New Britaniola, Old Newfoundland* (1628) was the first book of original English verse written on—or, for that matter, off—the North American continent; and Professor Galloway writes of its "rustic urbanity" and a "general literary quality not equalled in Canada until the coming of the Loyalists a century and a half later."

Our second poet was George Cartwright, a member of a remarkable eighteenth-century Yorkshire family. A brother, John, who had a distinguished career in the Navy, spent several years in Newfoundland as surrogate in Trinity and Conception Bays for Governor Palliser. While still on the Newfoundland Station he brought his elder brother George, then an unemployed Army officer recuperating from his services under Clive in India, to the Island. His interest in the country aroused, George returned to Newfoundland in 1770 and settled on the Coast of Labrador as a trader. During his ten years' residence, he kept a journal which, published in three volumes in 1792, was admired by Coleridge and Southey. He also composed a long poem entitled *Labrador: A Poetical Epistle* (1792), which he addressed to his brother Charles. It includes, as far as I know, the only verse description of the cod fishery:

> The Codfish now in shoals come on the coast,
> (A Fish'ry this, our Nation's chiefest boast)
> Now numerous Caplin crowd along the shore;
> Tho' great their numbers, yet their Foes seem more:
> Whilst Birds of rapine, hover o'er their Heads,
> Voracious Fish in myriads throng their Beds.
> With these our Hooks we artfully disguise,
> And soon the glutton Cod becomes our Prise.

Professor Cogswell finds the poem "enthusiastic and charming," and "completely without that sense of bleakness and isolation in the landscape that some critics have seen as characteristic of Canadian writing."

Our third poet was Henrietta Prescott. She was the daughter of Admiral Sir Henry Prescott, Governor of Newfoundland from 1836 to 1841. Her *Poems, Written in Newfoundland* (1839) are placed by Professor Cogswell in the tradition of Mrs. Hemans.

And finally there is E. J. Pratt.

There they are, our four poets: one for each of the four centuries of our settled history. Contemplating the meagre list, any pre-Confederate Newfoundlander must have mixed feelings. On the one hand, there is irritation at finding our four poets of Newfoundland described as Canadian at all; and yet mixed with this there is equal irritation at the omission of local favourites. Suppose we ignore living Newfoundland writers: where in Klinck is Margaret Duley? A prolific essayist and writer of short stories, she also wrote four novels between 1936 and 1942, one of them a best-seller in the United States, and all of them skillful tales written with a remarkable blend of wit and poetic insight. A true professional. Among our poets, where is Isabella Whiteford Rogerson, our leading Victorian poet, and Michael Francis Howley, the accomplished sonneteer and verse translator? And what of Jack Turner's wry verses from the trenches in the Great War? But most of all, where are those several hundred poets of Newfoundland who will never gain an entry in a dictionary of national biography because the details of their lives (and sometimes even their names) have long been forgotten, and whose work has become part of a folk poetry and now almost inextricably bound up with the anonymous inheritance of traditional ballad and song? What we need, of course, is an essay in *The Literary History of Canada* entitled "The Newfoundland Poet."

For where else is verse so natural, instinctive and admired a medium, and the tradition of composition so active, that an accident, a ceremony, a remark, immediately begets a poetic epistle? Does the Protestant editor of *The Public Ledger* have his ears cut off in 1835 by masked men enraged by his editorials? A ballad on the subject is immediately composed by the Catholics of Harbour Grace and Carbonear. Does the last British Governor leave the Island in 1949 unremarked for his efforts to promote Confederation? A touching poem of praise appears in the correspondence column of *The Evening Telegram*, only to turn out to be an acrostic, the first letter of each line spelling out in bold capitals THE BASTARD. Even the most ordinary event will find an anonymous poetaster in the crowd who can be relied upon to take pen in hand and address his fellows in compositions such as this, from the work of a man known only by the initials "O. R.," whose verse letters were from time to time printed in the local press between 1900 and 1910:

His Excellency the Governor

Sir—
In a dull week,
Enlivened only by sundry comments in the press
Upon the appointment of Judge Prowse,
The dismissal of Mr. Byrne,
And the retention of Mr. Fitzgerald,
The opening of the Legislature by your Excellency
Has made something in the nature of a diversion.
On Thursday when I stood outside the Colonial Building
With a number of persons
Who were doing their best
To kill time
Until your Excellency arrived upon the scene,
I thought many stupendous thoughts.
In the first place
There was the constabulary band;
Fine fellows with fine uniforms;

And I thought their music excellent.
Then there were policemen on horseback;
Why should a policeman ride a horse?
And when one comes to think of it, Sir,
Why shouldn't he?
'Tis a poor age, your Excellency,
When one has to kill time
By thinking such thoughts as these.
But to business:
When a man in the crowd inquired of me
"What came you out for to see?"
I answered him softly,
"Sir, I have come hither to catch a glimpse of the Governor."
Said the person in the crowd:
"Is this a habit of yours?"
I answered him truthfully,
"It is."
"But," said the person in the crowd,
"You will only see him for a moment."
To which I replied,
"I can't help that."

. . .

I hope
When you again proceed to the Colonial Building
Some day soon,
To close the House,
That I may be there to see you;
In fact, I will make a point of being there.

This example from the correspondence columns of the local press, represents a tradition of topical, and often satirical, verse. Indeed, if reports of the proceedings of the Learned Societies are widely reported, we are likely to see them made the subject of further contributions before these meetings are over.

But the compositions I wish to speak about more particularly, while related to these anonymous productions in their topical subject matter and (to some extent) in the audiences to which they were addressed, can be distinguished from them by the distinct literary tradition to which they belong, and, frequently, by their mode of publication. These are the songs and broadside ballads which were still being composed and sold in St. John's within living memory, and have still not disappeared in the Newfoundland outports.

The golden age of the St. John's ballads and composed songs were the decades between 1850 and 1914. A literary historian of Newfoundland might almost call it, "The Age of the Balladeers." Two of the most recent of the balladeers were Dan Carroll of Patrick Street, author of "The Master-Watch" and other ballads, and M. A. Devine,

one of a famous St. John's family of poets and antiquaries. Some older members are: John Grace, a seaman from the Riverhead who wrote that loveliest of ballads, "The Petty Harbour Bait Skiff." Johnny Quill, a shoemaker at Maggoty Cove on Water Street East who wrote "Betsy Mealey's Escape," describing the adventures of a St. John's girl who was shipped one summer for the cod-fishery in St. Mary's Bay and who ended up being cast adrift in a dory on the ocean; John Doyle, another Riverhead man, was the author of the ballad "The Huntingdon Shore," and possibly also of the perennial favourite, "The Star of Logy Bay"; Johnny Quigley, a native of County Wexford and a carpenter, author of "Jack Hincks," but most famous for his ballad "John Picco," about the Newfoundlander who once turned Quigley from his door in the old days (not wholly gone) when natives and "strangers" were conscious of their differences. In the present century, Jimmy Murphy was one of the most prolific of the balladeers; especially famous were his songs and ballads of the seal hunt. But the greatest of them all, by common consent, was Johnny Burke, the Bard of Prescott Street.

Burke was born in 1851; he died in 1930. He was one of four children of a well-known sealing captain and mariner. Johnny, for all of his adult life, lived on Prescott Street, named after Henrietta Prescott's father, the nineteenth-century Governor. He was a grocer by trade, though the small shop at the front of the house always seemed thinly stocked. Johnny, a bachelor (like many of the Newfoundland balladeers), lived at the back of the store with this sister Annie and her numerous overfed cats.

Mr. Justice Higgins, one of our foremost authorities on old St. John's, recalls that if Burke's shop always seemed deserted, it was because the crowd was usually in the kitchen, for Johnny loved company and lived to entertain. His theatricals and concerts were famous in his lifetime from St. John's to Topsail. But it is his songs and ballads that have kept his memory green. His popularity was immense, and the advent of a new Burke ballad eagerly awaited. Printed on one side of a single sheet, measuring about five inches wide and twevle inches long, they were sold at Burke's shop for between two and five cents a copy, or hawked through the streets by urchins.

Burke's subjects were almost invariably topical and local. Although, I recall one ballad about a fight between some Newfoundlanders and Canadians in Halifax, but most of them were about local events. Thus he gave us "Terrible Disaster on the South West Coast: Lives and Property carried away by the Tidal Wave," a 1929 ballad which began:

> Attention now good people all,
> And hark to what I say,
> About this sad disaster
> That we record to-day;
> That happened on the Western Coast,
> Around that rugged shore,
> Where families were swept away
> To see their friends no more.

Even the south coast was far afield for Burke; his favourite subjects were the St. John's events and personalities of his day: "Water Street Disturbance"; "The Sealer's Strike"; "The July Fire"; "The Stoppage of Water on Monday, August 1st, 1927"; "The

Terra Nova Regatta"; "Who Shipped the Moonshine to St. John's?" and so on. Hard on the heels of an event would appear a Burke ballad to be eagerly bought and read by St. John's-men and by visiting outharbourmen (and thus circulated among isolated fishing villages throughout the Island) even in the days when there were a dozen newspapers to serve a small town. It is clear that, as late as the 1920s, Burke's ballads were serving as the news service provided by his sixteenth- and seventeenth-century English and Irish forerunners.

But Burke's ballads had an individual quality which makes them quite distinguishable from those of his Newfoundland contemporaries and predecessors. They are marked, for example, by an intimate knowledge of his society, and the fineness of his balance between identification with and description of that society. When a neighbour named Bride McGinnis, an early Women's Lib adherent, ran for public office, Burke wrote a ballad, "Vote for Bride McGinnis: New Moon Twice a Week and Spring Latches on Pudding Bags," which walks a tight-rope between satire and good-humoured sympathy. Nothing was too small to escape his notice—witness the ballads entitled "Mrs. Mullowney Was Three Weeks in Bed Since She Ate the Flipper Stew"; "Casey Taking the Census"; "Mrs. Brookin's Cat"; "Betsy Brennan's Blue Hen"; and "Mary Jo Slip Your Bloomers On" (a ballad about berry-picking). With the observant eye and ear of a village gossip, Burke missed nothing in a tight-knit community in which from every house you could either see or smell the harbour.

Some of it he transforms into little comic gems. Thus, a learned debate in The Newfoundland Historical Society on the site of Cabot's landfall becomes (in the ballad of that name) a mock debate among a group of St. John's-men as to who discovered Nagle's Hill up behind the University:

> Then up spoke old Bill Furlong,
> Saying this thing it is a joke.
> While a scramin' of his pocket
> For to try and get a smoke.
> Some men say 'twas Tommy Hurley,
> Others say 'twas Tickle Bill,
> But we know 'twas Tommy Littlejohn
> Discovered Nagle's Hill.

Like Trabb's Boy, Johnny Burke lurked for his contemporaries behind every corner, or walked intently behind and slightly to one side of his fellows, executing wild and exquisite parodies; and, when caught, turned an innocent, smiling face on his delighted victims.

In his best ballads, his style, so plain and simple in the ballads on news events, becomes rich in colloquial idioms, in images at once concrete and far-fetched, and dazzling in its delighted display of rhyme. There are especially good examples of all of these in the well-known ballad "When Your Old Woman Takes a Cramp in Her Craw, Give Her Cod Liver Oil." Burke glories especially in ridiculous catalogues of discrete objects. Here, for example, are some of the ingredients of "The Trinity Cake":

> Glass eyes, Bulls eyes and butter,
> Lampwicks, and linament too,
> Pastry as hard as a shutter
> That a Billy Goat's jowl couldn't chew,
> Tobacco and whiskers of crackies,
> If you like it or not you should take,
> Oh, it would kill a man dead, if it flew to his head,
> A slice of this Trinity Cake.

Or this, his masterpiece, "The Kelligrews' Soiree," which begins:

> You may talk of Clara Nolan's ball,
> Or anything you choose
> But it couldn't hold a snuff-box
> To the spree in Kelligrews.
> If you want your eye-balls straightened
> Just come out next week with me,
> And you'll have to wear your glasses
> At the Kelligrews' Soiree.
>
> Chorus:
> There was birch rind, tar wine,
> Sherry wine and turpentine,
> Jowls and calavances,
> Ginger beer and tea;
> Pig's feet and cat's teeth,
> Dumplin's boiled up in a sheet,
> Dandelion and crackie's meat,
> At the Kelligrews' Soiree.

And it ends:

> One-eyed Flavin struck the fiddler,
> And a hand I then took in,
> You should see George Cluney's beaver
> And it flattened to the rim;
> And Hogan's coat was like a vest,
> The tail was gone you see,
> "Oh!" says I, "the devil haul ye
> And your Kelligrews' Soiree."

W. H. Auden has somewhere remarked (I think in an essay on the *Illiad*) that a delight in cataloguing things is one of the marks of true poetry. E. J. Pratt was a schoolboy in St. John's in Burke's day; and it has sometimes crossed my mind that the Pratt of the "Extravaganzas" is, for all the world, Johnny Burke's true fellow-countryman—and fellow-poet:

> So to the distant isles there sailed,
> In honour of the ivy god,
> Scores of log-loaded ships that hailed
> From Christiania to Cape Cod
> With manifests entitled ham,
> Corned beef, molasses, chamois milk,
> Cotton, Irish linen, silk,
> Pickles, dynamite and jam.

Be that as it may, it was during those years around 1910 that a prolonged literary debate raged in the Newfoundland press on these very poets; and it led, of all things, to an essay in *Collier's Weekly*, entitled "Poetic Unrest in Newfoundland." "There is reason to believe," the writer stated, "that Newfoundland will presently produce as many poets to the square foot as any province in Canada." And then, he continued ominously: "A high critical standard is being formed." The evidence he cited for this were editorials in *The Twillingate Sun* and *The Western Star* attacking the "horrible compositions of James Murphy and his fellow versifiers." "There must be something about the condition of life in Newfoundland," one editorial mourned, "which prevents the blossoming of the poetical flower," and it concluded by recommending that the broadside ballads be used to hurl at the office cat. Johnny Murphy's reply was prompt and characteristically vivid: the literary productions of the genteel editor, he observed, "are as devoid of expression as the wooden Indian that stands before Jim Cash's tobacco store [on Water Street]."

I would not (if pressed) pitch the literary claims of the St. John's balladeers very high. But I wouldn't put them very low, either. Even the least gifted of them, Michael Murphy reminds us, have something of the joyousness of those old Irish village bards Crofton Croker described—scribblers with a vast fondness for rhyme, though with scant regard for syntax. Croker relates a story of the village schoolmaster who remonstrated with one of these bards about his grammatical constructions, and was answered with, and silenced by, the impromptu couplet:

> Who is Grammar?
> I say, damn her!

Many of them produced, almost miraculously, a few songs and ballads of haunting and enduring beauty. One or two of them—certainly Burke—created a considerable corpus of ballads which, at least for a St. John's-man, are as much a part of our consciousness and idiom as the greatest names in literature.

All of them provide an object lesson to the student of Newfoundland folk song who thinks that oral circulation of song is part of their definition. Maud Karpeles, the distinguished English collector who came to the Newfoundland outports in 1929, and whose last beautiful sheaf of traditional songs has just appeared, observes that:

> In Newfoundland, as in other parts of the world, singers do not distinguish between traditional and composed songs, and many is the time that I have tracked down a singer with a reputation for old songs only to be regaled with 'When You and I Were Young, Maggie,' or 'The Letter Edged with Black.' In

order to convey what I wanted, I used sometimes to explain that I was looking for songs that had not been put into books or that had no 'music' to them, which to the folk singer means the printed air. I was once caught out by this ruse: a singer, coming to the end of his repertory of composed popular songs, all of which I had rejected on the grounds that they were already in print, innocently remarked: 'Well, I can only think that some other young lady must have come along before you and got all the songs printed off.'

But perhaps the singer recognized what the scholar had missed: that the broadside balladeers and songwriters have in fact played a role, the importance of which is only now being widely seen, in the dissemination of folk poetry. The traditional songs and ballads of Newfoundland have been well studied; what I am suggesting is that this tradition should not be studied in isolation from the composed songs and ballads which are equally part of the popular culture; that in Newfoundland as elsewhere innumerable songs were spread through writing and reading (as well as orally), and that this strongly affected the oral tradition. The buyers of broadsides were, in fact, for the most part the very people on whose lips the folk song traditions were to be found. A composition such as "The Kelligrews' Soiree" is to this day sung by hundreds of Newfoundlanders to whom the name of Burke is as unknown (and in a sense as irrelevant) as that of the anonymous author of the traditional 'pure' folk-song "She's Like the Swallow."

The St. John's broadside balladeers provide another object lesson as well. In his now classic essay, first printed as the conclusion to *The Literary History of Canada*, Northrop Frye observed of Canadian writing that "even when it is literature…it is more significantly studied as part of Canadian life than as a part of an autonomous world of literature." If this is true, then the study of Canadian literature is incomplete without some recognition of the popular regional literature I have been describing, a popular poetry, it should be said, which is strikingly different in the experience it embodies from what has come to be the conventional reading of Canadian poetry. Perhaps we should add to this the suggestion as well that, as some recent folklorists and anthropologists (including one who works on the continuing Newfoundland outport tradition of ballad-making) have shown, the study of the song and ballad makers can give us important insights into the nature and functions of poets, and the making of poetry, in a society.

But I have gone on too long, and perhaps raised issues too complex to deal with on such an occasion as this. To Ben Jonson's remark that "a poet should detest a ballad-maker," Johnny Burke and his fellows would want us, finally, to answer in D'Urfey's comment a generation later: "The Town may da-da-damn me for a Poet, but they si-s-sing my Songs for all that." Either way, short, fat, merry-faced Johnny Burke could, perhaps, fill a chink in Klinck.

Betsy Brennan's Blue Hen

Johnny Burke

From the widow McKenny
I bought for a penny,
To lay a few eggs
    When the berries are ripe;
But some dirty crawler
From the hen house did haul her,
    My beautiful little blue hen did swipe.

May his whiskers turn green
When he eats a crubeen,
And may pork fat and beans
    Nearly make him insane;
May two dogs and a crackie
Eat all his tobaccie,
    The villian who stole my little blue hen.

Oh, this hen she had dozens
Of nephews and cousins,
The world round
    I would roam for her sake;
But some wicked savage,
To grease his white cabbage
    Walked off with my hen and my beautiful drake.

May her stockings fall down
When she goes out of town;
May the hair on her crown,
    She can't bob it and then;
May the girls from the Nor'ard,
Stick pins in her forehead
    The villian who lifted my little blue hen.

I bought from Port Saunders
That hen and two ganders,
But some dirty clown from my
    Hen house did steal;
My beautiful chicken I would have to pickin
On Christmas day for to have a fine meal.

May the ravenous baste
Burst her blouse in the waist;
May she not get a taste
    Of a dumplin or cake;
May a man from Freshwater
Go back on her daughter,
    That lifted my hen and my beautiful drake.

I would search the seas over
From Boston to Dover,
To find out the rover,
    And wouldn't stop then;
I would talk to Trepassey
To collar the lassie,
    Who pilfered my dear little beautiful hen.

May the measles and gout,
When he chance to go out
On his double chin mouth,
    Shove him down in the Pen;
By the curse of Belleoram;
May he never stop roar'n
    The villian who lifted my little blue hen.

May his pipe never smoke,
May his tea pot be broke,
And to add to the joke
    May his kettle not boil;
May he burst on cold tay
When he drinks any day,
    And his ton of foxey whiskers
May soon go to oil;

May his clothes be in rags,
And his trousers bread bags;
May he stagger from jags
    If he goes round the lake;
And may he have bunions,
As big as small onions,
    The scoundrel who lifted my beautiful drake.

Last Words of a Dying Man

Johnny Burke

> I'm dying, Kathleen, dying.
>> What was fading, now grows bright,
>
> Earthly dreams on me are flying,
>> Angels I shall see to-night.
>
> I'm dying, Kathleen, dying.
>> Now I hear one heavenly splash;
>
> I'm dying, Kathleen, dying.
>> I'm dying my mustache.

Excerpt from

The Report of the Chairman of the South Coast Disaster Committee, July, 1931

R. F. Horwood

To His Excellency, Sir John Middleton, Knight Commander of the Most Excellent Order of the British Empire, Companion of the Most Distinguished Order of Saint Michael and Saint George, Governor and Commander-in-Chief in and over the Colony of Newfoundland.

MAY IT PLEASE YOUR EXCELLENCY:

    By Resolution of a Public Meeting called by the Newfoundland Board of Trade, and held in the Pitts Memorial Hall, St. John's, on the evening of Monday, November 25th, 1929, under the direction of Your Excellency as Chairman, a Committee was appointed to deal with circumstances which had arisen as the result of an immense and destructive tidal wave which swept the South Coast of this Island, following an earthquake, on the evening of Monday, November 18th, 1929, in which twenty-seven lives were lost and property to the value of Four hundred thousand dollars, or more, was destroyed.

    The circumstances attending this disaster were most appalling. Suddenly, without warning, the ocean rose up and deluged the land, crushing the people's homes and their possessions in one common ruin for a distance of fifty miles along the coast. Forty towns and fishing villages, affecting a population of 10,000 people, were involved in grief and disaster. It was a time for action, a time for Newfoundlanders to show solidarity and sympathy, a time for service and sacrifice.

    It was under these circumstances that a Committee was appointed by this Public Meeting to deal with the conditions that arose as a result of what came to be known as "The South Coast Disaster."

Summary of
Highway to Valour

Lisa de Leon

Highway to Valour is a novel of dual romance both between Mageila Michelet and Trevor, and Mageila Michelet and her country. The story focuses on the life of Mageila shortly before and after a tidal wave destroyed her home and family. (A tidal wave did in fact hit the southern coast of Newfoundland in 1929; however, this story is not a re-creation of that event.) Mageila was the seventh daughter of a seventh daughter and thus possessed the mystical healing powers of such a heritage. Being away from home when the wave hit, she was spared while the rest of her family perished. The story develops around Mageila as she tries to regain her faith in a country, a sea, and a world that denied her a life she loved so well. Even though uprooted from her tiny, close-knit community, she never loses her desire to go back to a life of isolation and hardship, a life of simplicity where she can once again employ her healing powers on the rugged outport people who needed her.

Running parallel to this love is her love for Trevor, an Englishman, who almost displaces her strong country ties with his promises. Extenuating circumstances intervene and Mageila must make a choice.

Excerpt from
Highway to Valour

Margaret Duley

"What is it? What is it?" moaned Mrs Butler, and Mageila was reminded of second-meeting: rocking, rocking and singing of being washed in the blood, while the sea went on outside straining to reach the church.

"Just the sea, just the sea," she said, but she turned her back so that Mrs Butler would not notice her dread.

She knew it was the sea and something else. Now nothing could hold her. All the Butlers could die at her feet and she would still walk away to her own. If there was more, she must be with them when it came.

But Bertie Butler sat up like a small resurrection, with anxious deathlike eyes.

"Miss, what's that?" he asked fearfully.

Unconsciously delaying herself, Mageila put a firm hand on his shoulder. "Just the sea, Bertie."

"Tis loud, Miss," said the boy, imploring explanation with his eyes.

"But we don't know all of the sea, Bertie," she explained. "We never come to the end of the sea."

There was a wild roar and a pound as waves broke on the shelving rock.

"But it knows the end of us," muttered Mrs Butler with a hint of panic.

"I'm going," said Mageila without looking back. "Bertie, stay with your mother like a good boy."

"Yes, Miss," said Bertie, dumbly obedient.

It was on and over so quickly that she could never recapture the split second of infinite living. As she ran with down-bent head to challenge obstruction she collided with Mr Butler, charging with a loud "Lord Jesus!" on his lips.

"Inside," he roared, as if his frail dwelling could protect them.

Dumb from collision, she swerved but stood cloven to the rocks by what she saw. There was nothing in front of her but a wall of advancing water, and the awful clarity of her mind photographed the infinite grandeur of peril. The sea was upright, glossily taut and curved at the top like a reaping-hook. It was coming to take her, and she could not move; but even as she waited for the strike, she saw the wave break at her feet and spit in her face. Then it churned and boiled and receded, meeting another wave and propelling it back on the shore.

"Inside," roared Mr Butler, and she landed on the kitchen floor from the urgency of Mr Butler's hip.

Then the sea struck as noisily as a cannon, lifting the house with savage buoyancy and sweeping it inland until it toppled on higher rock. There was a sense of sucking round the house, of water sweeping in, of sea-strength being mustered for a higher life on its bosom. When it swept the house outward, they were in a boat that was not a boat and on a bottom that let in much water. Its icy feel round her body made Mageila leap with a wild sense of self-preservation. With the same mental clarity she saw Mrs Butler's open mouth, witless eyes, bare breasts, and arms relinquishing her child. On its way to the floor Mageila snatched the baby, then held it high on her chest. She saw Mr Butler seize Bertie with one hand and give a dislocating jerk to his wife's arm with the other.

"We'll ground agin, Miss. I've got the two of them. Can you leap for it?"

"Yes," she said, feeling a rain of objects falling round her head and hearing hot wood-ashes sizzling in the water.

They grounded and the floor felt ripped by rock. Mageila saw Mr Butler leap, dragging a grotesque woman and a limp obedient boy. But he went, seeming to fall into a foaming cauldron.

"Now, Miss," he called in a loud encouraging voice.

"I'm coming."

Self-preservation took her beyond herself, making the baby a featherweight in her arms. She felt the step underfoot, the cold air on her face; she saw the seethe of water, but she knew there was land. She went out high and wide and strong as an eagle. She felt the wild soar of herself and the strange primal exaltation of danger. She felt winged and beaked to help herself in the air. She remembered a dream of flying when she did not fall. But she did, terribly, shatteringly, crashing on rock, tearing her flesh, lacerating her knees as she made a last spurt to climb as high as she could. Then a spur of rock winded her and she lay gasping with breath that had to run out. She slumped face forward; but cold snow cleared her mind, permitting the effort of pushing the baby aside so that she would not lie on it. Then as if it was too defenceless she covered it with an arm, while all around her sea-sounds mingled with shrill human cries.

Letter to H. B. C. Lake,
Chairman, Earthquake Relief Committee, 1931

R. F. Horwood

H. B. C. Lake, Esq., M. H. A.,
Hon. Chairman, Earthquake Relief Committee, City.

Dear Sir:

Among the numerous claimants on the Fund controlled by the Committee of which I am Chairman, there are a number of cases that might be termed extraordinary because of the unusual and pathetic circumstances which mark them apart from the ordinary claimant who suffered property loss.

The principle which we have followed in the expenditure of this Fund is that of rehabilitation to fit the claimant for earning a livelihood. Most of the claimants present cases to which this principle readily applies, but the cases I am stating are those of claimants whose earning days are over and who must be cared for as dependents because of vital and property losses which they suffered in the disaster, and because of age or disability.

We should welcome the consideration of these cases by your Committee with a view of advising us what course might be followed, and for your better information I will give the circumstances attending each case.

1. This woman's husband was drowned in the tidal wave and she is left a widow with a stepdaughter, a daughter aged 11 years and two sons, one two years old and the other an infant. Her husband's property and fishing gear are left with an adult stepson to enable him to carry on with his occupation as a fisherman. As this case, with her children, will be a claimant for an extended period, and as the funds for relief must be expended and the work of the Committee terminated, it is considered advisable to purchase an annuity that would carry over ten years and with returns of $30.33 per month, with an expenditure of $3000.00.

2. This is a man of about 70 years old. He lost his dwelling, which it would be useless to replace for him. He lost his wife and four grandchildren in the tidal wave and his circumstances are such as will make him dependent as a result of the disaster. In this case it is recommended that the sum of One thousand dollars ($1000.00) be deposited in a bank in the joint names of the Minister of Marine and Fisheries (for the time being) and Magistrate Hollett, as Trustees for the amount, the Trustees to pay to the man such amount monthly, half-yearly or yearly as they shall decide in their discretion. Any balance lying in the bank

at the date of his death to be paid as he may direct by will, or in case of intestacy, to the next of kin.

3. This is a man of 83 years old. He lost a wife and all he possessed. He is not a case for re-domiciling and it is recommended that he get the same treatment as that of the case mentioned in paragraph 2, in the sum of Five hundred dollars ($500.00).

4. This man is 83 years old, crippled and, naturally, unable to engage actively in the earning of his livelihood. The recommendation is that a cash payment of $150.00 be made for his relief. He lost stage, clothing and fencing.

5. This man's estimated loss is $400.00. He is 52 years old, sick with T.B. for the past seven years, no prospect of working again. The recommendation is the same as that of paragraph 4, except that the sum be Two hundred dollars ($200.00).

6. This man lost a stage, store, etc., and was assessed $170.00. He has been sick for five years and is unable to earn anything. The recommendation is that a cash payment of $150.00 be made.

7. This man was assessed $742.00; his dwelling was damaged and he lost two stores as well as other goods. This man has been bedridden for seven years and can do nothing for his own support. A cash payment of $200.00 is recommended.

8. This man lost his wife and three children in the disaster, as well as his property, and since then he has been badly depressed in mind and affected by his great hardships. The Committee feels that every effort should be made to domicile him and for this purpose an expenditure of $1000.00 should be made, taking care that the title to the house is lodged in trust with Magistrate Hollett at Burin so that he may not be deprived of his property by any mistake of his own in selling or otherwise.

9. This man was a claimant on the Fund and, as such, had his dwelling restored at Burin, but he met with a second disaster in that the new house which had been provided for him was accidentally burned down and he became again destitute. A payment of $800.00 in materials is recommended.

It has occurred to us as a possibility that the funds lodged with the Earthquake Relief Committee might be found to be applicable to such cases and we lay them before you for the purpose of having your consideration in such cases with that end in view. The total amount of the claimants, as you will see, will be Seven thousand dollars ($7000.00).

Yours truly,

                        (Sgd.) R. F. HORWOOD,
                        Chairman,
                        South Coast Disaster Committee.

Included in the report was the following note:
The Government was pleased to recognize the worthiness of these claims and handed over the Fund to the Committee for expenditure accordingly. This expenditure has provided for these pathetic cases who would otherwise be unprovided for after rehabilitation had been completed.

Photograph depicting the tidal wave disaster on the Burin Peninsula, November 1929

The Recitation
Lucy McFarlane

It was December, 1955. An icy wind whistled across the Atlantic Ocean and blew whiffs of snow around the school. Inside, Fred knelt in front of the cardboard. Dusk was already casting shadows through the curtainless window and the wind rattled the pipes through the hole in the ceiling.

When the fire was lit, Fred pulled his oversized coat tighter and moved closer to the stove. He blew on his fingers through the holes in his gloves and rubbed them vigorously against his chequered jacket. He looked down over the neat rows of empty desks, the gray walls and painted floor and let his eyes sweep over the huge desk in the center of the room. A sudden gust of wind sent some loose ice clattering down over the shingled roof. Fred shivered and looked into the fire, but his eyes were drawn back to the desk again. A worn leather strap lay on top of a history book and beside it, a bell and a box of chalk. He rubbed his hands together again as his eyes rested on the strap, the memory of its bite still fresh from this morning's thrashing. Swinging around, he picked up the iron poker and viciously jabbed at the wood in the stove. He didn't want to think of her now. He just wanted to soak up the heat from the blaze. The thought of Miss Collier always left him cold inside.

Fred stood in front of the fire until darkness covered the small window above the desk. Slowly he moved toward the desk again, the sight of the strap rooting him against his will. His hand shook as he touched the leather. This was the symbol of Miss Collier's authority; the kind of authority that she had brought from the city. No one in their small outport had even questioned her power and aggressiveness, she was just there, sent by the School Board to teach in their one-room school. She had made her intentions known from the very first day. "I've been sent to this God-forsaken place to teach and that's what I intend to do! Just remember who's in charge here from now on!" she said, banging the strap on the desk.

Fred rubbed his fingers over the edge, feeling the worn leather, sensing the pain that it had inflicted over the past two years. He grimaced, thinking about Miss Collier, arm poised, bringing the strap down over the shaking palms of young girls and over the toughened sinew of half-grown boys. Tom had been her first victim. He wrote with his left hand, but Miss Collier insisted that he change to his right like everybody else in the class. Try as he might, Tom could not hold his pencil properly and each day Miss Collier would stand him in front of the class and strap his left hand until he could hold it out no longer. "Now, let's see if you can write with your right hand! Believe me, Tom, I'll do this every day until you can!"

Tom never learned to use his right hand and within a month, he had given up school to help his father. When Miss Collier received the note from Tom's father saying that Tom would not be back, she tossed the paper into the trash and said, "Some people are just not meant to be educated!"

Fred threw the strap back on the desk, sending the bell clattering to the floor. Why didn't Tom stand up to her? Why didn't Tom's father do something? Fred's thoughts flew back to young Jessie, who sat behind him in school. Shy and nervous, she would turn pale whenever Miss Collier would ask her to read aloud to the class. "You have to get over being shy, young lady. Hold your head up and speak out loud and clear!"

Every day Jessie would stand at the top of the school room trying to suppress the tears, shaking so much that her hands could hardly hold the book. And then one day the tears stopped and instead, her eye began to twitch. Over the year, Fred had watched as Jessie's face became a contortion of twitches. No one said anything about it and Fred just looked away when she spoke to him.

Fred gritted his teeth as he thought about the fear Miss Collier had spread throughout the school. He had seen some of the bravest boys cower in their seats whenever she called their names. Even Leo, the school bully who swore that he was not afraid of the Devil himself, paled every time he held out his hand to be strapped. It seemed as though she had spun a web of evil around everything—Fred could see it in her eyes. Sometimes he wondered what Miss Collier thought about. Often during school he'd look up quickly and find her beady eyes staring at him. He couldn't explain the sense of dread that swept through his body. All he knew was that it stayed with him in his dreams at night.

Fred moved closer to the stove and ran his hand through his short, curly hair. Even his hair reminded him of Miss Collier. It was just a few short weeks ago that she had suddenly come up behind him in school and without any warning, had demanded that he get a haircut. "I don't want to see you back in my classroom until you've had a haircut! Go home this minute and get those silly curls cut off!"

When he reached home, he had tried explaining to his mother that he had done nothing wrong, but his protests were pushed aside as he sat beneath the crude blades of her sewing shears. "You should count your blessings that you even have a teacher, young man! Do you know how hard it is to get a teacher to come to a place that's so far away from everything? You're depending on her, like everyone else here, for an education and you'll just have to put up with what she says!"

When he returned to school an hour later, Fred pulled a cap over his uneven hairline to hide the white patches of skin. Pushing the door open, he took his seat in the first row in front of Miss Collier. The scratching pencils stopped as Fred quietly took out his book. All eyes were upon him and he could hear Miss Collier take a sharp breath. He kept his eyes on his desk, not wanting to meet hers. "How dare you walk into my classroom without removing your cap!" she hissed. "Take it off this minute!"

The classroom was silent. Fred raised his eyes to Miss Collier's and they stared at each other for a moment. He watched the dark red colour seep into her huge neck. Her eyes narrowed to slits until it seemed to Fred that her face disappeared. All he could see were her eyes. The hairs rose on the back of his neck as she held his gaze and then, almost as though he could not control his hand, he reached up and dragged the cap from his head. Behind him he could hear Leo snicker and a few giggles could be heard from the girls. Fred's eyes faltered under Miss Collier's hypnotic stare and he tried to look away. He saw her mouth squeeze into a satisfied smile as she turned away without a word. Inside his clenched fist he felt the lead from his pencil dig deep into his palm and opening his hand, he let the pieces fall on the floor. Jessie scrambled to her knees and picked up the pieces. Fred ignored them as she tried to push them in his hand. When her face began to twitch, he looked away.

Fred shivered again and threw open the stove door to let the warm glow light up the room. The wind had quieted to a lull now and somewhere outside he could hear the thin, wavering howl of a dog. He pushed his hands into his pocket and a slow smile softened his face as he touched something cool. He pulled out a harmonica and held it in front of him. He blew a moist breath on the silver and rubbed it against his jacket until it gleamed in the firelight. Cupping his hands over the harmonica, he blew softly into the metal reeds. Fred played the notes of his father's favourite tune, "Oh, Susannah," and felt his tense body relax as he visualized his father's proud face when he surprised him. He had been practicing for months now, just so that he could find the right moment to show his father he could play. Fred tapped his foot in time with the tune, forgetting about the darkening shadows that crept in through the window, forgetting about the unhappiness inside him; he was living only for the moment, enjoying his solitude, his sense of achievement. Suddenly a voice from behind him jolted him. "Just what do you think you're doing?"

Fred jumped so quickly that the harmonica fell to the floor with a loud crash. Without looking up, he was on his knees reaching for the harmonica, but in an instant, Miss Collier's foot sent it hurdling down the aisle. "Stand up, Fredrick!"

Never taking his eyes from the harmonica, Fred slowly got to this feet.

"Just what do you think you're doing in my classroom?" she screamed.

"Nothing, Miss."

"Speak up, Fredrick, you're mumbling again!"

Fred kept his eyes on the harmonica. "Nothing, Miss," he said louder this time.

"You were told to light the fire, not entertain yourself! This is not, and I repeat NOT, a barroom!"

She was standing directly in front of him now and Fred could feel the moisture from her breath on his face as she spat out the words. He raised his voice as loud as he could and looked her in the eye. "It is lit, Miss. The fire is already lit."

She made a loud grunting noise and put her hands on her oversized hips. "And it's about time, too, Fredrick! There's only an hour to curtain time and the others will be here soon. Turn on the light!" she snapped.

Fred felt his face redden at the sound of his name. Miss Collier knew only too well how much he hated to be called Fredrick. He had not mistaken that pleased look on her face the first day of school when she called his name and everyone laughed. She had ignored him when he said that he wanted to be called Fred and when he had reminded her in private a little later after school, she had put her face next to his. "You don't like to be called Fredrick, do you?"

When he opened his mouth to speak, he saw her eyes narrow to slits and then steady themselves into a cold stare. Fred swallowed and said nothing and just before he turned away, he saw a flicker of something creep into her eyes. He wasn't sure exactly what it was he saw there—animosity, resentment, or maybe even hatred. Whatever it was, he felt it in every fibre of his body.

Miss Collier's voice penetrated his thoughts again. "I just hope you know your recitation for tonight! Remember, I will not tolerate any mumbling!"

Fred watched the fire cast a grotesque shadow along the wall behind Miss Collier. Her glasses caught the glow from the fire and Fred took a step backwards as she suddenly moved quickly past him. She stopped a moment and looked at him. When she got to the door, she stooped and picked up the harmonica. He could hear her heavy breathing as she laboriously straightened up, but he deliberately turned his eyes away. "I think I'll keep this for awhile, Fredrick. From what I just heard, you're not doing too well with it. This is such a useless instrument for a boy who can't even carry a tune!"

Then she dropped it in her pocket and walked out the door. Fred felt himself tremble with rage and throwing open the stove door, he thrust the poker into the flames until the heat from the iron burned against his hand. He felt the pangs of hatred churn inside his gut. This feeling had been festering inside him since the first day he met Miss Collier, but now he felt the rage inside him fight to get to the surface. How dare she take something that belonged to him! How dare she try to humiliate him by having him say a silly recitation that a child of six would say! He was fifteen now—a man, and he had his pride to think about. It was time that Miss Collier knew how he felt and he would start tonight! He would simply refuse to go on the concert and there was nothing she could do about it. But now was not the time to tell her. He would simply wait until his turn came and then calmly inform her of his change in plan.

Typical scene in a one-room school house

Feeling very confident backstage with the whole class around him, Fred walked back and forth helping prepare the stage for the first performer. He peeked through the curtain and watched the people file into the seats. He felt his muscles tighten as his parents walked in. He had not expected his father to be here tonight, not tonight of all nights! His conscience troubled him, for he did not want to embarrass his parents by making a fool of himself on stage, but yet, he had to prove to himself that he was a man. He dropped the curtain and feeling very much alone, he went to stand with the others.

Fred listened as the crowd clapped and cheered for each performer. Then Miss Collier was beside him. "Alright, Fredrick, it's your turn now!" she said. "I see your parents are here to see your great performance tonight. Your father should be very proud of you, don't you think so, Fredrick?"

Fred could not mistake that look of ridicule in her eyes and in a loud, clear voice so that everyone behind stage could hear him, Fred said, "I'm not going to say the recitation, Miss Collier!"

He heard her suck in her breath as she turned to face him. "I want you on stage right now, young man!"

"I said I wasn't going on," Fred repeated, trying to keep his voice very calm. "I just think I'm too old to say that recitation and I've decided not to do it, that's all, Miss Collier."

Before the words were out of his mouth, Miss Collier reached out and grabbed him by the arm, pulling him along with her as she walked. "So you think you're too old, do you now? Well, we'll see about that!" she hissed through her teeth.

In one quick motion, she waved for the curtain to go up and Fred found himself center stage. The audience quieted and the lights dimmed. Fred stared out at their heads, not knowing what to do. He cleared his throat and tugged at his starched collar and in one quick stride, he walked off stage. As the curtain swooped down behind him, Fred felt a sense of satisfaction as he strode past Miss Collier. Drips of moisture traced her top lip and she moved swiftly, planting her massive body defiantly in the doorway. "You won't get away with this! I won't let you do this to me, Fredrick!"

Furiously she pushed him toward the stage again, the force sending him staggering center stage. She yanked the chord from the curtain boy and before he knew what was happening, Fred found himself centre stage again. Dumbfounded, he stared at the audience as they looked expectantly toward him. He could hear a few loud whispers from below and instinctively, Fred's eyes sought his mother. Helplessly he watched her rolling and unrolling the bandanna in her hands, nodding her head as if willing him to start. Then a man's voice from the back shouted, "Come on, son, don't be shy now!"

The crowd laughed and Fred felt his ears burn with indignation. Fury welled up inside him and holding his head high, he walked off stage as the laughter grew louder. Young Jessie stood aside to let him pass and the others just watched him, not believing what was happening. Jessie ran after him and caught him by the arm. "Please…Fred, you've got to say it! You've got to go back out there…you just have to!" she whispered urgently. Fred pulled away from her as he saw the tears spring to her eyes. Before he could answer her, Miss Collier pushed Jessie aside and faced Fred. Purple veins pulsated along her temple and her face was dark with rage. He could feel her breath on his face, see her chest heaving with short asthmatic breaths. "You're not getting away with that, young man! Do you hear me? You're not getting away with it!"

Fred felt himself being forced against the wall and his arm being wrenched behind his back. He gasped in pain and tried to loosen her grip, but she grabbed him by the ear and pulled him toward her. He reeled forward as a searing pain shot along the side of his head, but Miss Collier didn't let go. She dragged him behind her and then, quite suddenly, she let go, sending Fred slumping to his knees. He felt his legs go weak as he collapsed on the floor and a wave of nausea gripped his stomach. Everything was so still that he could hear his own laboured breathing. Trying to steady himself, he put out his hand on the floor and got to his knees. Everything seemed faint and hazy, and when he finally could see clearly again, he blinked as he realized that all eyes were upon him. The curtain had gone up and he was center stage again.

Fred staggered to his feet, trying to quell the sick feeling in the pit of his stomach. The crowd began to whisper and mumble and Fred blinked, trying to focus on the faces below. Again Fred's eyes sought his mother's and he saw her cover her mouth and stand up. He felt confused, stunned and frightened and he pulled his hand against his face. When he took it away, it was warm and sticky with blood. He stared at his hand as the blood seeped slowly down over his white shirt and in a panic, he kept wiping it away. Frantically he looked for his mother, but she was not in her seat. He looked behind the stage and found Miss Collier staring back at him, her thick jaw set defiantly. Fred's eyes never left her face and then in a slow, deliberate movement, she reached into her pocket. For a minute, Fred's eyes faltered as he saw her take his harmonica from her pocket and hold it out toward him. And then it hit him. She had done this to him! He wiped at his face again and stared at his bloody hands. Over and over again a voice in his head told him that she had done this to him. He looked back into her eyes, half expecting to see some remorse, pity, or maybe even fear, but all he could see were her cold eyes, staring back at him.

She held out the harmonica to him again and he watched her thick lips mouth the words: "Say it!" Then she dropped the harmonica back into her pocket. Fred could see Leo standing behind her, mouth ajar, gaping at him, waiting for his reaction. When Leo realized that Fred was looking at him, he turned his eyes away and stared at the floor. Still standing in the center of the stage, Fred stood helplessly still, feeling an uncontrollable fear numb his body. Miss Collier's eyes bore into his, mercilessly cold, holding him in a paralyzing trance. Defeated, Fred felt the will to fight drain from his body. His mother and father appeared behind the curtain, but Fred turned his eyes away. He didn't want to see his father's face—he felt too ashamed, too numb. Nothing mattered now, not Leo, not the crowd below, not even his harmonica. Miss Collier had won and that's all that really mattered now.

Taking a deep breath, Fred stepped forward. From the corner of his eye he saw his mother move toward him and with all the dignity he could muster, he put out his hand and motioned her to stop.

He saw Miss Collier put her hand out to stop her. Closing his eyes to shut out the blurry figures below him, Fred opened his mouth to say his recitation. At first, his lips moved but no sound came out. He tried again. This time his voice was barely audible. The whole place became perfectly quiet as the crowd strained to hear what Fred said. Fred forgot about the people, he forgot about his parents; all he could think of was Miss Collier's recitation:

"A bob-bear sl-slept in h-h-his
bare s-s-skin
He f-f-found it ni-ni-nice and
c-c-cozy
But I sl-sl-slept in m-m-my
bare s-s-skin
Gee…I-i-i nearly fr-fr-frozee!"

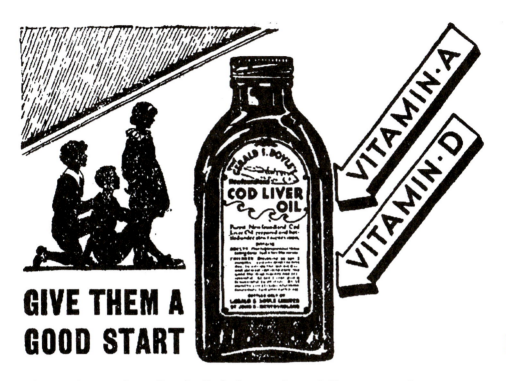

GIVE THEM A GOOD START

Sometimes the physical defects that follow an undernourished condition in childhood are outgrown — but not always. Why not make sure that your child gets an early start toward robustness? Cod Liver Oil is recognized the world over as one of Nature's most nourishing foods. Doyle's Pure Newfoundland Cod Liver Oil, because of its sweetness and purity and rich content of Vitamins A and D, strengthens growing children. Start your boy and girl on Cod Liver Oil. If a child is showing signs of malnutrition, such as frequent colds, coughs or sinus infection or other respiratory ailments, you will find Doyle's Newfoundland Cod Liver Oil most helpful in building up a strong resistance. Ask for

DOYLE'S NEWFOUNDLAND COD LIVER OIL

Advertisement from *Devine's Folk Lore of Newfoundland* (1937)

The Mummer

Tom Dawe

I was once the best mummer
in our cove.
I pleased the people
all the time.
And through the Christmas spell
I mummered by myself
across drifted fields
and tricky paths
above the cliffs
on raw nights
when sea voices whispered
in caves far below me.
I clutched my kerosene lantern
and felt my old accordion
wheeze against my ribs.
And in all those winter times
with my light coming to hers,
she always let me in,
though she never guessed me
and I did not lift my veil.
Not once did she guess
that all those tunes I played
of long-gone summer love
and never-forgetting
were just for her.
Though they danced and laughed
and shook the china on the shelves,
her youngsters could never know
how I played for mother alone.
Though they shone
with cake crumbs and syrup
on their happy faces,
I never played for them
in that salt-box house
where stove pipes cracked
and stars winked
on the snow outside.
And that big, lazy man she married…
least of all I played for him
snoring on the settle

in the chimney corner,
a red face so peaceful
with the tea-pot waiting
and long rubbers limp and steaming
by the blushing stove.
And in all those years
of forget-me-not tunes,
she never guessed me
and my veil stayed down.

Any Mummers Allowed In?

Bud Davidge

[Spoken]

"Don't seem like Christmas if the mummers are not here,"
Granny would say as she knit in her chair,
"Things have gone modern and I suppose that's
the cause, Christmas is not like it was."

[Knock]

"Any mummers allowed in? allowed in?"
(with ingressive voice)

[Sung]

Hark, what's the noise out by the porch door? Gran-ny, 'tis mum-mers, there's twen-ty or more. Her old with-ered face bright-ens up with a grin. A-ny mum-mers, nice mum-mers 'lowed in? Come in love-ly mum-mers, don't both-er the snow, We can wipe up the wa-ter sure af-ter you go. Sit if you can or on some mum-mers knee. Let's see if we know who you be. There's big ones and small ones and tall ones and thin, Boys dressed as wo-men and girls dressed as men, Humps on their backs and mitts on their feet, my bless-ed we'll die with the heat. There's

D.C.

Three Mummers on Winsor's Point, David Blackwood, 1979 , 20" x 32"

There's only one there that I think that I know,
That tall fellow standing over long side the stove,
He's shaking his fist for to make me not tell,
Must be Willie from out on the hill.

Now, that one's a stranger if there ever was one,
With his underwear stuffed and his trap door undone,
Is he wearing his mother's big forty-two bra?
I knows but I'm not gonna say.

"Don't s'pose you fine mummers would turn down a drop?"
"No! Homebrew or alky, whatever you've got."
Not the one with his rubber boots on the wrong feet,
He's enough for to do him all week.

"S'pose you can dance." "Yes." They all nod their heads,
They've been tapping their feet ever since they came in,
Now that the drinks have been all passed around,
The mummers are plankin' 'er down.

"Be careful the lamp, and hold onto the stove,
Don't swing Granny hard cause you know that she's old,
No need for to care how you buckles the floor,
Cause mummers have danced here before."

"My God, how hot is it, we'd better go.
I 'low we'll all get the devil's own cold."
"Good night and good Christmas, mummers, me dears,
Please God we will see you next year,
Good night and good Christmas, mummers, me dears,
Please God we will see you next year."

Excerpts from
The Winds Softly Sigh

R. F. Sparkes

Preface

Introduction	*What men or gods are these?* – Keats
Chapter 1	*I remember, I remember the house where I was born.* – Hood
Chapter 2	*Houses were built to live in.* – Bacon
Chapter 3	*And the Lord God planted a garden.* – Genesis
Chapter 4	*Of shoes and ships and sealing wax.* – Lewis Carroll
Chapter 5	*Whence is thy learning?* – Gay
Chapter 6	*O! this learning. What a thing it is.* – Shakespeare
Chapter 7	*What would life be like without Arithmetic?* – Sydney Smith
Chapter 8	*Let schoolmasters puzzle their brain, With grammar…* – Goldsmith
Chapter 9	*And the young and old come forth to play On a sunshine holiday.* – Milton
Chapter 10	*And they made it a day of feasting and gladness.* – Book of Esther
Chapter 11	*At Christmas, play and make good cheer For Christmas comes but once a year.* – Tusser
Chapter 12	*There is occasions and causes why and wherefore in all things.* – Shakespeare
Chapter 13	*On Sunday, Heaven's gate stands ope'.* – Herbert
Chapter 14	*What countless worshippers have sung in lowly fane.* – Hymn for St. Luke's Day
Chapter 15	*A man's religion is the chief fact with regard to him.* – Carlyle
Chapter 16	*Covering many a rood of ground Lay the timber piled around.* – Longfellow
Chapter 17	*Oh! this is the place where the fishermen gather.* – Scammell
Chapter 18	*I perceive that in all things ye are too superstitious.* – St. Paul
Conclusion	

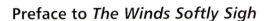

Preface to *The Winds Softly Sigh*

When I started this book, my purpose was to record for my children and their contemporaries some pictures of a way of life which has passed never to be repeated, in surroundings which have changed, never to be restored. I felt that it would be good for them to know something of "the pit from whence they were digged and the rock from which they were hewn."

The face of Youth is always turned to the Future and the eyes of Youth have the power to see beyond the far horizon the better world that they would build. King Harry was wrong when he said, "Old men forget." Old men must perforce remember, for when they have reached the three score and ten milestone of life, they may rest there awhile and look back over the longest part of the journey of Life and recall times, scenes and events. Youth has its vision of what is to be. Grandsires have dreams of the Past, and though at times, Youth may with heedless steps pursue its vision, is it not the duty of Old Age to show what lies behind? Thomas Hardy spoke well when he said, "If way to the Better there be, it exacts a full look at the Past."

I began this book then as a duty, but as the words grew into paragraphs, and the paragraphs became chapters, I found that I was writing for my own pleasure. I was reliving what I now know had been a happy childhood, passed in a pleasant place, among people who lived happy and contented lives and as I wrote, I seemed to recapture some of that feeling of security and sense of belonging which a child feels, though perhaps unconsciously, when he is a member of a loving family and of a community in which people live in harmony.

We in Newfoundland were, so to speak, late in entering the Twentieth Century. Whatever were the disadvantages attendant upon that tardiness, there were also many premiums attached. When the new volume of our history was opened in 1949 and we became citizens of youthful and virile Canada, the old way and time in which my generation had passed its youth was but a yesterday behind. It was still fresh in our memories. The new volume had been opened but the old one had not been closed. The story was there for any who cared to read.

It seems that not many did. Some few looked and, not liking what they saw, tried to tear out the pages; others made avid search for the ugly and unpleasant and, having found them, saw nothing else that was worthy or good. Surely, that is not the way to "exact a full look at the past." What we were is the origin of what we are, and our past, which included both "all time of our tribulation, and all time of our wealth," is now another scene in the tapestry of Canadian history and culture. It must therefore, however slightly, affect its colour and enrich its pattern.

There must be something of value in our past, some things worthy of discovery and salvaging, which might aid us on our way to the "Better." But old men and women die and take their memories with them. The years slip by and the past grows dimmer. The source of the stream of "what has happened" is fast drying up. If I have rescued some of the past, my reward is the richer.

Now that the book is finished, I hope that those who do me the honour of reading it will find pleasure in it, if nothing else. Some of those of my own generation, perhaps, will find their winds of memory softly sigh for the days that are gone. Some may accuse me of having painted a too brightly coloured picture because there is little of gloom or hardship in it. To those, I say that writing about the dark days of Newfoundland has, in my opinion, been much overdone and grossly exaggerated.

These pages contain a story of "humble livers in Content," written by one who lived and "ranged" among them. It is a story of a simple people who, though they had little of that which the sophisticated world calls "wealth," knew that "poor and content is rich; and rich enough."

To those who think that I have dealt too harshly with the present and too kindly with the past, I say that I am glad my childhood was spent in those days but I would not return to them if I could, and though at times I look back, I look forward as well, in the hope that Browning was right when he said "the best is yet to be."

Conclusion to *The Winds Softly Sigh*

One hundred and thirty years after our old ancestor had sailed his ship into the haven he sought, and founded the settlement that was to be our birthplace, my sister and I "sailed" out of it to begin a new life in a greater world. Could he have been there on that day he might have wondered at the steam-driven ship of iron that took us away. Boats moving without sails or oars, obviously propelled by noise, would have puzzled him. He might have doubted that the clicking telegraph key could really transmit words and thoughts around the world. So gently had Time dealt with his harbour that, apart from those strange things and the number of new faces, he might have picked up his tasks where he had laid them down, as if awakening only from a long night's sleep.

Fifty years after we sailed away, we returned to see what changes the long procession of the years had brought about. For one hundred and seventy-five years, the sea had been the only "road." We returned by motor car. Most of the old houses had disappeared and more modern styles stood on the old foundations.

Here and there were a few of the houses we had known when we were children, and their old owners, now well past their fourscore years, still lived in them, only a little less hale and hearty than when we knew them. One we found in his workshop making a pair of snowshoes, another was contemplating a trip to Greece and Malta where he had served in the Royal Navy in World War I. We visited two, well in their nineties, but still capable of taking a walk with swinging stride every day. The Psalmist to the contrary, their strength was anything but "labour and sorrow." They still tended small vegetable gardens round their houses, made their own jams and, so far as they could, refused to eat "that factory trash they be haulin' in by truckloads."

The one room school of our day had disappeared long ago. Now the grandchildren of those with whom we had toiled through Decimals and Practice and Vulgar Fractions, played their way through the New Mathematics with six teachers to help and guide them.

The "Aunt Ems" and the "Skipper Toms" who sang *Hymns A & M* so lustily when we were children had been a part of the dust of the cemetery for many years and a white-robed choir sang from a newer book in a larger and newer church.

The little grocery shop where once Skipper Ken had carefully and leisurely measured out a pound of peas, five cents worth of bull's eyes, with scoop, scales and weights, had given place to a self-service store where people bought pretty packages more often than they bought food.

In the houses, where once stood the water-gully with its bucket and tin dipper, was now a kitchen sink from whose shiny taps came both hot and cold water. Electric ranges had usurped the old Comfort and Waterloo stoves. With them had gone the woodbox and the settle, and a jarring telephone shattered the quiet of a Sunday after dinner.

No more did the population flock down to the Government wharf to see the coastal boat come in. Now, two or three came every week and there were no passengers to stroll around and stare at us quaint people and be stared at by us for the foolish questions they asked. Nothing now but freight, and that all in clearly marked and uniform containers; no boxes, crates and bales about whose contents we might guess and speculate.

The fishing boats were still there, but of the proud schooners only a few gaunt skeletons of bare ribs and broken keels lay rotting on the mud. The saw-mills were still there but gone were the water-wheels and the water turbines and the steam engines that used to power them. Now the smell of burning diesel fuel taints the fragrance of the new sawn logs.

The old lighthouse had gone, together with its old keeper, who, every evening at dusk, would climb its stairs and, with a stinker, light the lamp that would flash its warm yellow "Welcome!" to the entering ships. In their place, an electronic device switched on itself, and its cold, white light seemed to send out a warning, "Beware!"

As at the close of a bright and happy day we sometimes "with wistful eye pursue the setting sun," so my sister and I stood on Harbour Hill and recalled the days and the people of our childhood, now all passed into Time's great West of finished yesterdays.

When night fell, and the street lights came on, we knew that the twentieth century had come to our village.

Descriptive Passages from *The Winds Softly Sigh*

One of the saddest defects of today's society is the passing of the "home." A proof that most people now have no idea of what the word means may be seen in the advertising of the real estate agents who offer "Homes For Sale."

If you had the wealth of a Croesus, you couldn't buy a home. You may buy a house, or build one, but a home is something you create out of yourself, and money is no part of its fabric. The two words "house" and "home" are no more synonymous than "land" and "garden." A house, like a piece of land, is simply a bit of raw material. Add something of your heart and soul and in the course of time you may create a home or a garden.

If there are children in the family, the ideal house is an old one with an attic where there are closed trunks, boxes and bundles tied up with old string, where there are forgotten letters and cobwebs. What exciting times my sister and I had in the attic of our old house! One day I opened a trunk and among other interesting things, I found….

When a brash young dilettante asked the eminent painter John Opie, "Pray, Mr. Opie, may I ask what you mix your colours with?" he got the brusque reply, "With brains, Sir."

I have often thought that my great, great, great grandfather, and a few others like him, laid out their gardens in the same way: with brains.

He had left sturdy native trees standing in line of defence against the unkind East winds of Spring and the boisterous Westerlies of Autumn. To the North, broad shouldered hills, under a thick cloak of eternal fir and spruce, tamed the cold fury of the blasts of Winter. Then, having built the house and carved out the garden, they planted aspen and birch and mountain ash for ornament and delight and put in herbs and flowers for the good of both body and soul. Time and the loving care of women's hands did the rest.

When we were children the garden was indeed a lovesome thing. Great Grandfather's trees, their work well done, were slowly returning to the soil and little seedlings were creeping out into the sun and looking up at their parents reaching for the clouds. Caraway and tansy had long forgotten the hands that had planted them in clumps and were growing into thick hedges in which the hens hid and laid their eggs if you didn't keep strict watch upon them. In summer the grass meadows were lush and green and in autumn great piles of fragrant hay meant fat sheep all winter. The earth-covered cellar was a green hill of hops, source of leaven for bread, and I wonder how many gallons of beer had been brewed from the fruit of that granddaddy of hopbines.

When the rain poured down and all our world was grey, or when the drifting snow narrowed our world to the confines of the house, my sister and I found Grandmother and her chair an Eden of delight. With me sitting on her lap and my sister on her three-legged stool at her feet, she would take us into the land of fairies, of Jack-o'-lantern, of Tomassie the cat, of Peter Cottontail and, when her imagination flagged, she would tell us tales of when she was a little girl. I think that old lady knew every nursery rhyme in the English language. I took a great many of them very seriously and spent a good deal of time watching to see if a mouse would run up our clock. I even emulated that nimble lad who jumped over the candlestick, but I cannot remember having ever tried that walk to Babylon by candlelight.

Sometimes she told us stories designed to propagate Christian knowledge, moral rectitude and nobility of character. I clearly recall one evening when thunder roared and lightning flashed, that she told us the story of the wicked Bishop Hatto and his rat tower on the Rhine. All that night I could hear rats whetting their teeth against the stones.

So the timber for the house in which we were to be born was sawn and, with adze, axe and great jackplanes, the boards and beams were shaped. The groundpin and uprights were dovetailed and fastened together with treenails (trunnels) of pine and fir made on the spot. Holes for the trunnels were bored with a T-handled pod auger, a tool like a gigantic gimlet in that it had a long, sharpened gouge ending in a screw or "worm" to carry it into the wood. That tool was the ancestor of the modern and more familiar spiral auger. The expression, "back in pod auger days," meaning very old fashioned, refers to the time when pod augers were in use.

The boards were fastened with "cut" nails, more precious than gold because they had been brought from "Home." So the house grew until, finally, its roof was covered with shingles of pine and its chimneys were built from native stone, of which there was no shortage.

The spring rains, the gales of autumn and the freezing blizzards of winter would fall and beat upon that house, decade after decade, but through them all, the fragrance of a man's hearth and home would pour out of its chimney tops and through all those nights its windows would glow with the soft light of comfort and security within. Babies would be born in it and old people die in it as one generation succeeded another and, because it would know joy and sorrow, tears and laughter, the house would become a home.

When I was a small boy, our coastal boat was the *S.S. Prospero*. Every fortnight she came from St. John's and went on north to St. Anthony and across the Straits of Belle Isle to Battle Harbour, then she would retrace her route back to St. John's.

What a graceful and beautiful ship she was! Her all-black hull was relieved by large portholes with polished brass rims and her tall cowl ventilators were white with red throats. She had a transom stern, a raking stem with cutwater and bowsprit and tall masts. The funnel from which the coal smoke poured when her stokers fired up, was tall and slim with a broad black band at top and base. Stretched across the white in-between was the great red cross of St. Andrew, the patron saint of her owners, Messr. Bowring Brothers of St. John's.

An identical twin sister ship, the *Portia*, served the settlements along the south coast of Newfoundland. Bowrings always went to Shakespeare for their ship's names, but the Reid Newfoundland Company, whose smaller but otherwise similar ships served on the Gulf and the various bays, all bore place names of Scotland, the homeland of the Reids. The Company named its ships down through the alphabet, thus names like *Argyle, Fife, Home, Montrose et cetera* came to be household words.

Prospero's cook's galley was on deck amidships. From it the cooked food would be sent down by dumbwaiter to the serving pantry and dining room below. There were three long tables fore and aft in the beautiful mahogany panelled dining-room. Captain Abram Kean presided over the meals from the head of the centre table. Crusty old mariner he was; I assure you there was no tobacco smoking in that dining-room at mealtimes.

On the port side, between dining-room and the steward's pantry was the Ladies Cabin. I clearly remember once when I was four years old and travelling with my mother, that I fell and banged my head on its brass bound threshold. In spite of the first aid rendered by motherly Mrs. Cullen, the stewardess, I refused to be comforted and yelled several shades of blue murder. At last she went to the shop and brought me a bar of "Five Boys" chocolate and the pain disappeared as if by magic.

The *S. S. Kyle*, arriving in Newfoundland in 1913 from Newcastle-on-Tyne, where she was built

(untitled)
Rosalie Fowler

This morning I sat
indolent and limp
against a window pane
and watched a frantic sparrow
defying my lean cat.

The cat was taut
with leap and speed
and stealth and strength.
The bird had only poetry to wield
and lost.

Cats eat up grace with relish.
But they are poets too
and can create cunning
and flights of terror
with their eyes.

A small shudder
rippled down my flesh.

Do I have wings or claws?

The Tangled Forest, 1996
Hand Printed Lithograph, 4 5/8" x 7"

My work is the final stage of an event that goes through many changes along the way. I believe I am the recipient of the best and the worst of my art-making process, and the final material piece is a by-product, a testimonial of the journey, as it were.

I choose to live in remote wilderness places so the edge between myself and the world is more clearly defined. I observe the everyday transformation of the sea, the forest, and all that inhabit these environments. Subtly, all creeps into me and, while I choose traditional media, I allow what is in me out onto the surface. I experience what the process dictates and I work with whatever happens. Often in the past I was guilty of too literal an approach, but now I allow for the viewer to discover. Each piece reflects the season it was created, and portrays elements of the environment it was created near, but beyond that, my work is like a motion picture that takes me along as I work; it is new and fresh to me each day.

— *William B. Ritchie*

A Profile
Gilbert Hay

Inuit Art Quarterly

Gilbert Hay was born in Northwest River in 1951, but was raised in Nain where he now lives with his wife and family. Hay began carving seriously in 1972. Since it is his only source of income, he works at it almost every day: "I enjoy what I do. If I didn't, I wouldn't do it. I don't need any hassles from anyone and, as an artist, I'm my own boss to a large extent."

Hay has worked in ivory, whalebone, antler and soapstone, but prefers soapstone because of its price and availability: "It's softer than other materials and there's a variety of colours. It's cheaper and easier to get." He says that he never really knows what a piece is going to look like in the end. He begins each one by studying the stone and says that he hasn't got a particular style or favourite subject matter. "I have a broad variety of styles, suited to the customers' likes."

Hay, who is a past director of the Inuit Art Foundation, feels that interaction with artists from other cultures is important for the exchange of ideas and techniques. He has travelled a lot and has received grants which have enabled him to pursue his interest in other media such as printmaking, silk-screening and lithography. For these he must leave his community where such facilities simply don't exist.

Gilbert Hay at work on *Nuikkusemajak*, a soapstone sculpture, 1985 (completed sculpture to the right)

He has travelled to St. John's, Cape Dorset and even Montreal where he once took a six-month goldsmithing course with John Goudie, a well-known Labrador jeweller. Hay has also given workshops to children in Goose Bay and has had exhibitions of his work in St. John's and Calgary.

In March 1991, he received a scholarship from the Banff Centre for the Arts to participate in a five week session on neomythology. He considers that being in Banff was "almost like being in heaven." The contact with artists from all over the world, the intensive focus on artmaking and the availability of a wide variety of media caused him to take a serious look at his art and he started to wonder if he was "stuck in the stone age."

His travel experiences have all been very valuable to him: "I left Labrador to go around North America. Then I went home and found my culture. That experience enriched my art and brought me to a conclusion of a sort. Not every young Inuk can go outside and experience the world and learn to appreciate their culture and express it in their art."

Hay likes to hunt and fish when he can. He also raises dogs and is interested in traditional Inuit clothing. He learned to sew from his mother and has made kamiks, snowshoes and clothes for himself.

Hay says: "I have two different types of work: my own and what I can make a living on, the stereotypical Inuit art. I feel torn between these two worlds. I am raising my family and buying a house and also raising dogs and learning about the old-style clothing in an effort to keep my culture alive. I realize I'm losing something that is valuable. I feel I'm practicing my culture when I do my art. Everything happened very fast in Labrador. Dog teams disappeared in only two or three years. We got planes and speed boats all at the same time. Inuit art was sold to the South as a way for us to make cash, not as a presentation of our culture. We need the cash, but we have, simultaneously, to reach backwards and forwards—back to get a sense of our identity, and forward at the same time to connect with the rest of the world. Many Inuit are focusing on the cash and ignoring the potential they have in their art to communicate."

Tuckamore Festival of the Arts: Songwriting Workshop

Shirley Montague

It can be hard to imagine twenty students ranging in age from 13-18 and grades 7-12, participating in the same workshop. Though it did happen—honest!

In late April of '96 the first ever Tuckamore Festival of the Arts was held in the Bonne Bay area. There were forty different workshops offered including guitar playing, puppetry, sketching, and songwriting, just to mention a few. Many of the resource people came from the local region and students came from throughout the School Board area. I guess anything is more appealing than attending regular classes.

I was asked to conduct a songwriting workshop, and having facilitated one other songwriting workshop for a small group of students earlier in the year, I agreed to do so.

Students can be intimidating even to the most seasoned teachers. First, they want you to feel they're not interested, then they want to hide any interest that seems to be brewing. They then all want to go to the bathroom at the same time. Once they realized that, hey this isn't school, or we're not going to be graded or tested, and that they can all go to the bathroom at the same time, they began to participate.

After inquiring if anyone had brought any ideas and discovering none, it was time to post a few one liners on the flip chart to see if we could get anywhere near a song. Here were the starting points:

1. Why do you give your heart so easily?
2. I can feel the tension in the air.
3. Oh I had a dream last night.
4. Is that all you've got to say?

After they unanimously chose #3—"Oh I had a dream last night," we immediately worked on establishing a key and melody. Starting in a major key was definitely out of the question. I threw my trust and physical strength into an Em and 40 eyes lit up around the room. We were hopping!

We divided into two groups of 10 and the goal was for each group to write a verse. There were lots of giggles, a few paper airplanes and the usual. They were then left to their own creativity for about 20 minutes. Out of the corner of my eye I could see the odd relevant discussion. It was soon time for the exposé on the flip chart.

The song really began to fall into place. From that two-group session we had the makings of two strong verses. Together we worked on a chorus and another verse and completed the song, minus the fine tuning, ten minutes before closing time. Time for a few more paper airplanes.

Here's part of the result from the songwriting workshop at "The Tuckamore Festival of the Arts":

Oh I Had a Dream Last Night

Chorus: Oh I had a dream last night
And I hated you for spite
Saw you there in candlelight
Then I thought what a lovely sight

Oh I had a dream last night
About the feelings that I fight
Oh last night I had a dream
As I stirred in silent screams

Chorus: Oh I had a dream last night
And I hated you for spite
Saw you there in candlelight
Then I thought what a lovely sight

Though I found myself last night
Somehow something wasn't right
Though I found myself last night
I would change for you, I'd change tonight

Chorus: Oh I had a dream last night
And I hated you for spite
Saw you there in candlelight
Then I thought what a lovely sight

I feel pain deep down inside
Feelings I no longer hide
Oh last night I had a dream
Both confusing and serene

There is This Photograph

Carmelita McGrath

There is this photograph
taken when you were two,
or even younger;
certainly, your hair is full and thick—
no baby, you, no, a girl
staring confidently ahead;
in that second when the box caught you
you must have known
the focus of the world was on you,
only child.

That must have been
the slow summer of
1928; now,
sixty-odd years later,
it is where I go
to find you.

Each of us has touched that photograph,
has held it in careful hands, looked
into your straight dark eyes
to where the liquid light poured out;
we look for clues.

Someone asked me yesterday how you are.
I said, "Fine." I tell myself I have
this photograph; after that, something happened.

And, looking for you now amid the beds,
I learn that they have moved you,
and I consider going away
to the one sure place I can find you.

There is this photograph

of you in a cane rocking chair
one fine summer's day,
soft dress in photo is yellowgrey
small shoes extending just over
the seat, the rocker perched on stones
hauled from the beach. Behind your house
the sunlight was trapped below the hill
where the shadow of the cellar
missed the path
and the bees went cracked among the columbine.

You say you have worn holes
in your memory, can't construct
the whole picture. I have one
of a girl who is so whole and strong
that, if mercy holds, she will bring you back
to who you were; if luck is with you,
perhaps she Inhabits you still.

Percy Janes Boarding the Bus

Agnes Walsh

I was going to the Mall for a kettle
waiting on the number five,
when the number something-or-other
pulled up.

I was looking past it for mine,
when I saw him, an arm raised,
running softly.

I jumped to life, beat on the bus door,
said to the driver: "Mr. Janes.
Mr. Percy Janes wants to get on."

He raised a "So what?" eyebrow.

Mr. Janes straightened his astrakhan hat,
mumbled thank you and stepped up.
As the bus rumbled on
I continued under my breath:
"Ladies and gentleman, Mr. Percy Janes,
Newfoundland writer, poet,
just boarded the number something-or-other."

If this was Portugal,
a plaque would be placed
over the seat where he sat.

As it is, you have me
mumbling in the street
like a tourist in my own country.

Beneath the Dust and Stars

Boyd Chubbs

I embrace a wind and memory begins. A bell calls against the hill, around the harbour, announcing the carolled season. In the old church of St. Andrew's, beneath the depth and tongue of its timbers, I hear the tough breathing of organ bellows begin to warm with the psalms and molten voices around, across the stove, lifting the celebrationals, heralding the child and wonder.

O little town of L'Anse Au Clair, blood thunders through the memory veins, drives through the mouth and stays upon doors and prayers, layers and layers of pictures in the head: Mother with her hymns and miracles of berries and bread; Father on a bench, calling our names, waiting as the paper fell and the unwrapped jewels became a spell for the day and years.

Those are the gifts never lost or traded, precious gifts from the winter-coast, beneath that drenched Labrador sky, beneath that startling, dancing fresco of stars and dust, upon the beds of snow, massive constellations of the white rose come to earth where I hid and counted everything through the vital ribbon of hours: woodsmoke, chiselled links to heaven; purled labyrinths of frost in dense riddles upon the windows; laughter left from the long summer; tunnels and towers in the banks and mounds and slumbers; games without numbers; breath rhythms from dogs and other figures, where they passed the night around; low whispers of love and young committments; caravans of cinnamon, spruce and apple; fabled jesters making the cupboards rattle; spirituals from the kitchen remembrance and ovens of bread through the drumming heart and carnival head when such a gifted Eve happened.

> There, beneath the dust and stars
> in my ecstatic hiding
> I knew if I could stay forever
> I would see the reindeer riding

Teenagers

Aubrey M. Tizzard

There were several special interests which I recall as a young lad. These were special because for us there was a lot of fun. The first thing I suppose of interest to many people would be the teenage situation in a small village. For many years I went to church with my mother and father and older sisters. First my elder sister Eleanor broke away from the family when we left the church on Sunday evening and joined the crowd of teenagers that would walk the roads for a while and then sit on the Orange Hall steps or on some grassy dry mound. Then my sister Vina one Sunday evening coming from church broke away to join other teenagers; by this time, of course, my sister Eleanor had been going with a young man for a while, that is he had been walking her home but never came in house with her. In house, meant that the young man would walk the lady home and they would go in house together. After a little while the parents or guardian of the young lady would go to bed and leave the young couple alone with the lamp burning on the table. The first thing after the parents had gone to bed if it had not already been done was to get a lunch. A lunch would be bread and tea and raisin buns or sweet molasses cake. After the lunch the lamp would be turned down very low and sometimes the flame would be put out altogether and the couple would be courting in the dark for a few hours, maybe until around three o'clock in the morning. The parents would have been in bed by at least ten o'clock, so this would mean that the couple would spend five hours alone. That time would be usually spent lying on the couch in the kitchen; in the kitchen because no other room was available for such a meeting place, especially during the winter months. What happened on many occasions was the couple would lie on the couch and they would become so much involved in lovemaking or courting the fire in the stove would burn out and when no more wood was added, the house became cold and sort of forced the couple to part for the night, the young lady going to her cold bed and the young man going out to face the cold as he walked home. Courting was usually confined to two nights a week, Wednesday night and Sunday night....

I guess my love career was the most jumpy of all. I recall very vividly the first Sunday evening when I broke away from the family. We left the church together, that is, my mother, father and I; we walked to the main country road, which is about a hundred yards from the church. There they turned to the left toward home and I turned to the right—up the road. For awhile we walked the road up so far then back again, until the older folks had all gone home. 'We' means several boys around my age and older. After walking for awhile we sat on the Orange Hall steps; there were several boys and girls there. Some were already paired up or had been dating for some time, and others were anticipating the opportunity of walking someone home or being walked home by someone. I used the word 'dating,' but that was not really the word used, it should have been 'going out with.' 'Courting' was used occasionally but it was more or less

---

The setting of this essay is outport Newfoundland of the 1930s.

used in a hushed tone of voice. The interesting thing about 'going up the road' was that you could walk the road between Paul Rodgers' in Salt Pans (Hillgrade) and Reuben Adams' in Squid Cove, a distance of little more than a mile, and would rarely be seen because there were no houses on that stretch of road. No one couple, boy and girl, would walk past those houses in the daylight, therefore on Sunday evenings when we would leave the church, quite some time would elapse between the time we left church until we could pass those houses, unless it was a couple that had been 'going together' for some time and were close to marriage. This in between time was spent walking up and down the road, sitting on the Orange Hall steps or sitting on some grassy mound. If there was an occasion when it rained, everyone went home; there was nothing else to do and nowhere else to go.

    I must have walked the roads several Sunday evenings before I walked a young lady home. Who the first young lady was I cannot recall, and maybe the young lady did not know she was the first lady I had walked home. I do recall one evening we went to Boyd's Cove, several of us young boys, and I did walk home at Boyd's Cove a young lady. Then for a few Sunday nights after I went to Boyd's Cove and walked her home. However, it was just a friendly walk and a friendly conversation. I never seemed to get very serious no matter how many girls I walked home. I'd walk them home and that was that. Several of them became a little more serious and I would receive letters telling how much they cared. The first letter, perhaps you could call it a love letter, was in 1937. I had gone to Twillingate (Durrell's Arm) to write my Grade X Public Examinations and while there I walked home several evenings a young lady from Purcell's Harbour who was also writing the examinations, and when I returned home I received this letter from her. I answered it, and whether I did not express much love in it or whether she had found other interests I do not know, but I think that was the end of our correspondence. Another young lady I walked home on a few occasions who became very interested in me was a young lady who was spending some time

Pleasant Afternoon, Brad Reid, oil on canvas, 1997

with her mother at Boyd's Cove. Her father had died and when her mother remarried the children were put out with friends, and this young lady lived with a family at Back Harbour, Twillingate. The first letter I received from her was given me by her mother while I attended a picnic at Boyd's Cove. As she had to return to Back Harbour that morning, she had given her mother the letter for me as she knew I would be attending the picnic expecting to see her. I recall one night sometime later when I was staying with my cousin at Durrell's Arm, Mrs. Samuel Blake, that this girl walked from Back Harbour purposely to see me, but I was out. As yet courting or dating or going out with girls did not have much appeal for me.

During the winter months when I was growing up, when there was no Sunday evening service in our church at Salt Pans the young fellows and young girls would go to the Salvation Army service at Burnt Cove, a distance of about two and a half or three miles. There would also be young fellows and girls from across tickle: Kettle Cove, Black Duck Cove and Smooth Cove. This is how Vina became attached to two young men from across tickle, and she was not the only one. One particular night I met a girl from Smooth Cove and I walked her home. It was a cold night in the winter and I walked her to the door and said 'goodnight.' Some time later she went to Twillingate and found a new love. However, I was soon to make another trip across tickle; it seemed that Vina and I did find some attractiveness on Twillingate Island at the same places, Smooth Cove and Kettle Cove. Both my experiences came about by attending services at the Salvation Army Citadel in Burnt Cove. This time the pull was a little stronger and a girl from Kettle Cove and I were friends for quite a while. The following summer when she went to work in Twillingate, letters were exchanged back and forth when I could not make the trip to Twillingate to see her on a Sunday night. That trip would mean crossing the main tickle in boat to Kettle Cove and a five mile walk to Twillingate. I could not afford taxi fare. Then letters became less frequent and visits further apart until both ceased. Shortly after this friendship I began travelling to Merritt's Harbour to see a young lady whose mother nursed me when I was a baby. It was at our house then while Helen Adams was my nurse that she began going steady with Stephen Powell that would later be her husband. This travelling to and from Merritt's Harbour meant a trip by water to upper Merritt's Harbour, and sometimes this meant rough water and high wind and/or fog in the main tickle, and about three quarter of a mile walk to the Gut Arm where this girl lived. If the trip was not made by boat it meant about two hours walk over country road and cow path. This friendship lasted until the fall of 1942. Around the end of August 1942 I went to St. John's and for two months worked there with the E. G. M. Cape Co. During that time we corresponded back and forth regularly for awhile but by the time I came home, correspondence had ceased; she went her way and I went mine.

For about two years I walked several girls home, but there was never more than that; girls and marriage I didn't give a second thought to, until December 1944. I had just returned from Millertown where I had been working since September with the Anglo Newfoundland Development Co., Ltd. A few days after I came home I was in Alex Sansome's shop at Seal Cove, and the maid that Mr. and Mrs. Sansome had employed came in the store. She was a friendly sort of person and we exchanged a

few words. During the conversation I understood she had Thursday night off and I told her I would meet her 'up the road.' That was the turning point in my life and her life as well. I met her Thursday night with other girls coming around Seal Cove Pond. Of course, as the custom was, we all walked up and down the road for awhile, the girls on ahead and the boys following behind. Then we all sat down on Stumpy Hill awhile and talked and laughed and joked. However, when we heard someone coming we all scattered and hid in the bushes, the girls going one way and the boys another. I remember one such occasion sometime later—a group of us were hiding as we heard someone coming. But it turned out to be quite a joke on us. The person coming was my mother, and we were hiding in the bushes on a rise of ground and one of the group had just purchased five pounds of sugar at our store. She placed it down on the ground but instead of remaining where she placed it, it rolled out of the bushes to the road right in front of my mother. What a harrowing experience! But being the kind of woman my mother was she just passed on by as if nothing had happened.

    We continued walking the road for awhile and then one boy linked with his girlfriend, then another and finally Rowena and I walked along side by side. It was a beautiful moonlight night as we walked over the crispy snow and at the gate we said 'good night.' But before we parted there was a promise I would walk her home again after church on Sunday night. She kept her promise and so began the beginning of a matrimonial road that as yet August 9th, 1976 has not ended. Rowena, I discovered, was the daughter of Mr. and Mrs. Thomas Watkins living on Riding Point in Indian Cove. To walk there, which I did many times, was a distance of about four miles over a country road. By boat it was about three miles. Rowena stayed with Mr. and Mrs. Sansome for the winter and in the spring returned home to Indian Cove. I made several visits to her home on Wednesday and Sunday nights, as the practice was. Her parents and grandparents, that is her mother's father and mother, lived in a lovely home there on Riding Point, and I enjoyed every moment spent there. Her father was half owner of an eighteen-ton schooner, and after a little while going there he persuaded me to make the trip to the French shore with them in the spring for a load of codfish. With my interest in Rowena and my interest in the family it did not take much persuasion. It was an interesting experience and we returned around the middle of August with a full load of fish.

    My motor boat was used that summer for fishing on the French Shore, and it was decided that once our fish was out of the schooner and ready for drying or dried we would have the fall shore fishing in my motor boat again as it was a little larger than Mr. Watkins's boat. Around the middle of September all was in readiness and we began fishing. Rowena's grandfather, Theophilus Wheeler, fished in the front of the boat from the fore standing room, I fished by the engine room, as I was the engineer, and my father-in-law to be, Thomas Watkins, fished from 'back aft.' It was a jolly crew and we brought in a lot of codfish caught by handline, using squid for bait. Of course, this is not the main part of this story. The main part of the story for me was that I saw Rowena every day. I stayed at her place every night except Saturday night all during the fall's fishing, and slept on the daybed or couch in the kitchen. She would make sure I was nice and comfortable and warm before she went to bed every night. Grandpa

Wheeler was usually the first one up in the morning and when I would hear the fire crackling in the stove I would get up. Breakfast was usually a cup of tea and good home-made butter and bread, then off to the fishing grounds before daybreak.

Rowena spent some time that winter with Mr. and Mrs. Sidney Gosse; they lived in the bottom (head) of Indian Cove, about a quarter of a mile from her home. That winter I spent some time in Millertown with the A. N. D. Co., cutting and hauling pulpwood. We kept up our correspondence regularly as we were anticipating marriage in the spring. We were hoping to be married in May.

However, my father took very sick about that time and died on June 4th. On July 22nd, 1946 we were married in the little church at Hillgrade by Herbert Norman, a lay minister of the United Church of Canada serving the Herring Neck Pastoral charge.

Miniskirt

Alastair Macdonald

Child,
grown to the fancied daring
of sixteen:
eyes blacked, corpse-lipped,
hair down, farouche:
the whore-look of time past
hallowed today
by fashion-house decree
into a guise
for innocents;

self-consciously possessed
in brazen black and sexy shine
of metal,
patent gloss, and leather;
or slim or vast in shifts,
exposing knobbled knee
or thigh tremendous;
Picasso parody
of human shape
and line:

grotesquerie:
the calculated awkwardness
nose-thumbing at proportion
and stale authority;
the new-old flout which says
look, look,
only such youth as this
of mine
can dare;

with twitchings,
kicks, kinks, quirks,
you pass
along the sidewalks,
brief in skirts,
tapering in tights, eyes for the boys,
on teetering, tic-tac steps
on pinhead
heels;

or sit
in cafés, bars, and dives.
Child eyes
look out
from hanging screen of hair
and haze of rebel cigarette;
playing the game of temptress;
wanting,
yet afraid to be what you would seem.
Innocence
through bold stare
says "Is this right?
Is this the way of it?"
And laughter at the role
not quite believed in
breaking
the mask.

Seize, laugh;
enjoy
the smooth-skinned fun of it.
Not many years will pass
before
you cannot well afford
this luxury
of ugliness.

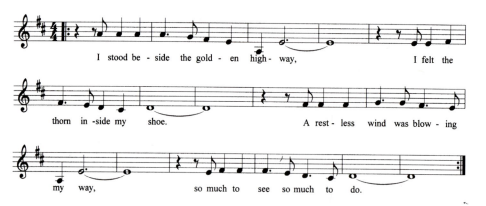

Halfway up the Mountain

Harry Martin

Slowly with feeling

I stood beside the golden highway, I felt the thorn inside my shoe. A restless wind was blowing my way, so much to see so much to do.

You said you'd share the load I carried,
You told me of the better way.
I said farewell to those who loved me,
I followed you a different way.

So where's this wind that blows the favours?
Where's this rain that washes clean?
I'm almost halfway up the mountain,
Stormy nights are all I've seen.

You promised me that there'd be sunshine
Somewhere on that mountainside.
I followed you, I sometimes tumbled,
I lost my way, I lost my pride.

So where's this wind that blows the favours?
Where's this rain that washes clean?
I'm almost halfway up the mountain,
Stormy nights are all I've seen.

It's still a long way up the mountain,
My days are long, my nights are cold.
Still looking for the things you promised,
My dreams and I are getting old.

So where's this wind that blows the favours?
Where's this rain that washes clean?
I'm almost halfway up the mountain,
I'm chasing someone else's dream.

Jim Wilson's Chum

Sir Wilfred Grenfell

Uncle Ike Wilson was a born rover. In his early days he ran away from his father's farm in England, being possesed by that inborn desire of so many English lads to go to sea.

This adventurous spirit, the desire to get out of the ordinary rut of life, the contempt for prosaic routine, even though it brought ease and plenty, and the determination to "do something," carried off Uncle Ike over sixty years ago, first as "scrub" on a small square-rigged wind-jammer, and later almost all over the world. At length he grew tired of the fo'c's'le, as so many others have, but nowhere did he find a place where it seemed possible to obtain on land a position with freedom enough for him.

Finally, having sailed from Spain with a cargo of salt for Labrador, whence his captain intended to bring fish for the West Indies, he thought he had found the poorman's paradise. Here was all the land he wanted, free to all comers. Here were fish in the sea and rivers, birds and bear and deer for food and furs, no taxes to pay, no social inequalities to remind him of his humble origin. Here men seemed free and equal, simple-minded, hospitable, while their livelihood depended only on their own resourcefulness.

So it happened that when the time came for the ship to sail, Ike was nowhere to be found, as he had taken care to remove himself far into the forest, where searching for him would be like hunting a needle in a haystack.

In due time Uncle Ike married, though somewhat late in life, and had one son. In order to have "plenty of room" such as he needed for his trapping he made his winter home far beyond the head of one of the many inlets of the coast; and as he was exceedingly clever at all kinds of woodcraft and animal lore, he had done remarkably well. His house, isolated though it was, had become proverbial for its generous hospitality. The numerous komatik teams which "cruise" the coast in winter—dogs being our only means of traction—never failed to make a little extra detour, sure of a good meal and a warm corner under Uncle Ike's hospitable roof.

It is not therefore remarkable, as his wife was the daughter of an old settler on the coast, that their son Jim should possess more than the usual quota of those natural abilities that go to make a valuable scout.

At the time of this story, Jim was still only fourteen years old. His hardy physical life had toughened his muscles, and already inured him to endure circumstances under which a "softy" would be about as useful as a piece of blotting paper. From his sailor father he had learned those valuable handicrafts which help out so invaluably in a tight corner. It was no trouble to him to hit the same spot twice with his ax, or to tie a knot that would neither come loose nor jam.

It was the very middle of winter. The snow lay deep on the ground, and everything everywhere, except the tops of the trees, was buried out of sight. On the barrens,

wind-swept and hard-packed, the least mark on the surface might be visible for days; but in the woods the drift only left light snow many feet deep, where any mark, or even an object, became hidden in a few minutes.

On the days between his long rounds over his fur-path it was Uncle Ike's custom to go into the woods and "spell" out such fire-wood as was necessary to keep the stove going at home. This incident occurred on one of these occasions. The old man had left at the first streak of dawn, as was his invariable habit, and had taken with him his team of six as stout dogs as ever helped to haul a sledge over ice. It was a glorious morning, and Jim had been allowed to go off on his little fur-round of some half-dozen traps—all his own. The price of whatever pelts he got was placed in his special stocking, that he might learn the value of things when he came to have a rifle and hunting-kit of his own.

Sundown is early in a Labrador winter, and Jim did not get home till so late that, with all his knowledge of the country, he was glad enough to see the twinkle of the cottage lights through the darkness as he sturdily trudged along the last mile homeward. For it had "turned nasty," the wind had shifted to the east, and it was snowing hard, which added greatly to the darkness of the evening. But that night Jim noticed neither weariness nor difficulty, nor did he feel the extra weight of the burden he was carrying on his back. To-day success had crowned his skill, and he was dragging home the very first otter he had ever caught all by himself. What a surprise it would be for Mother and Father! What a good time would be his by the crackling fire as the storm raged outside and he sat toasting his legs and telling of his adventure!

As he expected, a truly rapturous greeting awaited him when at length he entered the door, additionally demonstrative, he thought at first, because of his large otter. Soon he found, however, it was because Mother had been anxious, as neither of "her men" had returned and now she had at least one wanderer safe. Aunt Rachel was no longer a strong woman physically. Of late a weakness, strange altogether to her younger days, had forced her unwillingly to recognize that only by much resting between "spells" could she keep pace even with the few domestic duties which her small house made necessary.

"Get your things, Jim, and we'll have tea on the table by the time Dad comes. Cut more wood, please. We'll have an extra fire to-night. Dad will be cold after his long day's work."

"Right you are, Mother," said the tired Jim, forgetting his aching bones in the excitement of the occasion. He was outside in a minute, ax in hand, looking for another log or two.

Soon another hour had passed by. Still no sign of Uncle Ike. Everything stood ready, and the kettle was puffing out greetings from the hob.

"Better get tea, Jim. Dad may be kept by something. But he's always home before now."

The wind was howling outside, and Aunt Rachel's face was paler than usual, in spite of the firelight. Something must be wrong with Ike. The house was miles away from any neighbor, and it was utterly impossible on a night like this to seek help that way. Yet if anything had happened to her husband, he would never live till daybreak.

"What's that Jim?" she suddenly cried out. "Surely that's a dog outside!"

Jim, whose ears had not been so spry just for the moment owing to his being in the midst of his long-delayed supper, listened a minute. "That's White Fox's whine, Mother. I'd know it anywhere." And jumping up, he ran to the door, as he supposed, to welcome his father. But no father answered his call from the darkness: only a great, snow-covered furry animal lept up and kissed his face. "Down, Fox, down! Where's Dad?" But for answer all he got was a whine and what he took to be an invitation to follow her, White Fox having been the trusted leader of their team for three years past.

"Mother, it's White Fox all right. She's got no harness on. I'll go and see if the others are back, too."

A moment later and Jim was in from the dogpen. "They're all home but one, Mother. There's Jess and Snowball and Spry and Watch, all of them with their harnesses on and their traces chewed through. Father must be in the woods somewhere. But where's Curly, and how did they come to leave her behind?"

The anxiety was becoming almost too much for the poor woman. No help could be got from outside, and she couldn't travel fifty yards in that snow, herself, with the thermometer at twenty below zero. Jim was tired and young, ever so young to go out into the dark and storm and be of any use. She had him safe, anyhow. Surely it would only make matters worse to send him out again.

Jim had fed the dogs, and by all the laws of dogdom they should now be curled up and fast asleep in their cozy little house. But he had hardly closed the door when a scratching and the familiar whine outside said plainly that White Fox was not satisfied, and wanted something which they had failed to give her.

Again Jim went to the doorway. The bitter blast and snow drove into the porch and through into the house; but the great woolly figure of the dog showed up in the open space in the light which streamed from the cottage. As Jim looked into the eyes of almost his only real chum he could plainly understand her meaning, reading the message as well as if it were written.

"She does want me to go with her, Mother," he called from the porch. "What shall I do? I'm sure she has left Father somewhere, and wants me to go and help her fetch him home."

"Shut the door and come in, Jim. I don't think I dare let you go. You and your father are all I have on earth, and if you got lost too, I should never live through it." There was a momentary silence as the boy, with thoughtfulness beyond his years, stood listening.

Then once again came the familiar whine, ringing through the darkness of the night. White Fox had not given up her attempt to convey her message merely because she had met with two rebuffs. She knew well enough that the team would follow her if only she could persuade Jim to answer her call.

Still, absolute silence reigned in the cottage. Neither mother nor son spoke. Then again came the long piteous wail of the dog, and it seemed to the alert ears of the woman that now there was a tinge of disappointment in it.

It was she who broke the silence. "You must go, Jim. There is no help for it. That call would haunt me to my dying day if I left anything that could be done, undone.

God knows best, and it is He surely, and not White Fox, who is calling. Get on your things, boy. Take your father's lantern, and God help you!"

Jim was already half into his little oilskin suit, his storm cap, skin mitts, and moccasins, while his mother packed up a few little things which might be necessary in case an accident had happened. Indeed, he was already moving to the door when she called him back again. "Jim," she said, "it may be the last time I'll ever see you alive. Kiss me once more, and then we'll just kneel down ask God, Who loves you better than I can, to be with you to-night and bring you safe back with Father."

It was no set prayer that welled up from the soul of the poor woman; whether, indeed, it even took the form of words, she has long since forgotten. All that Jim remembers is that for some minutes he, of all people actually cried, though he didn't exactly know why.

At last the door had closed behind him, and—marvel of marvels!—Aunt Rachel, weary and exhausted, fell asleep in her chair, and in the God-given rest was able to economize her store of strength to meet the ordeal she had yet to face.

Jim, meanwhile, had found a spare harness and put on White Fox, tying the trace around his waist. Then he called out the rest of the team, tying their traces together and hitching them onto his arm. Having no idea of where he was going, there was only one thing he could do, and that was to follow the dog. So, closing his eyes, as seeing was out of the question and they were safer that way from twigs and brances after they got among the woods, he plowed his way as rapidly as he could, following all the time the tugging of White Fox's trace by keeping a strong grasp on the line.

Fortunately for all concerned, the spot of woods which Uncle Ike had selected for his winter's cutting was less than two miles from the house, and one mile of that was over a frozen lake, where, although the full blast of the storm made the cold the more bitter and hard to stem, yet the drift was packed, or altogether cleared away by the violence of the wind. Through the drogues of woods in the narrow gulches the young snow was so soft that the boy had almost to swim, and but for the tug, tug of White Fox's trace he could never for an instant have kept his direction, or even made progress. But White Fox stood twenty-seven inches to the shoulder and scaled nearly a hundred pounds, actually heavier than the boy himself, while every ounce of her was made up of bone and iron muscles.

One other element told strongly in the boy's favor, and enabled him to accomplish what must otherwise have been an almost impossible task: it never entered his head that the dog could be mistaken. He trusted White Fox as implicitly as he would his mother. Of course his chum knew better than any one else on earth what to do. If he could only last out and do his part, he knew well it was mere child's play to the dog.

Once and again, as he floundered through a deeper drift than usual, he became completely stalled, and it seemed impossible ever to extricate himself. He was nearly fagged out, and the cold and dark made the temptation to rest just for a minute almost irresistible. The excitement of the first hour had enabled him to call into play at once all his reserve strength, but now he felt he must sleep—only a moment of course, but just a minute's nap. In those deep drifts not even White Fox could have hauled so heavy a load. All she could do now was to return to her lagging master and kiss his

face, incidentally running to and fro and hardening a path for him on which he could crawl out of the bog of snow.

As once more they plowed along on their way scarcely a sound was audible: just the moaning of the storm, and now and again a rare whimper or snarl from one of the dogs as another got in his road. Indeed, the silence and darkness were almost visible, when suddenly, quite close at hand, a dog's call resounded from the bush, and White Fox leaped in the direction with such violence as to fling the boy clean off his feet, rolling him over once more in the deep snow.

But that he no longer noticed. That was Curly's sharp bark! Picking himself up and bracing himself for the effort, Jim shouted with all his might, "Father! Father! Father!" But the only answer was a howl in unison from all the dogs and the soughing of the storm through the firs and spruces of the grove they had entered.

Only for a moment, however, was there any doubt what to do. And again it was White Fox who brought the solution, for she hauled off into the bush at the side of the path, and began burrowing down into the snow. Jim followed, not without a sinking feeling at his heart, and in less than a minute he was kneeling over the prostrate body of his father.

"Father! Father! It's me—Jim!" But still no answer. Yes he was breathing— breathing loudly. And warm, too, where Curly had evidently been cuddled up against him. There was only one chance. Could he find the wood-sledge? If so, he might be able to save his father's life.

Curly was bubbling over with joy, and probably connecting Jim's arrival with the chance for some supper, after all. She was dancing all around and entangling her trace around Jim's legs, and positively forcing him to notice it. Seizing it with his hands, he followed it along. It seemed never to end, though really it was only thirty feet long, but it was entangled again and again in the bushes, and over it all the deep snow had fallen. True to the guess that the dog was still fast to the sledge, he found it at last, the sharp upturned bow jabbing right into his hand from the drift as he groped after it.

It must have taken another full hour to dig it out and haul it alongside Uncle Ike, to drag the limp and helpless body onto it, and then to so fix the lashings that his father could not fall off on the homeward journey.

A team of dogs going home on a night of that kind is almost as irresistible as a traction-engine, and Jim's only trouble was to keep the sledge right side up. That he somehow succeeded is actually certain, for in the early hours of the morning Aunt Rachel was roused by the sound of the dogs outside, and positively rushing into the night, she fell on the pitiful burden they had brought to her little cottage.

It was now her chance to call on her reserve strength, and that she certainly must have done. Buoyed up by his success, Jim's endurance did not fail him, either, and guided by the intuitive knowledge of a good housewife, the two were soon chafing Uncle Ike's half-frozen limbs as he lay before a gorgeous fire, rolled in warm Hudson Bay "four point" blankets.

Soon a little nourishment was forced between his lips, and he opened his eyes and gave anxious watchers a smile of recognition.

Uncle Ike was never quite able to remember how it happened. He had reached the clump, tied his team, and was cutting away, when suddenly he felt odd, dropped his ax, and could no longer stand upright. However, he had sufficient mental power left to reason that his only chance lay in reaching his sledge. The dogs instantly answered his call, but they were all fast to the komatik and were unable to reach him, as that was purposely tied to a stump. That was all he knew, except that one dog at last got near him as he lay, and, cuddling up close to him, kept him from freezing to death. The others in their excitement had chewed through their traces, or as White Fox had done, succeeded in slipping their harnesses.

Then White Fox must have hurried home for help, and the other dogs that could get loose had followed her as they were always used to do.

No, White Fox was not forgotten. Jim says that before he lay down to sleep he could not help just going out to give Curly some supper and taking a few extra little tidbits for White Fox. But he found her peacefully asleep as if she had done nothing unusual; and she slept that night as many a "better-off" being has never known how to.

First Fruit of the Tree

Irving Fogwill

He had not noticed the slow darkness coming on. His young friend and himself had been sailing boats—make believe—in the small stream in the park. They had used small pieces of wood. And it was not until it was quite dark that he had suddenly felt that it must be very late, and that he would have to hurry home. He said good-bye to his young companion and started to walk home.

His home was a mile and a half from the park. He was a very small boy—about six years old.

The long straight highway loomed dimly grey before him. He was a very happy little boy by nature, and now he sang to himself as he trotted along. While he sang he was thinking. He was always thinking about things, and he always sang monotonous refrains, even as he thought about things.

As he passed his school, which was on the highway, it suddenly occurred to him that he had stayed away from school that afternoon to play in the park. His daddy would not be pleased about that, he thought. Then a funny comforting thought came to him. He would soon meet his daddy coming to look for him. Nearly every night his daddy came to meet him. He came before he sat down to his supper. When they met his father would only say something about its being too late for little boys to be out. He would not be angry; but he would look sad and tired. He would take his hand and they would walk home together. He would ask his father about all the things he

wanted to know about. And his father would never say anything about boogie-men, wicked things that would carry little boys away—like Bernie's father did.

He remembered his father saying to his mother once when they reached home—his mother had seemed to be very angry—"No, Nell, don't say anything to frighten him."

"Aren't you going to punish him?" his mother had asked.

"No," his father had replied, "I'm not going to do anything to hurt the boy's spirit."

It had become very dark now and the little boy had reached the juncture of the roads where he left the highroad and turned up towards home. It was here that he usually met his father. He felt a sort of warm feeling and he looked eagerly up the stretch of the road. He could see no form in the gloom. Suddenly a strange feeling came over him, driving away the warm feeling he had had. He felt very cold, as if he had suddenly fallen in water. Some terrible kind of knowledge seemed to be trying to get into his thinking. He slowed perceptibly in his walking, and his singing trailed off into silence. A kind of fluttering thumping in his chest seemed to choke him. As the knowledge gathered to burst full upon him, a sequence of images raced across the vision of the eyes of his mind. He saw again that day—last Friday—his dad lying on the day-bed and his mother's face a funny colour like a newspaper with no print on it. He saw the oldish man with a satchel like his father's lunch box hurrying in. He had been sent to the kitchen then. After that he had been sent to his granny's. Then, two days later—on a Sunday—he had been dressed in his best suit by his Aunt Sue; and there had been a crowd of men in front of the house. After a while he had been taken into the front room, and some people were singing, but his mother was crying. Aunt Sue had told him that daddy had gone to Heaven. After that the men took the long brown shiny box with the lovely handles out of the house and put it on a carriage and he had walked behind that carriage a long way with his older brother Robert.

The sequence of images hurried upon him now. His slow feet dragged to a stop. Then full knowledge came to him in rememberings of words spoken in measured beat—ashes to ashes, dust to dust...the Lord giveth and the Lord taketh away. The little boy's face worked convulsively and seemed to become broken up and shapeless. As his eyes scalded over he started to run in stumbling, frantic haste, whimpering "daddy, daddy."

And finally, after a brief cessation of crying as if caught for a moment by a sudden idea, the small form stumbled on up the road, sobbing brokenly in definite and final panic. And through the shadows of closing evening the thin, piercing reed of young sorrow called "Mom! Mom!"

The Little Girl Learns to Swim I, 1993
acrylic and collage on canvas, 18" x 24"

The Little Girl Learns to Swim II, 1993
acrylic and collage on canvas, 24" x 18"

The Little Girl Learns to Swim III, 1993
acrylic and collage on canvas, 18" x 24"

When I begin to work there is an energy and excitement in the making of each new image. It is always an extremely physical process—whether drawing, painting or cutting a woodblock. I build and reduce, draw and redraw until I find that single image that creates the tension and movement I am looking for in my work. When it is resolved I feel that I have been a part of a process that has taken and given me energy. This approach to my art is linked with imagery that I feel expresses my fundamental view of life—that we are not separate from our landscape but that we are a physical part of the energies, cycles and movement in nature....

Whether I work with paint or print, neither is supplementary to the other, but quite independent, each with its own characteristics and strengths, each contributing in a different way to the development of the image.

In 1994 I had the opportunity to work in the small rural village of Soulignonne, France. The isolation of the studio and the solitude that I enjoyed there gave me the time to focus on my work that I had never experienced before. It was the woodcuts produced there that led to the development back home in my studio of [some] larger pieces....

When I produce a body of work over an extended period of time and I put each new piece away to move on to the next image, it is always a surprise for me to look back on them. They seem to take on a life of their own, separate from me, being left for others to assess and interpret what I have created. It is like a trail that I have left behind, but one that has marked my thoughts and presence.

— *Sharon Puddester*

The Death of a Tree

Gary Saunders

It's funny how people get attached to certain trees and hate to see them go.

Hard by the south wall of our house, its wide crown overarching the roof like a parasol, is a big elm we have come to love. With the house, it has weathered the gales of some ninety winters and the suns of ninety summers. In that time it has sheltered more than one family; ours is just the latest to nest under it.

But we thank whoever thought to fetch the sapling and dig the hole and plant this tree so many springs ago. For now on sultry Dog Days its rustling green canopy cools our roof, and in the depths of winter its warm beige bark relieves the wastes of white.

To be sure, it has its faults. Its autumn finery is somewhat on the plain side. Some summers aphids take over the foliage and rain down sticky honeydew to draw flies and begrime our white clapboards; but we can live with that. Some years its thirsty roots invade the septic tank, backing up the contents and forcing me to dig and curse till all hours. But once the hole is refilled and the grass resown I forgive and forget. It also stands too close to the house for comfort; but life is full of perils anyway.

All in all, it would sadden us to lose this elm before its time—which the book says should be a good five decades yet.

Unfortunately we could lose it any year now. Only ten miles away robust elms like ours began to die last summer. For Dutch elm disease has finally reached Nova Scotia, and it is spreading fast. As late as 1968 it was still possible to believe that the province might escape the destruction that overtook the elms of Quebec and Ontario and New Brunswick in the 1950s and 1960s. Then, in 1969, two diseased elms were spotted in Liverpool on the South Shore. Though both were promptly felled and destroyed and no more cases were reported that summer, between 1970 and 1974 the fatal symptoms showed up in the Annapolis Valley and then in six other mainland counties on more than a hundred trees.

Sooner or later it had to come, of course. Dutch elm disease has ravaged elms all over eastern North America since the 1930s, killing and deforming not only the familiar white elm—the only native Maritime elm—but five other New World species, plus all exotics except two Asian elms. This disease is potent. In New Brunswick it is still spreading and killing trees. New Brunswickers know the pain of losing beloved specimens and pleasant groves. Now it's the turn of Nova Scotians. So far Prince Edward Island has escaped, and Newfoundland has too few elms to need to care.

Like most plagues, Dutch elm disease has travelled far. But Holland was not its place of origin, despite the name. In common with the deadly blight that wiped out America's famous chestnut trees fifty years ago, it came out of Asia. The traffic of the First World War may have helped. In 1919 it appeared in Holland and in northern France. The Dutch pioneered research on its behaviour—and won the doubtful honour of having the disease named after them. By 1927 elms in the south of Britain were infected. Then it hopped the Atlantic, turning up in Ohio in 1930 and in New Jersey two years later.

Since then many more researchers have burned the lab lights late. Though they still have not found a practical cure, they have learned a great deal about how Dutch elm disease operates. For example they know how it kills. It works something like a stroke in humans. The circulation of vital fluids is dammed at some point and beyond that point the parts wither or die. Here the likeness ends, however, because in an elm the stoppage is caused by a yeast-like fungus that stimulates the tree's water-conducting vessels to seal themselves off. (British researchers suspect a poison at work, too.) When the vessels plug up in this way, the leaves on one or more branches suddenly wilt, take on fall colours in midsummer, then die and drop. As the fungus spreads throughout the water-carrying system, branch after branch sickens and dies, until the whole tree succumbs. Young trees may be killed in a month, large old trees may take longer. A few fight if off and survive.

While detection sounds simple, it isn't. Scientists also know that two other elm diseases display the same outward symptoms. This means that before they can confirm or rule out the presence of the causal fungus Ceratocystis ulmi, they must culture suspected sapwood material in the laboratory, a process that now takes about a week, and used to take longer. Moreover, C. ulmi can go undetected for years in aging trees. Elms die of old age like other organisms; after a while nobody pays much heed to their slow decline. Often it is the sudden yellowing of healthy neighbouring elms that announces trouble. By then the spores can have spread far and wide.

How it spreads is one of nature's ironies. A beetle smaller than a grain of rice is the chief carrier. This beetle feeds on the inner bark of live elms, and breeds between the bark and wood of newly dead elms or newly killed branches. If during feeding or breeding the sticky spores of Dutch elm disease are present, the insect may accidentally pick some up the way a dog picks up cockleburs. Then when it flies to a healthy elm to feed or to a run-down elm to breed, it may infect the tree. If a spore touches live wood, it can be whisked away in the sap stream to multiply and wreak havoc.

So the innocent elm bark-beetle, by trafficking in lethal spores, is killing its own food supply.

The disease can also spread underground via root contacts. This happens in Britain where elm hedges are common.

But the long-range transit is supplied by man. Dutch elm disease first entered North America, it is thought, in elm veneer logs from Europe. If so, somewhere in those logs were spore-laden European elm bark-beetles. Somewhere in Ohio they left their hiding places and flew through the New World air to a New World elm and found its bark to their liking. Perhaps on the way they met native elm bark-beetles—slighter in build, but otherwise almost identical in form and life habits to their Old World kin. For millennia these native insects had played harmless undertaker to dead and dying American elms. Now, armed with the seeds of destruction, they helped hasten the spread of the fungus.

Ohio being just across Lake Erie from the elm heartland of Ontario, it seemed only a matter of time till the disease reached Canada. Yet it was in the province of Quebec that the symptoms first appeared, fourteen years later in 1944. Ships unloading

elm-wood crates near Sorel likely brought the malady from overseas. In fifteen years Quebec had lost more than 600,000 elms in an area bigger than Nova Scotia. By 1946 Ontario elms had been infected from across the Quebec border. And in 1950 the Niagara peninsula and Windsor area were hit by the inevitable incursion from the United States. Closing in thus from two fronts, the disease fairly raced through Ontario's elm-rich counties until in 1963 it embraced an area the size of the Maritimes.

This shows how fast it can move at its worst.

Shall we then lose all our elms? Is our familiar and well-loved white elm, that queen of shade trees, to go the tragic way of the American chestnut, which today survives only as scattered great ghostly trunks ringed with a few miserable green shoots?

Few experts would be so pessimistic as to predict this. The chestnut blight was an extremely virulent, entirely windborne fungus that caught America unaware at a time when knowledge of tree diseases was limited. Dutch elm disease, though very potent—especially against white elm—is almost wholly insect-borne, it spreads more slowly, and its mechanics are much better understood.

Today the problem is more of mobilizing our knowledge and resources to fight back. This governments at each level are trying to do. At the federal level, the Canadian Forestry Service does excellent work in monitoring the disease, disseminating information, and researching methods of prevention and cure. They have succeeded in developing an injection that can protect individual elms for a short time; but the method is laborious and costly. More promising is their work on controlling overwintering beetles by spraying the lower tree trunks in late summer. In one Ontario study a one percent solution of chlorpyrifos virtually prevented overwintering of beetles.

Provincial governments help where possible with detection, and in some cases tree removal and planting. When the town of Kentville embarked on a massive tree removal scheme two years ago, the Nova Scotia Department of Lands and Forests assisted. Towns like Fredericton, Truro and Windsor have organized tree commissions for better detection, education and sanitation. In fact, Fredericton has over fifteen years of experience in elm-saving, and has made a standing offer to give the benefit of that experience to any town that wants it.

The key word that keeps cropping up in any discussion of Dutch elm disease is sanitation. Sanitation means just that: keeping the trees clean, so that the beetles have no place to breed or to pick up the deadly spores. This in turn means constant vigilance to spot the first signs of old age, storm damage, or sudden wilting, and it means following up with prompt removal and destruction or spraying of suspicious material, year after year.

Such a program requires expertise and dedication—and dollars. Caring for small trees is not so bad. The average homeowner can manage it with simple tools and techniques. But the white elm is by nature a large and fast growing tree. (One specimen near Trigonia in Tennessee is more that 160 feet tall and eight feet across.) Most of our street elms were planted before 1900 and are now mature giants. To prune or fell such a tree amid hydro and telephone wires with traffic and pedestrians

swirling below demands the skills of a B. C. lumberjack and tree surgeon combined. These skills don't come cheap. Taking down one large specimen can cost over $500. George Goodall, president of Goodall Tree Expert Company, of Portland, Maine, estimated in 1974 that the town of Windsor should budget $15,000 a year to control the disease on its two thousand elms.

But if a town or city can muster the concern and the money, it can save ninety per cent of its elms or better. Fredericton is proof of this. When I first went there as a forestry student in 1954, I was struck by an elegant sign proclaiming it "The City of Stately Elms." Stately was right. Along Queen, Regent, Westmorland and many other streets, stood magnificent colonnades that met overhead and hid the sky. Dutch elm disease had not yet arrived. From up the hill the city all but vanished under a sea of foliage, with only a scattered church spire poking through to get one's bearings by.

Then in 1961 the fungus struck two trees. Next year two more caught it. In 1964 there were fourteen new cases. By 1967 a total of sixty-four trees had been infected—out of a population of some 7,500 elms. By any standards this was a remarkably low infection rate. What could have been an epidemic was held to little more than a minor rash, while elms up and down the Saint John River Valley died wholesale. Today Fredericton still has most of its stately elms.

The key to this success was sanitation, which happily had been started on a small scale in 1952, before Dutch elm disease even reached New Brunswick. But sanitation did not begin in earnest until a tragedy struck. One squally Sunday morning in 1964, as people filed out of St. Paul's United Church after service, a branch fell from an ancient elm and killed a girl. Her death brought home the realization that trees don't last forever. So Fredericton's older elms were removed, and by the time the disease arrived, its remaining trees were fairly healthy. After that it was mostly just a matter of spotting infections and treating them promptly.

In sharp contrast is the experience of Woodstock, where the first known occurrence of Dutch elm disease in New Brunswick was reported on a single elm in 1957. Like most elmy Maritime towns, Woodstock had enjoyed her trees and never noticed how old they were getting. Meanwhile the disease was at work only fifty-five miles away in Maine. Then when the fateful signs appeared in her very midst, Woodstock delayed removal of the stricken trees too long, despite the urgings of people who knew better. So when the town did start sanitation, C. ulmi had a head start.

In the same period when Fredericton lost only sixty-four trees, Woodstock—with a much smaller initial elm population—lost 872.

The lesson is clear for any Maritime town that prizes its elms. Even if they don't have Fredericton's enviable assets—a wealthy citizenry, two great forestry schools, plus a regional office of the Canadian Forestry Service—they can still do much. Especially in Nova Scotia and Prince Edward Island, where time is on their side.

But what about the elms of the countryside? Unfortunately, they are apt to fare much worse. Because they are scattered over wide areas and much harder to watch than urban trees, the onset of trouble is much easier to overlook. To monitor and treat roadside and farmyard elms alone would be a formidable task. As for wild forest

elms, it would be well-nigh impossible. This in turn makes successful urban sanitation harder. Elm bark-beetles can't live where all elms are dead. They will strike out for the nearest green or dying trees. Fredericton, now an elm oasis surrounded by dead trees, finds itself beset by increasing swarms of beetles, "Lookin'" (like the boll weevil) " for a home."

For the rural elms the best we can hope for is that in time they will develop a resistant strain. Something like this happened in Britain. Although there was a national felling and sanitation campaign during the 1940s and 1950s, the outbreak seemed to subside partly of its own accord, as if it were running into a more stubborn breed of tree. Maybe after two or three decades the same thing could happen here—or be engineered genetically.

However, there is a catch. Sometime in the 1960s a new and extremely aggressive strain of C. ulmi entered Britain and sparked a new epidemic that is now killing even tough rural elms that survived the 1930s outbreak. Ironically, that strain almost certainly came from North America. So the breeder of stronger elms might only be buying time. Genetics wields a two-edged sword.

It is autumn again. Again, in what may be its final normal leaf-fall, our ninety-year-old elm is preparing for winter. Down past the window, tawny and tattered, looping and tumbling, its leaves hurry earthward. Watching them fall, and pondering the strange love affair we have with trees—our genuine individual affection for them versus our collective destructiveness, our capacity to heal versus our capacity to kill—I am moved to ask, with the writer of that truly sad and sadly true lament:

"When will we ever learn?"

The Death of an Elm

Herbert Pottle

It was a landmark for two generations,
    Where lovers loitered long;
    Under its welcome shade
    Elders exchanged their histories;
    Emblem for all, the faithful elm—
Sylvan cathedral of community.

But it stood straight in the iron path of progress;
    It was trapped in a sea of planning,
    Islanded in solitary confinement;
    An anchored bench of gravel ringed its base;
    And a sea of cement froze like an icecap
Tight to its throat in the silent forever of permafrost.

Then the long slow cortège of decline descended;
    The breathing came in spasms;
    The blood, bereft of nature,
    Limped its lessening course and fell;
    So one by one the limbs were paralyzed,
And the spectre curtsied to the winds in effigy.

Soon came a day, the day of dissolution:
    The last rites of the buzz saw—
    Preparing the uncouth body,
    The slicing of the prostrate torso,
    The splattering of the spinal cord—
In multiples the corpse makes final exit….

Now passers-by tread where the elm tree grew;
And some lament, forget, or never knew.

Alder Music
Gary Saunders

I must say I like alders. Except for the times I've been in a hurry and they barred the way, alders have given me nothing but pleasure. And not only in the campfire. Everything about this remarkable tree-shrub is congenial to me; its appearance, its attributes, and the company it keeps.

I'll admit at first glance it looks unkempt. Devotees of its more elegant cousin the white birch could be excused for thinking so. The crooked stems curve and sprawl, seldom achieving an upright trunk, let alone tree stature. The mature bark is a nondescript grey-brown. Its wood is brittle and of no commercial value. To the uninitiated, the alder's only claim to attention is the cute mini-pine cones on the upper twigs. Sometimes these find their way into floral arrangements.

Yet we have maligned this humble and harmless dwarf tree beyond measure. Farmers revile it for sneaking into worn-out pastures. Foresters would plow them up and plant larch—though some would grudgingly admit that an alder swamp makes a dandy firebreak. 'Alder swamp.' For many, the very words conjure up visions of swarming mosquitoes and smelly ankle-deep muck.

Isn't it time we made amends? Or at least came to terms? Extermination is out of the question; the alder is far too stubborn and successful. We'll just have to live with it.

As usual we can trust the intuitions of children. While a real forest intimidates them, an alder thicket is just their size. Its springy branches make an ideal jungle. As kids we would watch a Saturday matinee featuring Tarzan of the Apes, then troop off to one such thicket to spend the entire summer afternoon dodging ivory hunters and fierce leopards in its risky mazes. In winter, when the swamp would flood and freeze, we played the same games on skates. If I could spare the land I'd plant an alder jungle next to the house just for the children.

Wildlife seems to have the right idea about alders too. On April evenings over most of eastern Canada the winnowing of snipe is as much a sound of Spring as robinsong. As often as not, the snipe's home ground is an alder swamp nearby, where it probes with its long bill for earthworms and other tidbits that live in the rich soil. Woodcock, with their similar habits, are even more partial to alders.

Or come in summertime to look and listen. As your eyes grow accustomed to the bottle-green light under the leafy canopy you may catch a glimpse of the olive-sided flycatcher darting after a mosquito and calling its loud "Quick Three Beers." Or you may see a yellow warbler flash like a sunray among the branches. And if there's a brook nearby, you may spot a speckled trout lazing in the cool shade while turquoise-and-jade dragonflies rattle their wings in pursuit of gnats.

Autumn is so-so in the alder-woods, if you hanker for colour. There's no fanfare at all. The leaves just curl and fall while still green. Presumably the plant recycles what it needs from them as they lie on the ground in a crunchy brown carpet, smelling deliciously tea-like from their high tannic acid content.

Beavers, intent on laying in winter stores of bark to eat, mostly bypass alders in favour of aspen. But for building dams and lodges they make it their standard

construction material. Skillfully weaving and thatching the flexible stems together, the big rodents fashion walls which at the onset of winter freeze rockhard, proof against the strongest meat-eating prowlers.

By November the alder groves seem deserted except for an occasional itinerant jay or crow. The arrival of snow one night only heightens the look of abandonment. Sifting down among the bare branches, it muffles the only notes of colour remaining, until the little glade becomes a study in dark-on-light, more line drawing than three-dimensional reality.

Morning tells a different tale. Everywhere the fresh sheet is eloquent with the typography of animal activity. Over there in boldface capitals I read of the nervous midnight browsing of snowshoe hares. Nearby, in lower-case characters around a dismantled spruce cone, is the same statement by a red squirrel. On this mound a few tiny asterisks tell of a chickadee's quick visit. In the deeper snow bordering the swamp are the exclamation marks of deer tracks. This dotted line needs no signature to declare that a fox was here. Finally, in fine print at my feet, some notes from the underground; weasel ellipsis overprinted on the delicate quotation marks of a field mouse making for the sanctuary of its undersnow tunnels. Picturing that labyrinth of weather-free thoroughfares, I can believe that it got away.

As I said, I'm fond of alders. And the more I learn of its attributes—nitrogen fixer, scented firewood, healer of wounds, diarrhea and sore eyes, natural bonsai forest—the more I cherish it.

As a kid I liked it for more mundane reasons. An alder fishing pole was good for a whole season. The powdered leaves, rolled in brown paper, made quite a good smoke if you could get it lit. With a supple young shoot you could flick iris pods or potato balls at blinding speed toward distant enemies.

Of those childhood uses only one has survived: making whistles. Surely this is one of the least sinful things a grown man can do in the spring. Especially when he does it for children. There's poetry in it.

Last May while leading a Grade Five nature walk I stopped to discuss an alder thicket—and made the tactical error of showing the class how to make a whistle from the sappy green stems. I didn't want the art to die out in suburbia, you see. But for the rest of that hike I did little but make whistles and try to supervise their flashing pen knives.

It's hard to guarantee uniform pitch in alder whistles. You get a variety of notes. Straggling back toward school, we sounded like an orchestra of spring peepers tuning up. My Great Truths of Ecology didn't stand a chance. The kids were making alder music. Pan would have smiled.

Talking to Trees

David Elliott

> I like talking to trees
> And they say they like talking to me.
> Their speech delights me:
> The heavy utterance of elms and pines,
> The sensible remarks of maples,
> The banter of birches,
> Even the idle chatter of the giddy aspens.
> There was an old spruce who taught me much poetry,
> And in a far country an oak tree
> Told me the meaning of patience.
> But especially I loved the old poplars in my back garden.
> How courteously they would interrupt their meditations
> To answer my greeting.
> I told them about us mobile folk,
> And what strange lives the unrooted undergo.
> They told me stories of air, wind, water,
> And the slow riding of the midnight world
> Toward the stars.
> They died last winter.
> This week I cut them down.
> Some day, through various stages of ashes and dust,
> We shall be back in earth together,
> And resume our conversation.

Julie-Ann

David Pitt

I am yaffling on Skipper Tom Milligan's old flake down by the sail-loft on an August evening, and I'm coming up the second last row. Right in front of me, working the last row, is Julie-Ann, Skipper Tom's granddaughter, and kneeling down to pick up the yaffle I am looking up a little under her bob-tail skirts. She isn't wearing stockings and the backs of her legs are reddish brown from all the sun and wind of the summer. They look very smooth and soft like lovely silk, and I am powerfully tempted to reach out and touch them. I almost do but she moves on, not that I really would have if she didn't. So I pick up my yaffle and carry it to the fish-pile in the middle of the flake. Coming back to my row I pass Julie-Ann bringing her yaffle to the pile too. She says, "Lor', Jim, we're near done! This old flake sure takes a mite, what!" I grin back at her and say "Yeah," and go back to my row. Soon she comes back and bends over again right under, or rather over, my nose. I can't help looking and I see where her pink bloomers are pinching red rings all round her thighs. But now she squats down, and I see the yellow hair all down her back, just parted a little in the middle where I see her skin so white and smooth, and I want to touch that too but I dare not—no, but I wish I did. I think Julie-Ann is the prettiest girl I know. I don't know very many girls, but I've seen pictures of them in books and in the catalogue my mother gets to send away to buy things out of, and none of them is half so pretty as Julie-Ann.

I think I am in love with her but I wouldn't say so out loud to anyone, least of all to Julie-Ann. She doesn't know it, naturally, and I don't think she is in love with me. She's friendly to me though, but what does that signify? She's friendly to everybody. But perhaps she wonders if I'm specially fond of her. After all I don't love to be yaffling Skipper Tom's fish. We've lots of our own to yaffle, and across the cove I can see my own ma bending down to pick up a yaffle, and when I go home I dare say I'll catch it for not coming round to help her and Tobe and Liz take it up before sundown. I don't care though. They all get paid for making the fish, thirty cents a quintal, share-and-share-alike. But I don't get anything for helping. I'm only thirteen, and they figure I don't need pay at my age. But helping Julie-Ann, especially when we're all alone, just the two of us, on the flake, is better than getting paid. I don't suppose she gets paid either though she is fifteen. But it's her grandpa's fish. So's ours, but we're no kin of his, so we get paid for making his fish. At least the others do.

She goes to stand up with her yaffle, but she's made it too big and she loses her balance and falls right back against me. I have an armload too and it spills all over the flake as I catch her and hold her for a minute while she rights herself laughing. "Good Lor', Jimmy boy! Lucky you were behind me. I mighta took a tumble! What a clumsy goat I be. Here, let me pick up your yaffle." I am on my knees all round with fish, hers and mine, and she brushes the white dusty salt off her skirt and kneels down beside me. Her face is almost touching mine. Her head does touch mine once. "There," she says when we're done. "But hurry, sun's almost down."

   I carry the yaffle to the pile while she picks up hers and brings it toward me. One more apiece and it'll be all up. I could go on all evening yaffling fish with Julie-Ann, especially when there's no one else here. Today I'm being lucky, tremendously lucky. Her ma and her aunts and her brother Tom, who usually do most of the yaffling, had to go off somewhere in the trap-skiff—to a funeral I think. They've been gone all day, and no one left to look after the fish and things but Julie-Ann and old Johnny Stykes who works for them when he's not drunk or disappeared somewhere. Today he's probably both, because he hasn't been about all day, and the crock is gone from the fish-shed bench. Yes, I've been tremendously lucky today, but now it's almost done. We're coming back to the pile with the last two yaffles, and there's only the tarpaulin to put over it and weight it down with some beach rocks.

   I take one side of the tarpaulin, which is not really a tarpaulin at all but a piece of an old schooner foresail, and Julie-Ann takes the other, and we spread it out between us and bring it up over the pile of stowed-up, half-dried codfish—all good Labrador heavy-salted and a heap of fine eating for somebody somewhere come winter. We fold the old sail-canvas down around the sides and put beach rocks on the edges to keep the wind from lifting it off in the night, and put a few more on top just to make sure. The sun is getting low down now, almost touching the top of Tickleace Island, and the water all down the Reach is turning pinkish and red with a bluish tinge. I can feel a little small breeze coming off the water, and it smells sweet because it is blowing in from the blackberry islands across the Reach.

Yaffling fish on a rooftop

The blackberries are ripe over there now, and I wish I was there picking them with Julie-Ann. Perhaps she will go there with me tomorrow or the next day, if Tobe will let me have the punt for a couple of hours. It's only a half-mile row, but I'd best be asking Tobe for the punt before I'm asking her if she'd like to go blackberry picking with me. She might say Yes, and Tobe might say No. Then again it might be the other way round. I must think some more about this. It would be tremendously nice though to go there with Julie-Ann, just ourselves. Perhaps a storm would come suddenly up the Bay, and we'd be caught there all evening, all night even, and have to take refuge in the old tumble-down house that they call Paddy's Range—though I don't know why. It's a spooky place and the windows are all broken, and the door doesn't close all the way, and there's the wrack of an old graveyard right beside it, but it keeps out the rain. I know because I was caught there once last summer in an awful rain, myself and two other fellows. We stayed there an hour or more, and didn't get a drop of wet on us. But I don't know how it would be in a real bad storm and at night. But I shouldn't mind if Julie-Ann was there too. Ah but I don't suppose anything like that will ever happen. Yet, it could, it could! It would be tremendous, I'm sure it would.

I'm standing by the fish-pile looking out over the Reach and the islands, and thinking all this as fast as a wink, and Julie-Ann is dusting the salt-powder off her skirt and knees and thinking, I dare say, about something very different from me, when all of a sudden there comes a tremendous yell, more of a screech I guess than a yell, from down by Skipper Tom's old root-cellar in the garden by the sail-loft. I turn about quick and so does Julie-Ann, but not because we don't recognize the sound. Sure enough it's old Gran Milligan in her long black jersey dress and her white apron, steadying herself with her twisted old stick, and yelling to us like somebody wild. "What's she want now?" says Julie-Ann, and she picks up one of the beach rocks as if she is going to fling it down at the old shape in the garden there. But I know she really isn't.

"I don't know," I say, because I don't. But I'm a little bit scared of old Gran. She walloped me once with that stick of hers for climbing the old, twisted, branchy tree by the woodshed to get a few of the little, hard, wormy apples that grew high up. I didn't really want them. They were no good to eat. It was mostly to show off to Julie-Ann, who said I could never reach the top ones without a ladder. But old Gran came out and caught me just as I was coming down and walloped me twice or three times across the bum with her old stick. Julie-Ann just laughed and ran off somewhere, perhaps thinking I'd tell old Gran it was she put me up to it. But I wouldn't do anything like that to Julie-Ann. And another time old Gran sicked the dog after me for throwing stones at the old black spitfire of a biddy-hen she keeps in the back-kitchen garden. It's a fierce old hen (reminds me of old Gran) and would fly at me like a hawk going after a mouse if I didn't drive it off. I only wanted to go in where it was to get my sponge-rubber ball that had bounced off the shed and over the garden fence when we were playing rounders on the open space across the road. It's not really any wonder I'm a little scared of the old shape.

Julie-Ann puts her hands up to her mouth like a trumpet and yells down. "Yaw, Gran! What's the matter down there? You yellin' at we?"

"Come down yer this second, you two young whelps, 'fore I come up to 'ee," the old biddy yells back, jabbing her stick in the ground. We know she can't come up to us; her old legs would never make it now. But we know we had better obey her quickly just the same.

So we both run across the flake to the ramp going down to the fish-shed. "What you s'pose she wants, Julie-Ann?" I say as we trample down the ramp, trying not to sound scared at all though I am, a little bit.

"Lor' knows," says Julie-Ann in a not very nice manner. I don't think she likes old Gran very much, though she is her own father's grandmother. Yes, I really mean it. Not his mother—his grandmother and nearly one hundred years old at the least and looks every day of it. I don't like her much either, especially when she looks hard at me with those little blackberry eyes, sunk in so deep in her old wrinkled face. Julie-Ann runs on ahead of me, not because I can't run just as fast, but because I don't want to get there first, and she comes to where old Gran is standing with her hands on the crook of her stick which is stuck in the ground in front of her. Julie-Ann stops before she gets too close and I stop a distance behind her. Julie-Ann stands there, looking, I think, just a little like Gran herself except that Julie-Ann's hands are behind her back and she is tremendously prettier. But I suddenly think that maybe long ago this old woman looked like Julie-Ann, and then I think—I don't know why, but I think awful things sometimes—that someday Julie-Ann may look like her. I almost shiver, but I see that old Gran has pulled her stick out of the ground—it wasn't in very far—and is holding it up as if she's going to take after Julie-Ann and maybe give her a swipe with it. And I'm thinking now that maybe I ought to cut and run behind the cellar and over the fence and scoot down round the fishing-stage before something happens. But I'm thinking also that I want to know what is going to happen—if it does—so I stop where I am, about half a gun-shot away, and I bend down and make out to tighten the laces in my boots—not laces really but pieces of fish-line which is better than real laces any day and don't cost anything. I loosen one lace and do it up nice and tight and listen all the while to what's going on.

"Jewlan"—that's what old Gran always calls her—"Jewlan," she says in that old scritchy voice of hers, "what be the divil got into 'ee maid, that makes 'ee treat me like 'ee do?"

"Treat 'ee like what, Gran?"

"Takin' t'ings off'n me dresser whenever me back is turned, me combs and me brush and—where be 'em now? Tell me straight er yer pop shull know it the vury minute he lights to home."

Julie-Ann doesn't say anything at first, but tosses her head back a little which makes her hair shake out in the breeze and old Gran is going to say some more, when Julie-Ann says, sort of loud and I think not very nice, "What should I want with your old combs and things? I got all them things o' m'own."

"Then why don't 'ee use 'em an' lave mine be?"

"I never touched 'em an' tha's God's own trut'. P'rhaps 'twere Tom er A'nt Tess er—" Julie-Ann laughed, I suppose at the thought of Tom, her brother (he's about twenty now), wearing Gran's combs.

"Never you mind tryin' to put the blame on some un else. I knows 'ee, Jewlan." The old woman shakes her stick toward her, but Julie-Ann only laughs again and runs into the house without so much as a look over her shoulder at me. Old Gran, with her stick still raised, gives me a look that is not very nice, as if she wants me gone and good riddance.

I would like to wait a little and see if Julie-Ann comes out again or looks through the back porch window or her bedroom window which is also at the back. (I know because she told me once. I've never been in it of course, though I would tremendously like to see where she sleeps.) But I daren't wait to see if she comes back or looks out. So I take off and hardly stop for a breath till I'm all the way home. I think to myself it has been a lovely day, all day—almost. Lovely to be with Julie-Ann! Heavenly to be with Julie-Ann! If only the old witch hadn't came out to spoil it all at the end.

As I am falling asleep, I wish I hadn't called her that, even if it was only to myself. So I say my prayers.

But I have a very strange dream. I dream that I'm out on the berry islands with Julie-Ann, and she and I are lying on the grassy slope by the old graveyard. It is nice and warm and sunshiny, and I'm thinking I could probably kiss her now and she wouldn't mind or slap me or run away. And all of a sudden she jumps up and says, "Jimmy boy, I'm goin' in swimmin'." "But," I say, "we didn't bring any swim-suits." "I don't care. I'm goin' in with nothin' on." And she takes off all her clothes right there and runs down to the landwash. She stops and turns round to face me, all naked and white, and motions me to come on down. I start to pull off my clothes, so excited I can scarcely move, but nothing will come off, as if it was all grown onto me, like bark on a tree, and I feel like a tree grown into the ground. But then I see that Julie-Ann has jumped into the water and I wrench myself free and run down to the water's edge, but I can't see her anywhere. I look and look, feeling frightened and more frightened, because I'm almost sure she's drowned. Then all of a sudden a body comes up, stiff and pale, and I'm sure it is Julie-Ann because the face is like hers—yet different somehow. I look more closely and then I see that it is not Julie-Ann after all. It is old Gran Milligan—dead, but staring at me with her little blackberry eyes. I give myself such a start that I wake myself up, so wide awake, and frightened, that I can't go back to sleep any more.

I think about it as I lie there in the half-light of morning coming on, shaking a little still. I try to remember and to forget at the same time. I want to remember Julie-Ann—especially when she turned and waved to me before she jumped in. She looked so lovely and white and shining—like an angel I think, now that I have time to see it all again in my mind awake. But I want to forget her jumping in and old Gran coming up. That I never want to see again.

I've heard tell that some dreams have meanings in them, or they are like tokens of things to come. I wonder if that is true, and what my dream might be meaning. But when I'm up and dressed and downstairs with the others, I soon know what it means. My mother tells me that old Gran Milligan died last night in her sleep. I don't know why I do it, but I start to cry, and my ma and my brother and sister look at me as if I'm

crazy. Perhaps I am—a little. My ma says, "Surely you're not crying because that poor old soul passed on? 'Tis a wonder she didn't go long past. Pretty near a hundred, she was, poor old thing. 'Twas time the Good Lord took her up." I rub my eyes with my sleeve, and Ma says, "Come on, Jimmy boy. I'm sure you weren't that fond of her. Dry up your eyes, for shame on you." I try to do that. But I can't tell her that I'm not crying because old Gran is dead, but because Julie-Ann isn't. My dream might have worked the other way, but it worked the best way for me and Julie-Ann, though I do feel sorry for the poor old woman and wish I hadn't called her a witch in my mind. Perhaps that's why she came up from the water to frighten me in my dream.

In the afternoon, after thinking about it all morning, I set out to walk round to Skipper Tom Milligan's house—to pay my respects, I tell my ma, but really, of course, to see Julie-Ann if I'm able. And I do. When I reach the house and go round to the front, very slowly and quiet, as I think you should when going up to the house of the dead, I see Julie-Ann, sitting in an old hammock on the verandah. She doesn't hear me coming up the front steps because I am treading so softly, and I'm seeing her in my mind as she was in my dream. Then I see that she is looking through one of those catalogue books I mentioned before, where you can send off and buy all sorts of nice things they don't have in the stores around here. I think she doesn't look very sad and her eyes are not red at all. And I say to myself that I'm right to think she didn't like old Gran very much. But maybe I'm wrong. After all, old Gran was so very old and had lived so very much longer than most people do. There was really no need to be grieving a lot. But I am thinking it sort of odd for her to be looking so pleased with the things she is finding in the catalogue. She looks up and sees me then, and smiles—oh, a lovely smile—and I ask her how she is and she says, "Fine an' dandy, Jimmy boy."

I say I am sorry to hear about Gran, but she only says, "Well, she was awful old and had to go sometime." But she doesn't seem very sad.

Then she picks up the catalogue and starts to look into it again. So I ask her what she is looking at. And she says, "Know what, Jimmy boy? Old Gran—you won't believe this—but she lef' a note, wrote out in her own old shivery-shaky hand, tellin' us all what she was leavin' to us when she passed on. Yep she did! And y' know what? She lef' me—this part is a little funny, considerin' the huff she was in las' evenin'—she lef' all her combs and brushes to me! An' all her jewelry—not an awful valu'ble lot—but not bad, some of it old and nice. She wrote down that she wanted me to be a fine lady some day—marry a handsome, rich man too I s'pose, though she didn't write down that. But that ain't all! She lef' me five hundred dollars! All of that to just me! No one knew she had more than a hundred or two. So—I'm looking at what I might send away and buy fer m'self. What d'you say to that, Jimmy boy?"

I am very surprised by what she tells me. But I can't feel upset any more about her not being sad. I think though that now she's a little bit rich and can buy fine clothes and things she won't ever think of me any more, not that she ever did very much, maybe. Perhaps, like old Gran said, she'll want to go off somewhere and be a fine lady. I begin to wish old Gran hadn't left Julie-Ann her jewelry, or all that money. I feel myself beginning to think bad things again about the old woman. I am thinking all this when Julie-Ann jumps up and throws the catalogue into the hammock. Then she

takes me by the hand. Oh!—I don't think she ever did that before! And she says, "Come in and see the poor old soul. Laid out on her bed she is. The men are makin' her coffin, but it isn't done yet."

So, still holding Julie-Ann's hand—so soft it is and warm I almost feel a little faint—I go with her to old Gran's room, at the back of the house, not upstairs because she couldn't climb stairs any more. The room is dim because the blinds are half down, but soon I can see all right. And there on the bed I see her lying, almost as I saw her in my dream, though now her eyes are closed and she doesn't look scary any more. I look away from her and around the room where she slept and died. I see her poor old clothes on nails in the wall and laid on a chair, and her worn-down shoes half under the bed and a white chamber-pot beside them. I feel very strange and sad. And then on the dresser I see her combs and brushes that are Julie-Ann's now, and some very old pictures of faded people. I look again and see in one with a fancy, crinkled frame, a girl with long hair and a very old-fashioned blouse and long skirt, and then I see that it is Julie-Ann I think.

"Julie-Ann," I say, "look, what a strange, old-fashioned picture of you!"

And she laughs—a lovely laugh, but I think a little too loud and lightsome with old Gran lying there dead—and she says, "No, silly boy, that's not me. That's old Gran when she was a girl! Is it really like me? I don't think so." Then she pulls my hand and turns me round toward the bed again, and says, "Just look, Jimmy. She can't yell at us no more."

I lean forward a little to get a better look, because the light is not very good and I have never seen a dead person before—except in that dream. And then, as I lean forward a little so does Julie-Ann, and all of a sudden without a word she kisses me—right on the very mouth! My heart gives a tremendous leap, and I almost fall. But she steadies me and laughs.

And then, though my heart still races from the shock of the kiss, I suddenly shiver, and a strange feeling flashes over me, for I seem to see in the pale, old face on the bed before me the very face of Julie-Ann.

Barrens (for three Dylans)

Jeff Baggs

Delicate Purple Prose
   its sweet inebriating flow
     spilling o'er pursed lips
       trickling blood of september berries
         touched once by frost

 and twice by rain-numbed hands,
   their lifeblood dearth seeking fiery hearth
    to delicately warm

   Divine, joy-stained fingerprints
     that they might reach to touch
       but squeeze not tightly
     lest sweet microcosm be quashed by carelessness.

     Learning to touch but not to squeeze
     Yearning still for another dizzying taste
       before the sparkling winter comes to call
       and purple numbness silences us all.

The Great Fire of '92

W. J. Kent

The great fire of July 8th, 1892, which laid waste the whole of the eastern portion of the city of St. John's and by which over $20,000,000 worth of property was destroyed, 12,000 people rendered homeless and several lives lost, will long be remembered, and will mark an important period in the history of Newfoundland.

Just before 5 o'clock on the afternoon of Friday, July the 8th, an alarm of fire was sounded, and the firemen, hurrying to the scene of the outburst, found the flames proceeding from the stable of Mr. T. Brien, at the head of Carter's Hill, on the Freshwater Road. Unfortunately, the water-pipes were being cleaned that day, and though the water was turned on again at 3 o'clock, it had not reached the higher levels of the city when the fire started. The flames therefore made headway before water was procurable; and, as a very high westerly wind was furiously fanning the fire, it began to spread rapidly.

The locality was a most densely populated one, containing a large number of residences of the laboring classes, and masses of glowing wood blown hither and thither by the wind set ablaze a number of houses within an area of two hundred yards. By 6 o'clock an idea of the magnitude of the outbreak had spread through the city, and a large crowd gradually assembled to aid in the saving of property which was becoming endangered, and to remove into places of safety furniture of the houses in close proximity. While it was seen that the fire was of more serious character than usual, no fears were entertained, even at this time, for the safety of the city generally, and it was believed the stone buildings of the main streets would withstand the fury of the flames; so beyond assisting in the immediate neighborhood, no thought was given to the great portion of the town.

The Church of England Cathedral and Gower Street Methodist Church were made the receptacles of large quantities of valuable property, and the most cherished possessions of these around were piled in these places of fancied security.

About 6:30 two wings of flames were steadily descending the hill, the western one burning in a direct line down Carter's Hill to the water's edge, while the eastern swept diagonally through Long's Hill, swallowing everything in its way. The Methodist College was situated on the east side of this hill and stood pre-eminent among the public buildings of the city. It included a magnificent hall, furnished with a splendid and most valuable organ, the gift of the late lamented Hon. C. R. Ayre. The College was one of the most thoroughly equipped educational establishments in the country and was an object of much pride to the denomination. Soon a thin column of smoke was seen arising from the tower, and within a short time the whole place was ablaze. The flames quickly spread to the primary school and Methodist boarding-house near, and to the magnificent Masonic Temple which crowned a rising eminence within a few yards. This hall was erected only a few years ago at a cost of $40,000, and was a noble evidence of the generosity of the Fraternity in Newfoundland.

A very short time sufficed to number these edifices with the things of the past, and after wiping away the Presbyterian Manse, the fire raged furiously down the hill and quickly fastened on Gower Street Methodist Church. Within a very short time this building was a ruin, and the Parsonage was also in flames, together with the Orange Hall, immediately opposite. But a few yards off stood the Rectory of the Church of England Cathedral, the residence of Bishop Jones, and directly fronting it was the Anglican Cathedral of St. John the Baptist itself. Stretching forth its horrible tongues the fire quickly turned the Rectory and the Girls' Orphanage adjoining into a flaming mass, and with one fearful rush the demon of fire seized upon the doomed Cathedral, and sooner than tongue could tell the immense edifice, a gem of gothic architecture, the masterpiece of Sir Gilbert Scott and the pride of every Newfoundlander, was a seething mass of flame. With a crash, heard even above the din of the elements, the roof fell in, and the result of the labors and offerings of generous thousands for many years vanished in the cloud of smoke and dust.

Having worked its will upon the Cathedral, the fire now rushed to the group of buildings congregated together at the foot of Church Hill, and soon St. Andrew's Presbyterian Church, the Athenaeum and the Court House were throwing masses of fire into the sky, though the Union Bank bravely withstood the assaults of the enemy. The Presbyterian Church was valued at $30,000; the Athenaeum, which contained a most beautiful hall, a library of 5,000 volumes, the Surveyor's, Government Engineer, Superintendent of Fisheries' Departments and the Savings' Bank, at $59,000, and the Court House at $80,000.

The Commercial Bank, not far distant, succumbed a few minutes later, and the Telegraph offices had been consumed long before, the operators having to fly from their keys. Communication was thus cut off with the outside world.

Consternation now seized the populace as they saw with terror that the stone edifices were no more able to resist the attacks of the fire than the flimsiest wooden structures, and those whose houses were endangered fled, panic-stricken and breathless, beyond the reach of the conflagration, with that which was most valuable of their possessions. The western section of the fire ate its way swiftly and surely down to Water Street, throwing out, as it swept along, offshoots which seized upon and consumed the Star of the Sea and Total Abstinence Halls, Tasker Terrace and numerous other substantial buildings within that area.

The height of all the above-named important buildings placed them in the direct power of the gale, and burning masses of fire were blown incredible distances, to drop in unexpected places, and render frantic the already bewildered people. Thus many places on Duckworth and Water streets were ablaze before the intervening sections caught, and Saint George's Barracks, on Signal Hill, about two miles from the outbreak, was burnt before the Court House. All along Water, Duckworth and Gower streets the residents were deluging the roofs of their houses with water in the delusive hope of staying the flame, while their wives and families got together at the street sides their portable possessions. All efforts were of no avail.

William Campbell's builders' supply store caught fire early in the evening. It was a wooden building erected as a shed after the great fire of '46, and being filled with inflammable materials—paints, oils, tars, &c,—did not stand above a few minutes. One after another the houses and stores on Water Street took fire from the burning brands which were flying through the air. Before nine o'clock the walls of James Baird's liquor and grocery store tumbled in and just after, the extensive warehouses of George Knowling were seized by the devouring flames. The first part of this premises to take fire was a warehouse at the rear, which Mr. Knowling was having enlarged to meet the growing requirements of his trade. Carpenters had been working there that day and had left their tools in the building, little thinking that when they returned in the morning the whole place would be a smoking ruin. The flames spread rapidly from the burning warehouses to the dry goods store fronting on Water Street, when it was seen that the whole premises were doomed. Costly silks and satins were regarded no more than the cheapest cottons, and people rushed to take freely what they pleased. The stock destroyed on this premises alone amounted to over $160,000. Quicker and quicker the flames advanced, gaining strength and power with every foot; the solid masses of flame, sweeping pitilessly through the streets, soon formed an impassible barrier. With the strength of desperation the unfortunate people fought till the last moment, and it was only by the sacrifice of their burdens that many of them were saved, while the crash of falling chimneys and walls was as the sound of a mighty bombardment.

Like the line of march of a retreating army the thoroughfares were filled with goods, abandoned because of impossibility of conveyance, and fabulous sums were offered for carts and vehicles. All the arteries which led from the water to the higher portions of the town were crowded with the terrorised mob, and the screams and cries of the women mingled with the wailing of children, the shouts of men and the trampling of animals, the whole being intensified by the ever-freshening mass of livid fire and the glare of the burning buildings, contributed to make a scene, the like of which it is not often given to the lot of many to witness.

When the magnificent warehouses, stores and shops of Water Street were within the power of the fire, the flames fed by accumulated contents, consisting in many instances of most inflammable materials, such as kerosene oil, butter, lard, gunpowder, and alcohol mounted to immense heights, and the whole horizon was one mass of lurid light surmounted by a thick pall of heavy smoke.

About 10 o'clock the fire worked up Garrison Hill, and along Queen's Road, where the Congregational Church was situated; and although a wide street intervened, it was also doomed, and its bare walls alone stand in position today. In a spacious plot of ground, bounded by four wide streets, stood, just under the Roman Catholic Cathedral, St. Patrick's Hall, perhaps the most spacious and imposing public hall in the city, constructed of free stone and heavy stone from local quarries, covered with cement. This building contained a large hall, four elegant school rooms occupied by the Christian Brothers, giving accommodation to 400 children, and a basement just being prepared as a billiard-room. It was thought that its isolated situation would save it, and every preparation had been made for its safety. A length of hose had been laid along the roof, and the Brothers who worked heroically thereon, directed all their efforts to the protection of its western front, as the fire worked its way up Garrison

Hill. For over an hour the unequal fight continued, and at last a small patch of fire stuck under the overhanging wooden cornice of a roof window, and the water being unable to reach it, the flames quickly effected an entrance to the building. Its complete demolition was henceforth a matter of time, and within an hour it was a total ruin.

The safety of the Mercy Convent and with it Georgestown, Monkstown and the whole collection of magnificent structures which compose the head-quarters of the Roman Catholic denomination, was threatened, but after a brave fight, the danger was overcome. A few yards lower down a collection of buildings on Rawlin's Cross also jeopardized the above flourishing suburbs, where numbers of those who had been previously burned out had taken refuge, and, as the flames gradually increased, in consequence of the burning of a large liquor store at the Cross, the feelings of the multitude may be better imagined than expected.

With the assistance of many volunteers, the firemen and police succeeded, after a severe exertion, in successfully combating the flaming elements. The flames which threatened this point had not come directly along Military Road, but had crossed Prescott Street lower down, and had then eaten their way up the hill to that portion of Military Road which lay between the head of Prescott Street and King's Road. A gallant fight had forced the flames to pass the Terra Nova Bakery and the Electric Light Works, and it was for a considerable time hoped they would be saved. But the tanks of water in the pipes was turned off to be used upon another locality, and soon it was seen that the long and gallant struggle had been all in vain. Both buildings were engulfed in the flames, their contents were entirely destroyed, and the city, save for the glare of burning stocks of coal, has been in darkness ever since.

Another severe struggle took place at the head of King's Road, where the security of a portion of Military Road depended on saving the Drill-shed, and already overtaxed energies were expended in fighting the flames. At the same time another corps was busily engaged at the western extremity of the conflagration, preventing it extending its ravages into the west-end of the town. Dougherty's foundry, and several dwellings at the foot of Theatre Hill were torn down to make a firebreak, while at O'Dwyers Cove an eventually successful struggle nearly resulted in the loss of one or two lives.

All the shipping at the wharves had to make for the stream, and there anchor, out of reach of the flames, and all the wharves, in many instances with valuable contents, were destroyed. The coal hulk of the Coastal S. S. Co., moored near Chain Rock, took fire early in the night. The streamer "Sharpshooter," belonging to Messrs. Harvey and Co., and a large vessel lying at John Woods and Sons wharf, were burning at the same time.

All through the long night the crowds continued passing and repassing—those who had friends gladly availing themselves of the welcome shelter of their houses, while those who had no better places settled themselves and their belongings in Bannerman Park, the R. C. Cathedral grounds and even by the road sides waiting for day to break. Few there were who closed their eyes that night—the homeless, too heartsick and too weary to seek relief in slumber, while those more fortunate found themselves burdened with relatives and friends or gave way to natural excitement engendered by such an occasion, and wandered aimlessly from place to place, fascinated by a scene at once magnificent and awe-inspiring.

When morning broke the thick clouds of smoke still ascended from the burning ruins, and it was hours before it had cleared sufficiently to admit of a view of the track of the desolating scourge. A walk through the deserted streets demonstrated that the ruin was even more complete than seemed possible at first. Of the whole easterly section, scarcely a building remained. In the extreme north-east a small section of Hoylestown was standing, protected by massive Devon Row, but the remainder of St. John's East had vanished. Of the immense shops and stores which displayed such varied merchandise and valuable stocks gathered from all parts of the known world; of the happy homes, of artisans and middle classes, where contentment and prosperity went hand in hand; of the comfortable houses were laboring classes sought rest and refreshment; and of the costly imposing structures and public buildings which were the pride and glory of the people, scarcely a vestige remained; and St. John's lay in the morning sun as a city despoiled of her beauty, her choicest ornaments, presenting a picture of utter desolation and woe.

Since the fire, temporary shelters have been erected in Bannerman Park and other public places, and substantial provisions provided. From the Dominion of Canada, the United States and from Great Britain generous donations of food, clothing, lumber and money have been received, and arrangements for the relief of the people are being fully carried out. The total number of individuals burnt out, as far as can be ascertained, is 12,400 of which 2,700 are sheltered in Bannerman Park, 65 in the Drill Shed, 190 at the Railway Station, 154 camped near Quidi Vidi Lake, and the balance in private dwellings and school houses, Monkstown, Hoylestown and the suburbs.

St. John's after the fire of 1892

The 1921 Fire at Nain

Martin Martin

1921 is a date not to be forgotten for it was in that year that Nain caught fire. All the mission buildings were destroyed by fire, in that year, 1921.

At that time I was cod-trapping at Natsatuuk with William Barbour's crew.

The *Harmony* had arrived in Nain and all the able-bodied men were told to go to Nain to unload the freight and the winter's supply of food. Consequently, a lot of people came in to work. When the *Harmony* was unloaded, it left in the morning travelling north towards Hebron. It was a beautiful morning. It was warm, a little hazy, and the sun was shining brightly.

Before we had to go back to our fishing place, we tried to get to the store, before dinner, to buy our provisions. There were so many people also buying their supplies that we were not able to leave before dinner. We just left without going to the store because we were in a rush. We were fishing at Natsatuuk and our work there came first.

When we got to the western end of Uigumigali, by that island, someone saw smoke. We stopped to watch where it was coming from because it was just getting bigger and bigger. When we realized that it was coming from the direction of Nain, we started heading back to Nain.

All the Inuit who were able to work were away at their summer places. They were all spread out around Nain; some were at close places, others further away.

When we came in sight of Nain, we saw that Nain was burning. When we saw that, we unloaded all that we were carrying in the boat on a rocky bank on the landward side of Nuvutannak, on the island facing Nain Harbour. With great speed we proceeded to Nain.

As it happened, the store was on fire. Because there was such a wind from the west, the flames from the fire were shooting up and were being blown to the missionary houses. The roofs of the mission houses were caught afire. Before we reached Nain the roof of the church was in flames. When we reached the wharf we all started running to our houses. I just kicked the door open to our house and began taking all the things which were most important to us down to the beach. My wife and I carried everything to the water-line of the shore. When all the possessions which we valued most were out of the house, we went to see the fire. The heat was too great to go near the church. The fire was still raging and as I wanted to see the store, I went over there. The day before the store had been full of everything, but we saw nothing as everything had been burnt.

Also burning were big puncheons, huge barrels of seal oil, rendered from seal-blubber, readied to be transported by the *Harmony* on its way south. There were also many, many barrels of trout ready to be shipped out on the *Harmony.* Right there from by the store there was a river of flames right down to the water's edge from the seal oil that was burning.

There was no food left.

All the *Quallunaak's* [whites'] possessions were swallowed by the fire.

Not one Inuk house caught on fire that time that there was a fire in Nain.

These things can be replaced, that we understand.

All these things I saw with my own eyes and perceived with my own credibility. This is not just a story.

Letter Written by Torsten Andersen, Makkovik, Labrador, 1901

My dear brothers and friends,

It is now a long time since I heard from you in our old Norway. I thank God that all of us are still alive and healthy, but I begin to feel my age. However, it is no wonder as I was born in the year 1834.

We receive letters each year from our relatives who live in the United States, and find there that they are all in good circumstances.

I will now send you a photograph of me and my wife. She was born in the year 1837 of English parents, who lived here on the coast for many years. We were married in 1859, so that we naturally both seem old, but the time speaks to us all in Labrador as well as in Norway. We have had ten children, who are all still alive to this day, but there are only three of them who are not married. One, a girl named Berta Andria, plays the organ in our church, and the piano and the harmonica which we have in our house. My two unmarried sons are known as good hunters in the winter, and fishermen in the summer. However there has never been such bad fishing on this coast as there was this summer, although the fishing was good about two hundred miles south of us. The point from Davis Inlet was taken out of the coast, so that the fish could not come to land. As a consequence, I am afraid that there will be poor living for many people around here in the coming winter.

When I think of the days of my youth, I still think I can see the old places where I used to go, when I was a shepherd on the Saeter (summer farm), and many places where I and Anders used our fishing rod in the Buvas River, and other places in Begna Valley. Yes, it is now about fifty years since I left my place of birth.

I'm still a merchant in this place, but it is not easy to make money with trade as there are so many poor people among us and I find it hard to see families with small children who have not much to eat. I cannot hold back, but must give them something and thus goes many, many dollars from me, one year after another. But I do not think about it as long as we have enough for each day.

Be so kind as to write to me, when you receive these lines, and let me hear about all the old places in Begna Valley. Who is now owner at Haugsrud? Is there much timber on Huget? Have you many new boats on Begna River? Is there a railway now through the Begna Valley? Is Oslo now a big city, and how many inhabitants does it have?

All right dear brothers and friends…

My address:
Mr. T. Andersen,
Mission Station, Makkovik,
Labrador.

Letter Written by Catherine O'Dell to Her Daughter, Mary Jane

Pinware River
Jan. 7, 1888

My dear Mary Jane,

I am happy to have this opportunity of writing, hoping you are well and happy. How anxious I am to have a letter from you to know how you are getting on. It is now five months since I left you and only received one letter from you, that was in September. I received one from Mrs. Scully in October. I am writing in hopes to hear how you are.

We are all well home thank God, except Uncle Hughy. He was paralyzed in the right arm and leg in the fall, his leg is getting better and he can walk around. I don't think his arm will be any better.

Edith Lilly died the sixth of this month. Her mother and sister are very sorrowful about her. She got a cold last fall going to Lance-au-Mort.

We have lots of company here this month. There were seven or eight families of Mountaineer Indians come out here and the leader of them is brother to old Mitchell that lived seven or eight year with your father. They are always at our houses. They have lots of fur, beavers, otters, martens and all kinds. The people in the river are making all kinds of trade with them every day. They have over $300 worth of fur and no shop or place to buy food nearer than nine miles east or west. If I had brought some goods from St. John's when I was there I would have sold them. Your Uncle Mike, Steven and Uncle John are making trade. They are up there now preparing to go away. They are talking of buying a stock of all sorts.

Father MacCarthy was down here a fortnight ago for a while. He made the first mission. He stayed at our house. He had Mass every morning in the school-room. The place was crowded with people. The Mountaineers sang vespers Sunday evening and came next morning to Mass. They sing grand. Father MacCarthy was delighted with them, and with the river, too. He said he did not think there was any such place on the shore. He saw a wedding and funeral and Indians all the same time. He said it reminded him of the town.

I must not forget to tell you that Lottie O'Dell and James Bolger were married that morning after Mass. He looked down the river and saw Poor Edith's funeral going with a large attendance of mourners. It looked very sad.

Next morning he called out the names of the persons to lead the different crews to cut sticks to make the house in Pinware for the priest to live in. On the following Monday it was very frosty and rough, the men assembled nevertheless and each one trying to outdo the other. In two days they had it all lodged by our door on the river and two flags flying over it. Rich and Ned O'Dell went up yesterday to bring the priest down here to see it according to orders. These two days I could not get a chance to write, we were so busy. The mailman is expected here every moment. I thought I would not get a chance to write, if the priest had come I would not. Ann Marie have not time to say her prayers. She has her letter waiting for a chance to send it. You must excuse all this news. Mark is the only one that has good times, when he sees the rest so busy he takes it easy. He joins me in sending love to you.

Hoping to hear from you very soon. Give my love to Mrs. Power and all my friends. I have not room for their names, the mailman says that my letter is overweight, I can't put any more paper in. I wrote to you last mail in December and to Miss Scully. I hope you got them and answered them. If Ann gets time to write she will tell you some more news.

Your affectionate mother,
Catherine O'Dell

Troubled Waters

H. M. Heather

When the Customs cutter ran into Stag Harbour, Corporal Tobin hit the beach running and kept on going till old Jos Hiscock slammed the door in his face. Somehow or other the Corporal, who had ready ears for a rumor and a nose that could smell out a smuggled bottle from under a quintal of fish, had got an idea that the glass of toddy Jos mixed for himself at bedtime came out of a bottle without a Liquor Controller's label on it. The Corporal was only a young fellow but he made up in energy what he lacked in years. He was in his office at eight o'clock every morning, and Mrs. Harris, who kept the boarding house at Westport where he had his headquarters, said that he sat in his room at nights studying lawbooks till after midnight. Certainly he knew all there was to be known about how laws are broken. Before he came to that part of the coast, folks around there had the reputation of being pretty well behaved. There was no thieving or fighting, or damaging another man's property. But after the Corporal arrived in the district, somebody always seemed to be getting into trouble for not having a gun license, or letting his dog run loose or some other thing that no one ever knew was n offence against the realm until Corporal Tobin said so. Of course, the crime he really hoped to discover was smuggling. No doubt a good many illicit bottles came ashore under jackets and inside rubber boots, but the men who knew about these transactions never talked, and those who talked knew nothing. But whatever the explanation, there Tobin was, hoping to make a really big haul which would win him another stripe for his sleeve, and transform him into a Sergeant.

When Hiscock's door slammed in his face, he hammered on it for half a minute and then shouted that he'd have the law on them anyway for obstructing an officer in his duty. So Jos came shuffling as slowly as he dared, fumbled a while with the key, and finally opened the door a couple of inches. Tobin pushed his way in.

"Bring out this liquor you've got hidden away," he said.

"What liquor?" asked Jos. "If it's a drink you're after you've come to the wrong house. There hasn't been a stain in the place since Christmas."

"None of that now," snapped the Corporal. "There's smuggled liquor in this house, and I'm going to search until I find it."

"Search away," invited Jos with a hospitable wave of his hand as he sat down in the rocker by the stove to watch. "There's only one thing," he added, taking out his knife and cutting himself a chew of tobacco, "my poor old woman's sick upstairs. I'd be obliged if you don't disturb her."

The Corporal didn't answer but started poking into cupboards, peering under the stove and rooting through a barrel of dirty linen that stood ready for the wash. He didn't miss much in the kitchen or parlor but still he didn't find what he was looking for. He was pretty red in the face by this time, and stopped to loosen the neck of his tunic, and pull out a handkerchief to wipe his forehead. Jos rocked placidly in the corner, the squeak of his chair keeping time with his jaws as he chewed. But when Tobin finished mopping the back of his neck and started for the stairs, the old man was out of the rocker and scuttling through the door as nimble as an emmet.

"Didn't you hear what I'm after telling you, Corporal?" he said, spreadeagling himself across the stairway. "There's a wonderful sick woman up there."

The Corporal's frown showed that he was in no mood for arguing and Jos reluctantly moved aside. Tobin looked under the beds, and into the cupboards of the first two rooms without reward and then hesitated for a moment outside the closed door of the old woman's bedroom. But he quickly made up his mind. With silent determination, he laid his hand on the doorknob and went in. He pulled back the curtain which shut out the morning light, letting the sun pour in across a chair hung with hastily abandoned clothes and on to the bed where the old woman huddled out of sight beneath a bright patchwork quilt. Then he stood in the middle of the room with his thumbs hooked into his belt and slowly pivoted around, running a professional eye over each individual floorboard to make sure that none of them had been pried up recently. There was no evidence there. Old Jos standing in the doorway saw the baffled look on the Corporal's face and a wicked gleam shone in his watery eye.

"Well, my son," he said sympathetically, "that's a dirty trick they played on you, sending you away out here so early in the morning. I wonder who was the scoundrel did a thing like that. Why, my dear man, there's been neither drink nor sup in this house since me birthday."

The Corporal grunted and swung towards the door but as he did so a glint from the bed caught at the corner of his eye. He ran his hand over the rumpled coverlet, threw back an edge and brought out three clear bottles of gin, three dusky bottles of rum and four of golden whiskey.

Half an hour later he came out of the back door lugging a knobbly sack. He stood on the step looking round for someone to carry it to the boat but a strange calm had come over the settlement and there wasn't a man to be seen. A few women stood in the doorways, and four or five children played in the middle of the road, but the men who usually worked about the stages or stood in groups outside the store had disappeared completely. Corporal Tobin fancied he saw a head move behind a rock on the hillside, but it might have been a goat or a grazing sheep. He shifted the bag to his other hand and set off down the hill to the harbor. When he got there and came clanking and gurgling round the end of a shed, he found that the cutter was anchored fifty yards away from the end of the wharf. A man in the stem waved and shouted, "Can't come any closer, sir. Tide's dropped." Tobin carefully set down his burden, rubbed his bloodless fingers and yelled back, "Can't you come in anywhere?"

"No, sir. We're right in the channel. Shoal all round."

"Well what the devil are you waiting for?" shouted the exasperated Corporal. "Send off a dory."

The man on board threw up his hands.

"It's gone sir. Look!" he pulled a trailing end of rope from the water and held it up. "Cut! We were all down below having a mug-up."

The Corporal gritted his teeth and turned on his heel. He would have to get hold of a dory and row it out himself. But when he looked around the harbor he realised that all the boats, like their owners, had mysteriously disappeared. The high-nosed dories which generally bobbed beside the jetties or lay drawn up on the beach were nowhere to be seen. Only their ravished floats rose and fell with the ripples, trailing their empty lines.

By this time the noon-day sun shining hot in a blue sky was making the Corporal's shoulders prickle with sweat under his neat tunic. He walked to the edge of the wharf and looked across the sparkling water to the group of men who gazed back at him from the cutter's deck. It was only a short distance to swim and the sea looked cool and inviting. He had started to undo his belt when he remembered the sack at his feet and realised that he would have to abandon the booty, which was going to mean so much to his career. Slowly he refastened his buckle and turned to look at the cluster of houses, which clung around the edge of the bay and climbed unevenly up the side of the hill. He knew that from every house a hidden face was watching, but outwardly the whole village lay asleep, drugged into unconsciousness by the warmth of the summer sun. Even the playing children had vanished from the street and only the smoke that pencilled the air above each roof showed that the settlement was not actually derelict.

Desolation descended on Harry Tobin. There was nothing for him to do but stay in that inhospitable place, with invisible eyes shooting daggers at his back, until the tide rose and the boat was able to come alongside. He hitched up an overturned bucket and sat down to consider whether he could have made a more diplomatic approach. He was on the point of deciding that an extra stripe was a poor exchange for wholesale unpopularity when a voice hailed him from the road. He raised his eyes and saw a pretty girl in an apple-green dress coming through the door of one of the fish-sheds. She looked entirely out of place in those surroundings.

"You there," she said in a crisp voice which revealed no terror at the power of the law. "Come over here."

Corporal Tobin's neck crimsoned but with a humility which surprised himself he got to his feet and walked towards her.

"I suppose you want a boat," she said.

He nodded briefly.

"There's one in here then. Help me to get it out."

He followed her into the shed where she pointed to a jumble of lobster-pots and nets which hid a small flat-bottomed dinghy. Between them they lifted it out and carried it down to one of the jetties where they pushed it off into the water. The girl climbed in and held it steady while Tobin went back for his sack of bottles and lowered it into the boat.

"I'll row," said the girl. As the Corporal hesitated, she added impatiently, "Hurry up or they'll be down to stop you."

He climbed cautiously in beside his bundle, while the light flat swayed with his weight. As soon as he was seated she pushed off and rowed strongly for the cutter.

"Thanks for helping me out," he began.

"Don't thank me," she said shortly, "I just don't believe in monkeying with the law." She looked at the sack between his feet.

"That isn't really Uncle Jos's liquor," she said. "It's my cousin Tom's. He's getting married tomorrow and of course he thought he had to have a drink in the house. I told him he would only land us all in trouble."

The Corporal decided to change the subject.

"You're not from Stag Harbour, are you?" he ventured.

"Oh yes I am," she said decidedly, "I'm Mary Hiscock. But I've been working in Halifax for the last five years. I'm only here for Tom's wedding."

She stopped abruptly as if realising that she was fraternising with the enemy. There was silence until the flat bumped gently against the cutter's bow and edged along her side.

"Haul her in, now," the girl ordered.

Tobin stood up carefully and reached for the cutter's deck. Mary lifted her oars on board but as she did so she spooned up a bladeful of sea and the stern of the flat spun round. Tobin staggered, clawed helplessly at empty air and belly-flopped into the water while Mary scrambled to her feet with a scream and a lurch, which made the small boat balance for an instant on its side, and then turn over completely.

The girl went with it and the men who were reaching out to help Tobin left him abruptly and clustered by the rail peering into the troubled water. A head broke the surface and the girl swam smoothly towards the shore.

Tobin climbed on to the deck and peered through the ripples at a scattering of bottles on the sea floor.

"Can any of you fellows dive?" he demanded.

The men shook their heads.

"We might get them at low tide," suggested one.

"Not a chance," said another. "It's still too deep. You'd want a diving suit to go after that lot."

There was a long silence. Tobin glanced across at the beach where Mary was demurely wringing out the hem of her dress. With a resounding oath he crashed his fist against the cutter's rail and turned on the crew.

"What are we waiting for?" he barked.

The engine sputtered into life. Corporal Tobin stood on the deck in a widening pool of water and gazed darkly upon Stag Harbour.

"No witnesses; no evidence; no case," he muttered. "I've made a proper fool of myself and got nothing out of it at all."

A distant flicker of apple-green caught his eye and the gloom gradually lifted from his brow.

"I'm not so sure though," he murmured. "It's a poor wedding with nary a drink. If I chanced along with a bottle or two of Screech tonight…I wonder what would happen."

Advertisement from *Devine's Folk Lore of Newfoundland* (1937)

Squarin' Up

A. R. Scammell

O the fish are all caught and the squids are all jigged,
And the traps are cut up and the schooners unrigged,
All hands round the counters are drivin' the smoke
While Jacob, he's splicin' some left-handed rope.

'Tis squarin' up time inside the big shop,
The clerks are kept busy and right on the hop,
The men are awaiting the bookkeeper's sum,
For they all want a bottle of Hudson Bay rum.

Now Skipper John Wilkins strolled in to divine,
If his credit was good for a few slips of twine,
He got such a fright when they gave him a "ran,"
That he bought a boloney for Aunt Mary Anne.

Then Skipper John Wilkins, half-brother to John,
He asked them the side that his balance was on;
And chuckled, "Here, sonny, come tend to my needs,
A pack of those raisins without any seeds."

Skipper Harry his brother was the next to go in,
With the baccy juice dribblin' down over his chin,
And when he went home he was all in a charm,
With a box of Black Jumbo tucked under each arm.

"Say, Jimmy," said Uncle Joe Brooks to his son,
"Have you got enough left to buy that new gun?"
"I've just got enough when I've squared up my bills,
For a couple of boxes of Injun Root pills."

Uncle Dick Nichols gave his old lips a wipe,
And asked Billy Coles for a loan of his pipe,
He got some "Black Richmond" from young Tommy Hayes,
And he smoked till his whiskers went in a blue blaze.

Grandfather Pelley went stark staring mad,
He swore all the oaths that he knew, till bedad,
His son wouldn't recognise him as his pop,
Till he bought him the best pair of shoes in the shop.

'Twas all because Roberts had no "Gillett's Lye,"
Which Grandmother Pelley had asked him to buy,
The way that old codger took on was a sin,
And just at that moment, the Parson walked in.

All hands who were laughin' at Grandfather's pranks,
Were quiet as mice when they saw Parson Banks,
And Billy O'Toole, he was frightened so bad,
That he swallowed the last chew of baccy he had.

The Reverend man looked around at the crowd,
"What's the joke boys," he said, "you were talkin' quite loud
Just before I came in, who was makin' the noise?"
And he looked Uncle Pelley right square in the eyes.

"Well Parson," said Grandfather, sheepish enough,
"I cannot deny I was cuttin' up rough,
Cause Billy O'Toole has had toothache all day.
An' begor, I was tryin' to charm it away."

Now come all you men who have squared up your bills
With not enough left to buy Injun Root pills;
 If you must have enough to keep body and soul,
The only thing left is to go on the dole.

"There's five dollars comin' to you, Mr. Knee."
"I don't want it, Sir, that's no good to me,
Share it up 'tween the Parson and Dr. Carew,
For I wants to keep on the good side of them two."

"If I got to niggle on six cents a day,
I'll be wantin' the doctor by the end of next May,
And maybe the Parson will have to come round,
To help me 'square up' 'fore I goes underground."

This is an example of Newfoundland paper money, *circa* 1857.

This is an example of Newfoundland paper money used when the change was being made from stirling to decimal, *circa* 1882.

This is an example of the paper money used in Newfoundland after the currency was firmly established as decimal and it was used up to Confederation, *circa* 1882.

The Coil That Binds, The Line That Bends
Pam Hall

The Coil That Binds, The Line That Bends is both object and process, both work as a way of seeing or knowing. As a sculptural form it is both the result of a long and laboured process of making, and the enabling tool, means, or vehicle for another, longer process of encounter, of engaging with the earth in a direct, yet non-intrusive way.

The Coil emerged both physically and conceptually from one of the last remaining primitive interactions between humans and Nature…the fishery of inshore Newfoundland. It is constructed from part of a retired fishing net, and bound by hand into a long, heavy, red line which has been "drawn" from the sea to make transient marks upon the land.

Since The Coil's "birth" in 1988, the fishery has undergone significant trauma… the biological and ecological sending shock waves through the economic and cultural elements of one of the oldest traditions of a place. What began as a retired fishing net starting a life beyond the fishery, has ended up as one of hundreds lying idle all over Newfoundland. What began as a celebration and reflection of a harmonious relationship with Nature, has become a solitary echo of some mystery we have not yet deciphered. It began as a line drawn from an abundant sea, and has become an ambiguous reminder of scarcity….

Although urban living and modern technology have increasingly fragmented and regimented our ways of knowing, and have distanced us dangerously from the natural world, there remains for me, especially within the physical and cultural environment of Newfoundland, not just echoes and reminders, but strong and daily encounters with a natural world both alive and untamed…and in the current context, still mysterious, misunderstood, and humbling. The preoccupations of my work in recent years have been focussed upon finding ways to know, express and re-enchant that world…to empower it once again as an acceptable source of knowledge and to find my own place within it.

Laying down the line beyond its source in Newfoundland, on Vancouver Island, in the ancient dry sea-bed of the Alberta Badlands, and in Japan, another island fishing culture, seemed like a natural progression. It was an instinctive journey, an act of following the leading line…from the first sunrise to the last sunset, from wet to dry, from island to inland, from East to Farther East.

The Coil is both an echo of my own female experience in the physical world, and an object building a history of its own. The two-dimensional works which have emerged from the process are like entries in a diary…like shorthand which encodes the experience without struggling to capture it or re-present it. These 2-dimensional works, the Biographical Notes, are the location where the physical experience becomes symbolic, where the memory of the past interaction becomes the navigator of the next…they are both tracks which reveal where the process has been, and maps which hint at where it might lead.

(1993)

caught~bound
by the tools of the trade

nets to entangle- tools to ensnare
one role to nourish- one to impair
to harvest, to feed, to ravage, to bleed
to consume and deplete, or renew and repair

The Coil: *counter-clockwise from top right:*
Wrapping the hold of The Whispering Sea, North Atlantic, 1988
Coming ashore at Eli's wharf, Quidi Vidi, Newfoundland, 1988
Spiralling on the rocks at Harling Point, Vancouver Island, 1990
Amidst the hoodoos near Drumheller, Alberta Badlands, 1991
In a Japanese garden, Tokyo, 1993
Biographical Note *from the Japanese site work, 1993*

Come In
Grace Butt

>Come in,
>come in, and shut the door on the world's weather.
>
>Take off your coat:
>my room is small, and two will make it warmer.
>
>To clasp me
>unglove your hands.
>
>And here, on the porch shelf,
>lay your pride
>before you take the few steps across the threshold
>to where I live.

Full Circle
Nadine Browne

>Baby is not trained
>and has accidents, but that's
>fine, so does Grandpa.

eye
Mary Dalton

>and this is me
>watching TV
>
>and this is the video
>of me watching TV
>
>and this is the video
>>of the photos developing
>>of me watching TV
>
>this is TV
>watching me

Praise
Boyd Chubbs

> Praise is a paper fire
> a loud torch leaping, a flaming rush
> raising, pushing the room
> then, nothing but a thin sound
> an ashen rumour across us
> The permanent lights retrace
> across the prints, books and face

Lies for the Tourists
Mary Dalton

> That rug was hooked by a sweet white-haired grandmother
> For love not money.
> That fish is fresh, caught by that strapping young feller
> With not a care to worry him—he loves the sea.
> That harbour the sun gleams bright on is so-true-blue—
> No poison here.
> Those children playing in the crooked streets—so friendly
> So quaint—
> Are fed on the milk and honey of our simple island kindness.
> Those starlings strayed in from the mainland,
> Their mad cries an alien sound on our shores.

Brigus, *circa* 1915

Vocabulary

Alastair Macdonald

its better now
for we
schoolage guys
you dont have to sweat
what was called
vocab
like in olden days

three words
like n stuff
check
four
n stuff like that
is all

n youcn vary—
n stuff like
n like stuff
n like like
n that stuff like
like n that stuff
n like stuff that

thisll do
for anything
you have to explain

n theyll last you
into adult life

Al Pittman and Tom Dawe: Island Poems

Terry Goldie

> Hurrah for our own native isle, Newfoundland!
> Not a stranger shall own one inch of its strand!
> Her faces turns to Britain, her back to the Gulf,
> Come near at your peril, Canadian wolf!
>
> – nineteenth century anti-confederation song

This image of Newfoundland as a feisty country protecting its independence is a very common one. Today, more than thirty years after confederation with that Canadian wolf, the concept of Newfoundland as a nation, both within the province and outside of it, is still a common one. Thus when one speaks of insularity, the tendency is to see it in political terms, a place which looks inside rather than out, except in the sense that the defenders of a garrison look out from the parapets.

But insularity must also be seen in its most literal sense in that Newfoundland is an island. The encircling sea which must be crossed in order to make contact with the rest of Canada and the rest of the world is a simple fact. Thus any analysis of psychological or political insularity must always retain an awareness of the geographical.

In "Stranger at Hemlock Cove," Tom Dawe records the reactions of the local people to the new teacher, "Reading stuff by poets with queer ideas / like men are islands and such…" The error, perverting John Donne's "No man is an island," produces a line which would apparently follow the Newfoundland experience and which is perfectly suited to the isolationism of the modern poet, one of the identifying features of modernism.

In *Realism in Our Time*, George Lukacs states that in realism, the characters' "individual existence…their 'ontological being' as a more fashionable terminology has it—cannot be distinguished from their social and historical environment. Their human significance, their specific individuality, cannot be separated from the context in which they are created. The ontological view governing the image of man in the work of leading modern writers is the exact opposite of this. Man, for these writers, is by nature solitary, asocial, unable to enter into relationships with other human beings." In realism, individual characters are isolated but they are only individuals: "Besides and beyond their solitariness, the common life, the strife and togetherness of other human beings, goes on as before. In a word, their solitariness is a specific social fate, not a universal *condition humaine*."

That isolation is a real physical and political fact in Newfoundland seems obvious. This should be even more true for Newfoundlanders from the bay, from the outports. In his study of Newfoundland literature, *The Rock Observed*, Patrick O'Flaherty makes the following observation:

> If life in the outports seemed to men like Bartlett and Smallwood to be limited and poverty-stricken, it can easily be imagined what habitués of the best

society in St. John's thought of it. By the end of the nineteenth century the capital city's dominance over the social and economic life of the country was complete. Whatever "leisured classes" Newfoundland could boast of possessing were located in St. John's East in close proximity to the elegant home of the governor.

Even for Tom Dawe and Al Pittman, growing up in rural Newfoundland after the war, this series of removals from power is quite extensive. Just as Britain and the United States seem far from insignificant Canada, so does Toronto from insignificant Newfoundland, and St. John's from insignificant outports.

Both Dawe and Pittman might appear to have this attitude in their reactions to resettlement, the government policy in the sixties which moved Newfoundlanders from small outports to "growth centres," in hopes of emulating an urbanized vision of the good life. In "Stage," Dawe looks at the result:

> No put put of the motor boat,
> no waiting women placing boughs,
> no children playing in the cliffs,
> no cod-oil doors with painted moons,
> no meadows green through caplin,
> no sound-bone talk from tired men…

> But one grey fish-stage
> leaning seaward
> from the cold sloping rocks
> below the meadows
> of the unmown hay…

Pittman's last play, *West Moon*, takes this ghostly reaction to a more literal extreme as the inhabitants of the outport cemetery realize that resettlement will mean no relatives living near to tend their graves and remember them.

In Dawe's "The Madonna," he looks at a church abandoned in a small island community. Yet even without people it has a presence, as the walls "loomed strong":

> And there were certain still nights
> when the ocean pulsed in calm
> and duplicated every-season's moon.
> On such nights
> the firm church-steeple seemed
> to waver down on a ribbon of tide…

The title of one of Pittman's earliest books, *Seaweed and Rosaries*, suggests a similar connection between faith and the bay. In one of his poems to the abandoned outport, "St. Leonard's Revisited," he wandered

> and came again to the cove
> as they did after rosary
> in the green and salty days…

"The Madonna" is a lament for the vandalism which some young men perpetrate on the statue left inside the church but it is no simple defence of the Roman Catholic faith. The religion here, as in Pittman, is not denominational or dogmatic but an association between tradition and the island experience.

The young boys in "The Madonna" come to the island as outsiders but there is always a suggestion of some danger in the human element resident on the island, in both Dawe and Pittman. In Dawe's "Inuk," the people of Hemlock Cove reject an Inuit arrival. In Pittman's *A Rope Against the Sun* there is a series of harsh and unnecessary conflicts. This atmosphere of hostility can extend to the buildings themselves, as in "Island Estate of St. Andrew's." Pittman takes a compatriot to an isolated, dark and withdrawn house, representative of an almost gothic danger. He ends, however, with nature in opposition:

> from there on the top step
> stand in deep shadow
> your back turned
> to the great dark door
> observe what perfect patterns
> the bright whitecapped waves make
> as they glisten silver in the sunlight
> all the way to the thin horizon
> and beyond

Dawe's "House on the Coast" presents a similar image, although the house is by no means foreboding. The important point is that its abandoned state leaves room for a clear interaction between the parts of nature:

> There's a plain old house on a coast
> with evening now in its upper panes
> and no smoke in the on-shore air
> to blur the lines
> of seven sea-gulls wheeling
> the horizon definite
> over rock edges and pools
> and the empty pebble-beach.

In this, as in so many of their poems, there is a clear connection between the different elements of the island, all brought together at that point where land, sea and air meet. This atmosphere is often improved by the absence of man as in Dawe's poem. This is perhaps related to the association between death and the sea, as in Pittman's "Driftwood":

> A grey portion of bone
> ignored perfectly by insects. Oblivious
> perfectly to the heat of the sun. The shift
> of sand. The grip of ice. Rain. Wind.
> Time. Imagine us cast up here in perfect
> communion with this driftwood.

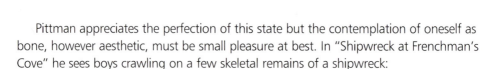

Pittman appreciates the perfection of this state but the contemplation of oneself as bone, however aesthetic, must be small pleasure at best. In "Shipwreck at Frenchman's Cove" he sees boys crawling on a few skeletal remains of a shipwreck:

> do they find
> some perverse comfort
> in knowing that you too
> were killed by the sea
> like so many of their fathers
> before them

For the Newfoundlander, the sea must be an image of danger as well as of beauty and completion. In "Driftwood," Pittman brings both together. In *A Rope Against the Sun*, the reef in the harbour attains supernatural significance in the fear which it instills in the people of Merasheen. But they are still tied to the sea. The fishing society has decayed but it remains as a heroic myth. The old drunk, Joe Casey, hollers out praise for various ships, "toasting the first in a long list of drowned seamen he'll pay tribute to before he joins them in his drunken dreams." Jack Connors is likewise withdrawn from active life but his past greatness is always recalled: "At that time, the children played at make-believing they were Jake Connors, skipper of the *Swallow*, and most renowned fish-killer in the bay."

In "On the Full Tide," Dawe reflects on his own childhood, and the importance of the acceptance of the old fisherman, "holding the thorns from lobster pots/and wrinkled like ice kelp/across the nets of fall":

> I always felt that
> he smiled at me then
> as the pure surf smiled at me,
> as the ringing cliffs
> as the sea-birds
> as the children smiled at me.
> And it was good.

Although the human life on the shore can be evil, and although nature is always on the point of destroying the fisherman, there is a connection between the wholeness found in nature and the power of the fisherman which, at times in a vicarious way, provides a potential for the poet in his relationship with island and sea.

As a rule, the interaction between beach and sea appears beneficent but it can easily change, particularly when, as is so often the case in Newfoundland, the point of contact is not a beach but rough rock or cliff. In "Evening, Bareneed, Conception Bay," Tom Dawe notes the following:

> The cold wind
> creeps unmarked
> through an ancient picket-fence
> and eats the salt-stained grass
> already dead

> on a skull of rock
> above a misty bay
> spilling itself
> on the teeth of kelp-ringed crags.

Pittman sees a more overtly dangerous transition:

> from here on the headland
> there is nothing
> between us and the world's dark end
> but infinite distance
> black and immutable as death
> the night encloses us
> as we cling to each other
> in darkness
> and fall like broken insects
> from the sky

At the same time, this treacherous cliff can provide an inspiring balance. Once again it is a product of that close interaction among three elements, land, sea and air:

> you walk knowing you
> walk with angels
> angry on either side
>
> it is something you'll do only once
> between here and wherever it is you're bound
> and they only if

There is a mystic elevation to this position which is very different from the state of being totally immersed in water, from the drowning that is always a possibility for those who fish in the cold North Atlantic. In one of his poems, Pittman combines his thoughts on that potential experience with the change which he has experienced in maturation:

> Once
> when I was drowning
> I held on long enough
> to say the Act of Contrition
>
> If today I were drowning
> I wonder what I'd do
>
> I can't remember
> the Act of Contrition
> and besides
> I'm not nearly the sinner
> I used to be
> when I was eight and a half
> years old.

As in the earlier examples, the water has a power which is comparable to but clearly removed from that of the traditional church. As an adult, the potential for drowning remains but the ritual is forgotten and the concept of sin has been displaced. There seems to be no established set of values, a moral gap that is found in much of modernism.

A number of years later, Pittman finds a reply to his quandary. The island fear, the isolated drowning, remains at both points in the first poem, regardless of religious belief, but in the second work this has been altered:

> Once
> when I was drowning
> I held on long enough
> to make an act of contrition
>
> that was long ago
> when I knew what to be sorry for
> when I knew how to confess
>
> that was before we made
> an unholy sacrament out of our love
> a brutal religion out of our innocence
>
> now as I go spinning down
> for the last time
> I struggle in the flood
> not for any absolution
> but for your approval
> of my perfect death

The lack of capitals shows how the religious ritual has even less power. But a sexual connection has overcome both the absence of religion and the fear of drowning. There is a positive link between the sea death and the lover.

It is difficult to find a similar mystical sea change in Dawe's poetry. There is a reasonably clear difference between those of his poems which consider religion and those which concentrate on the physical island. In "The Madonna," as noted above, there is an important connection between bay and church but this does not seem mystical. Perhaps an exception might be found in "Evening, Bareneed, Conception Bay." It ends,

> Beyond
> across the bight
> a slow mist hangs
> in a wooden cross
> in a block of window-light.

Another example, although a rather pagan one, might be his reaction, thinking back to an old man who always used to believe in the man in the moon:

> Now we are scattered men remembering
> back along a fish-spine row of years
> to the time on that coast of his belief
> when the moving herring-schools
> mooned in the long night tides
> and tangled in this waiting nets
> just yards below his quiet house
> where he slept.

Similarly, Dawe does not seem to find the sexual fruition at the island edge suggested in some of Pittman's poems. The latter's "Song Also," to Pat Lowther, a poet from British Columbia, provides a lovely example of the multiple connections of the island experience:

> Take me to your island.
> I'll speak so softly
> you'll have to feel my words
> whispering on your skin.
> Coming from my own island
> I know very well how sound
> carries across water.
> I'll come in the blackest night
> of the year and walk with you
> through the twisted trees
> to the sea.
> And we'll collect
> whatever jewelled creatures
> you want to wish up
> out of the onyx ocean.

The romance is linked to the island as a place which possesses all the possible sensations of nature, as in "Sea-Lovers":

> The green-backed sea
> refused to run
>   a longer course
> and lept
>   the island's edge
>
> And satisfied
> with doing that
> rolled in contented waves
> over the grey sand
> and kind of lazily
> came
> to cool our four feet

>   as we made love
>   to it
>   far better than
>   we ever had
>   to each other

Here the insularity of the individual comes to the fore. But although each is unable to make the full connection to the other, there is potential for something approximating a completion, with nature, with that mixture of waves and sand at the shore.

The land-sea interaction has an importance which goes well beyond a metaphoric relationship with sex or religion. Part of the sensibility out of which Dawe and Pittman write is represented in their works for children. Both Pittman's *Down by Jim Long's Stage* and Dawe's *Landwash Days* make attempts to bring modern children into contact with life at the edge of the sea, with fish as friends and playmates. In his "Author's Note," Dawe writes:

> When I was just a conner-catching youngster living in Conception Bay, Newfoundland, my friends and I spent many long, summer days in the landwash. For us, this was all the area on the shoreline, especially that marvellous world around the tide-marks where all kinds of creatures lived. It was here in the ways of the fish, the flight of the birds and the clouds, the buzz of the flies, and all the other mysteries, that we formed our first view of the world: here was the meaning of everything.

This image of the landwash interaction as a communal one, to be made with friends, is primarily limited to the vision for the child, however. In the adult poetry, the tendency is to seek the island edge alone. Even when a friend accompanies or, as in "Sea-Lovers" and a number of other Pittman poems, is an equal participant, there is a separation. One might speculate that the dream of contact with another island-lover in the poem to Pat Lowther is only possible at the impossible distance which extends between Pittman's Newfoundland and Lowther's Gulf Islands.

Even alone, the poet's connection with the landwash seems limited. It remains for another element of nature, the gull, that bird which participates in land, sea and air, to achieve fully, as in Dawe's "Gulls and Ice":

> The harbour
> once ice-congested
> succumbed to an Arctic thrust
> and threw its margins
> upwards jaggedly
> to pierce the eggshell horizon
> undulating the whole
> on immaculate whites
> and close-up watery greens
> in a matrix
> of melting spring sky
> seeming to cast itself

> gracefully awry
> in wheels of wavering flight
> as sea gulls
> in a new-creation light.

The power and danger of the sea is intensified by the ice in the harbour and the resulting direct antagonism between the sea pushing the ice and the shore holding it back. In the end once more, however, there is a lift up into the air, in which the image is compared to the gulls. The effect is linked to the gulls "in a new-creation light," a feeling of epiphany through this apparently angry contact at the shore.

I mentioned before that even this subtle suggestion of a mystical, religious experience of the shore is unusual in Dawe. It is much more common in Pittman, and in "Sea Gull" he extends the image of this bird as a particular participant in the island coast:

> Something sacred he seems
> raised for worship
> above the grey sea altar
>
> poised on priest wind hands
> he awaits
> the genuflection
>
> a certain concern for eternity
> kneels me on the salt wet rock
> and seeming satisfied
> with that small penance
> he tips one wing in casual benediction
> and moves on seaward
> to command another's adoration

Both Dawe and Pittman seem to find some kind of harmony in nature but in neither is it simple pantheism. The physical joining of land, air and sea presents suggestions of a possible harmony in opposition to their natural tendency to isolation. The gull is such a suggestion of the possibility but it remains quite removed from the very human considerations of the poets.

The means of overcoming the individual limitations is to become more a part of the island. Both poets seem to fit into Lukacs' definition of modernism in that their isolation is a contemporary malaise rather than a product of their environments. They may lament resettlement or the failure to achieve harmony between different religions and different races but these concerns do not present the cause of insularity.

Paradoxically, moreover, rather than the political isolation and geographical isolation increasing insularity, it seems to have little effect. It might be possible to see the St. John's-outport division as the cause of the resettlement lament, but this is seldom if ever a direct concern for the two poets. As to the geography, the island is never a limiting frame, with the sea cutting them off from important places elsewhere. Rather it is a source of connections, as in Pittman's observation to Pat Lowther about how sound carries over water. It is a dangerous place, where the sea meets the land, but it is a necessary place if one is to recognize all the potentials in that restoring nature. This can be seen in another poem about a gull, Tom Dawe's poem, "The Tickleace is Ticklish":

> The Tickleace is ticklish
> It seldom comes to land,
> It sleeps upon the ocean waves
> It does not like the sand.
>
> It comes ashore to make a nest
> But does not stay for long
> It sits upon an iceberg top
> And squalls a ticklish song.

There is always a tendency to attempt an escape from the island and from those essential but ambivalent experiences at the edge of water. In "Winter '72" Al Pittman shows two men hibernating in an outport house, apparently contented companions, but existing for faraway fantasies, like a "spangled princess." "Crewlike," they hide in their stationary ship, this "sea room house." Their fears of the winter sea are clear:

> outside and above the boiling cove
> above the age-old fish-storied stages
> (resisting still in their trembling old age
> the never-say-die seaweeded sea)
> the sky crawling gulls claw
> at the white confusion of the whistling wind
> scratch their screeching frenzy
> on the impenetrable windwall of our alliance.

The final dream, however, releases them from exotic visions and from fears of their winter island:

> like a cocoon from which we will uncurl
> when thank god the sainted sea windows
> releasing us weak-winged
> into the salty and seagulled sky.

The insularity of the poets, in the psychological sense, is a major factor in their poems. But it is the insularity of most contemporary poets, the insularity of what Lukacs calls modernism, the insularity of removed and often anxious contemplation. The insularity is not bred by a rejection of an oppressive mainland, nor an oppressive St. John's. Resettlement is presented as one more image of man's failure to maintain what is good. Rather than a defensive, pugnacious reaction against those who were in charge, it is the reaction of the poet who appreciates the beauty and harmony of rural life and who is depressed by its absence.

The one escape from this insularity, created not by the island but by modern life, is the island as physical being. Rather than being a cause of isolation, the island is a potential saviour from its pain. The individual contemporary poet, all too aware as the rest of his breed of that "universal *condition humaine*," to which Lukacs refers, finds a possible hope in that energetic point of connection at the island's edge. The gull, who survives and prospers in his ambivalent stance between land and sea, provides a possible key. The island might defeat that isolation which Dawe so carefully repulses in "Connections":

> And we can sleep through this night
> if we group and connect
> our comfortable similes and such
> as stays against
> disconnection.

For most contemporary poets the defeat of that disconnection seems impossible—but for the island poet it might be only a landwash away.

Excerpts from
No Man's Land
Kevin Major

Publisher's cover blurb for No Man's Land

Kevin Major reaches a new milestone in his career with the publication of No Man's Land. Set in France during World War I, it pulls us into the lives of the young men of the Newfoundland Regiment at rest in the village of Louven-court, preparing to set out for the trenches and what will come to be known as the Battle of the Somme.

Second lieutenant Alan Hayward and his brash fellow officer, Clarke, together with young Martin and the other men heading into battle, wait out the hours to the final whistle. Longing for their homeland, frustrated by the lack of knowledge about what lies ahead, they stand resolutely on the firesteps as their pocket watches tick away to zero hour.

A classic war novel, the book is equally effective in its portrayal of the camaraderie and unnatural quiet before the storm, as in its graphic account of the fight to make it through the barbed wire and sweep of machine-gun bullets across no man's land.

Two hundred and seventy-two young men from the Newfoundland Regiment who went over the top on the morning of July 1, 1916, lost their lives. The regiment suffered more casualties than any other unit on the battlefield and the island from which it came lost many of the men who would have been its future leaders. No community in Newfoundland escaped the consequences of the regiment's attempt to drive the enemy from Beaumont Hamel. It was the single greatest disaster in the island's history.

Chapter Eight from No Man's Land

There were sixty-six of them, fresh that morning from Rouen. When Hayward and Clarke arrived, they were sitting about on their packs, having just been scrutinized by the colonel. They looked an eager lot, despite the tramp of the last few miles from the train station.

"Whelps," Clarke said under his breath. "Someone should have told them they had to be weaned before they could join up."

He led Hayward to a couple of the youngest looking ones. "What part of Newfoundland are you from, men?"

"Trinity Bay, sir."

"Both of you?"

"Yes, sir. Him and me are cousins."

"And what brings you to this part of the world?"

"Pardon, sir?"

"Why are you here, then, Private?"

"The war, sir. We're here to do our bit."

"Ever hunt seals?"

"Lots of times, sir. I woulda had a berth on the *Stephano* this spring if I hadn't joined up."

"You know, this is a lot like sealing. Only the seals have guns, and they're just as smart as you are."

They looked at each other and laughed heartily.

Hayward knew their response would only sharpen Clarke's tongue even more. For the sake of the men, he diverted Clarke's attention to the sight of the colonel conferring with the commanding officers of the regiment's four companies. "They're splitting the pot."

They were about to join a group of other officers standing nearby when Hayward was approached from behind by one of the new men.

"Excuse me, sir."

He faced a private who looked to be no more than seventeen.

"Do you remember me, sir?"

He did look vaguely familiar, yet Hayward couldn't think where he had seen him before.

"Neddy, they all used to call me. Edward Martin. I lived up the street, in number 39."

"My God, Neddy Martin."

"Ned, sir, that's me name now."

"The fellow who almost broke his neck slidin' down the hill back of Kelly's Brook?"

"Yes, sir. The same one. I still got the scar." He pushed back his hair to show Hayward.

Hayward's mind was suddenly flooded with memories of growing up on Maxse Street. "He gave himself some smack," he said to Clarke. "We all thought he was dead. He came around just as we got him home."

"I was hoping I'd find you here, sir."

"But you're not old enough, are you?"

"Don't tell anyone, sir. A lot of us got away with it. I wasn't the only one."

"I bet you didn't want to miss out, did you, lad?" said Clarke with a slight smile.

"I made sure I wasn't going to be called a slacker. There's a good many of them a lot older than me, sir, marling around the streets in St. John's. It's people like you two, sir, that I want to be like. I think one day I might be an officer."

"That you will," Clarke said. "All it takes is persistence, and a good stretch of luck…."

Chapter Twenty-Four from *No Man's Land*

When Hayward and Clarke went their separate ways they knew the next time they could hope to see each other would be on the battlefield. They were silent in their handshake, and tried to look at each other as if nothing would change.

Hayward called, after Clarke had turned away, "We'll go for another swim."

Clarke glanced back, for the moment the familiar grin across his face. He turned the corner, and was gone.

"Sir." It was Bennett. He looked worried. "The men are very anxious, sir."

"The wait will soon be over."

"We're going, then?"

Hayward's look confirmed it. The corporal's face stiffened even more.

"The word has to come from the colonel," Hayward said.

"The men just want to get to it."

Hayward looked about at his men. They all were eyeing him.

He had a word for each of them, the encouragement that was his duty. There was not the fire that had sometimes been in his voice, though he would not have them think anything but that there was a job to be done and they were the men who could do it.

"Sir," said Smith, "she'll be over and done wit' soon."

Hayward expected more, but Smith went by, not able to stand still.

"He's on about hes wife and youngsters," Moss confided. "It's different when it's only yerself."

"You got it all figured."

"If yer number comes up, it comes up. There's not a damn thing can be done about it. No sense broodin'."

Hayward wished it was as simple for all of them. Their wait was in dense, impenetrable silence for the most part, though their minds had to be racing like his own. The few words that passed between them shrugged off the strain, foolery smack in the face of mountainous seas building ahead.

"The Hun knows better than to get saucy with a Newfoundlander."

"Gaff the buggers, I say, and fling 'em back where they come from."

Hayward gave word that the tot of rum due each man be passed out. Most took it eagerly, downing it in one gulp, savouring the burning warmth. Some others, Martin included, took their time, as if they had no stomach for it, the final rite that marked with certainty their plunge over the top.

When the order came to stand-to, Martin was on his feet and onto the firestep as quickly as the next man, his rifle at the ready, bayonet clamped to the muzzle, pointing skyward. His will to get through it was equal to his grip on the rifle. He would get through and, if he had to, go face to face with them in their trenches.

He was all but rid of the voices from home. He would be part of the Great Push and they'd not forget it. A fine time it would be when he'd go on and on how he was right in the midst of the charge.

By now his fear had turned to rock in his stomach. He clenched it and riveted his attention to the lip of the trench and the leap that would take him up and over. With three regiments ahead of them, and the hammering from the artillery, what chance was there for anything to be in their way? They said it was machine-gun fire they'd heard, but no one knew for certain, and it had passed off now whatever it was.

His eyes closed and his forehead pressed against the trench wall. He prayed God would get him through. The prayer he repeated silently again and again, without lull, until it became part of him, until it was all that filled his mind.

The weight of his pack dragged mercilessly at his body. It became a penance, a sacrifice, whatever His will might be. As more minutes passed the effort to open his eyes had gone. He sank away to His protection.

"Steady, Ned! On your feet, lad."

It was Hayward's voice. Martin opened his eyes and discovered he had slumped down on the firestep. He struggled back upright, with Hayward's help, his rifle clenched as firmly as ever. He said nothing. His head pressed against the trench wall again. His eyes shut.

"Six minutes, Ned."

He could feel a hand gripping his arm. When he looked it was Hayward on the firestep shoulder to shoulder with him, standing-to, pistol in his other hand.

Smith was on the firestep to his right, and Moss next to him, the trench bridge between the two. They stood eager for the whistle, their tin hats strapped tight, their jaws set. They uttered a gruff few words, making sport of what the next few minutes would bring. There was no thought now to anything but the regiment.

Martin could hear others on both sides of him, pitching droll insults at the Hun and betting on who would be the one to get Kathleen, the St. John's beauty who rumour had it wanted to marry the first of the regiment to get the Victoria Cross.

Martin straightened up more and tried to stretch the aching stiffness out of his shoulders. Hayward took some of the weight of his pack while Martin repositioned it to something less painful.

"The sledgehammer," he muttered, when he had the full weight of it again.

"They all have their reasons."

"What good will it do us?"

"It gives you trouble out there, sling the bloody thing to hell!" The anger slashed the air.

Martin froze, unable to look into his face.

"Ned," Hayward said, a forced calmness in his voice. "You'll not do anything foolish. You'll have your go. You'll do your bit, lad. Don't be thinking about anyone but yourself. There's plenty more to fight after this one."

"Me mother'll see me back," Martin said. "She will, sir."

Hayward nodded.

"Yours too, sir."

He nodded again.

"A great day on the saltwater, what, Mossie?" Smith called out.

"Yes, and that it is so."

"Feel that sun on yer face, bud. Nuthin' like it."

Smith started to hum one of their old favourites while in the background the corporal declared them down to the last minute.

Beaumont Hamel

Frederick Andrews

Walk slowly here,
Be reverent and fervent,
For here upon this noble plain
The youth of our fair island
Bled in twain.
That grim July dawn,
When sallied forth twice 400 strong
Into the valley unknown,
Their charge was fine,
Their strength as nine;
In battle-dress arrayed they fought,
They bled, they died.
When shall their honours die,
Or that great bloody charge deny?
Sooner Orion burst in two,
Or the rushing water kiss the dew.
"We few"—we gallant few,
We three score six and two—
The remnant of that glorious stand.
Never! shall we forget that band,
Or the famous charge in "No Man's Land."
Their names are written in deeds of gold
Across the island strong and bold.

The Ballad of Beaumont Hamel

Jim Fidler

Beaumont Hamel,
Beaumont Hamel,
Ecout l'appelle,
Beaumont Hamel.

A Nation brought down to its knees,
'Neath a foreign sky far across the seas,
For the sake of all our liberties,
Beaumont Hamel.

In an empty book of history,
Void of circumstance that was ne'er to be,
Cry the only two words there to see,
Beaumont Hamel.

As they laid our young men down to rest,
And the trumpet sounded its last address,
All a nation's hope perished in her breast,
Beaumont Hamel.

Oh, how vivid is the spectreous hag,
In the colours of the empire's flag,
I see only red in that treacherous rag,
Beaumont Hamel.

And now every year on the seventh's first,
As the flags unfurl to the fireworks,
We can only pray we have seen the worst,
Beaumont Hamel.

Romance In the Twentieth Century

Robert G. MacDonald

These boys in the trenches in Flanders
Mud-soaked, bedraggled, half stifled with gas-stopping helmets,
Boys from the Highlands, boys from Canadian plains,
Chaps from English cities, artisans carrying repeating rifles,
(A couple of years ago 'twould be odd enough to see them)
Irish boys from Erin's green Isle:
They are all of them knights to-day,
Knights as true and as bold as ever figured in Mediaeval tales,
Because their work, their job, is to avenge the honor of a Maiden
Ruthlessly trampled on, shamefully violated,
The beautiful Maiden, Belgium—
This is Romance in the Twentieth Century.

These lads on Gallipoli's ridges
From the Isles of the South, from the Austral Continent;
(Can't you see the Maori touch in their dark faces, the little limbs, the flash of the eye?
Has it struck you that some of these others were keeping sheep little more than a year ago?)
Lads from the Isle of the North—you can almost see the roll of the fisherman in their walk to this day;
Half mad with the heat, half blind with the glare, tormented by flies and by vermin,
Clothed in stained and worn khaki garments.
Do you know what they are doing?—here's romance for you—
They have come from the ends of the earth, from the corners of the globe,
And their work is to wrest the Holy Shrine of Saint Sophia from the Infidel
To take possession in the name of Jesus Christ of the Holy Sepulchre,
To drive the Turk out of Europe.
This is Romance in the Twentieth Century!

Prelude to Doom

Irving Fogwill

The iterated idiot round of words
Dribbles and mouths its talk of peace;
The lie writ large upon old masked faces.
Intent and wan the Scientist makes
His new gun and deadly gas, bat-blind
To God, to love, to human brotherhood.
Fashion he must, engines of death,
Besides food of life, at his masters' bidding.
His masters—the old men, the wolfish old men,
The foolish old men—who never learn.
The old men who cheer their sons to death.
Old men of all lands, teaching youth hatred;
Teaching youth to murder youth for a flag.

The old men, the grave old men,
The suave and polished old men,
The old cynical souls of old men,
Flinging in our teeth the old lies,
Building anew the foul old lies,
The old idiot, weasel lies.

There they sit, the grave old men
Secretly sit and spin the old lies,
Weaving the bloody web of war,
Waving the same old flags—the old men—
Bidding youth to die for the same old lies.
The old and grinning skulls of war.

The skulls of old men, skulls of withered death,
Asking youth to die when youth should live;
Teaching youth that its last strangled breath
Be gasped in some red hell; nor—plaintive—
Must youth question the myriad dead.
The myriad, heaped-up, useless dead.

And so mankind prepares to die.
Soon sons of mothers will march to kill
Sons of mothers on other lands. The sky
Will echo and echo again the despairing cry
Of dying youth. How awful to spill
This precious blood—and, O God, why?

Bill

Jack Turner

Bill, the Bomber, is down in the mud,
    Shot to pieces and bleeding fast,
He played his cards in the game of games,
    But he's come to the end of his stack at last;
He bet on his cards for all they were worth,
    Now his last check's up on a losing hand,
And he's cashing in at the game's grim end,
    In the shell-swept reaches of No-Man's-Land.

Bill came down from the frozen North,
    From the lonely land where the corpse-lights glow,
Spurred and stung by the tales of war,
    That filtered in from the land below;
Tales of torture and filthy lust,
    Tales of horror and deeds of shame,
Till he left his claim and his trapping line,
    To take a hand in the greatest game.

His mukluks and parka are cached away,
    And they've dressed him up in a khaki suit,
They've taught him to see with a soldier's eye,
    They've taught him to drill, and to march, and shoot;
He, who had shot that he might not starve,
    He, who had run with the dogs all day,
Learned to shoot as a soldier shoots,
    Learned to march in a soldier's way.

They took him over across the sea,
    And set him down in a ravished land,
Where the trenches twine through the war-tilled fields,
    And the Hun is held in an iron band;
Doing his bit with his heart held high,
    Taking his chances as they came round,
And now he's lying between the lines,
    And his blood drops red on the reeking ground;
He prays for the greatest gift of the gods,
    The touch of death that will end his pain,
Then sleep steals down on his weary eyes,
And his soul is back in the North again.

He feels the fang of the frost in his flesh,
    As it stabs through the parka's fold,
And the scorch of the storm-whirl sears his cheek,
    With the touch of its biting cold;
He hears the crunch of the wind-packed snow,
    As it grinds 'neath the snow-shoes' tail,
And he knows he is back in the North again,
    At the start of another trail.

Back to the land where he'd fought, and failed,
    And risen to fight again,
Fought and fallen, but battled on,
    In the strength of his sweat and pain;
Broken and beaten, but undismayed,
    Fighting the fight to the last,
One lone man 'gainst the lone wolf-land,
    Braving the biting blast.

Daring the devils that ride the storm,
    The fiends that reive in the snow,
Going gay to the jaws of death,
    As only the brave may go,
Hurling a taunt in the wolf-land's eyes,
    Laughing in death's dark face,
A lonely atom that takes its stand
    In the midst of infinite space.

Back in the grey old North again,
    With the flat snow stretching wide,
Back in the land of the stunted pines,
    Where the wolf and the Husky bide,
Back where the Frost King's grip is strong,
    And the winds, his courtiers, race,
Back where men rattle the dice with fate
    And gamble for gold or a grave.

Then the flame of the past leaped through his blood,
    Like the flame of a sacred arc,
And the wail of the wind was a welcome home,
    To the land of his heart's desire,
The Huskies howled in the driving storm
    And the howl of the wolves replied,
From the shadowed thickets of stunted pine
    That blackened the mountain side.

Then mush, you sore-footed brutes, mush on,—
    The tugging malamutes strain the trace,
And the whip's sharp snap is the crack of doom,
    As it rings and echoes through silent space;
The coarse snow shrieks 'neath the speeding sled,
    And heading into the rising gale,
Strong in the strength of his heart and hands,
    He's mushing off on his last long trail.

Bill, the Bomber came back to the trench,
    A mud-stained tunic over his face,
By the light of the first faint flush of dawn,
    They dug him a shallow resting-place;
They looked at the wounds where his life leaked out,
    And their oaths held more than a hint of prayer,
For they knew that he'd suffered the pains of hell,
    Waiting for death in the darkness there.

Then they bared his face for a last good-bye,
    Ere they laid him down on his couch of clay,
And he seemed to sleep, as a man may sleep
    At the end of a long and weary day;
Never a mark on his face to tell,
    Of the age-long hours of a night of pain,
But the smile of a man, who, the long trail past,
    Is come to the home of his heart again.

Seeking Recruits

Compiled by Fred Adams

This is the proclamation which appeared in February 1940 in the St. John's area seeking recruits for the British Army.

Proclamation

BY HIS EXCELLENCY Vice-Admiral Sir Humphrey Thomas Walwyn, Knight Commander of the Most Exalted Order of the Star of India, Knight Commander of the Most Distinguished Order of St. Michael and St. George, Companion of the Most Honourable Order of the Bath, Companion of the Distinguished Service Order, Governor and Commander-in-Chief in and over the Island of Newfoundland and Its Dependencies.

HUMPHREY WALWYN,

(L. S.) Governor

BRITISH ARMY
JOIN THE ROYAL ARTILLERY AND FIGHT FOR KING AND COUNTRY

The War Office through the Secretary of State for Dominion Affairs has asked Newfoundland to call for volunteers to serve in the Royal Artillery for the duration of the war. Newfoundland men will form one complete Heavy Royal Artillery Regiment, and as far as possible, other complete Heavy Royal Artillery Regiments. Volunteers are required to be up to the following standards:

General Requirements

Age—20 to 35 years.
Height—At least 5' 4"
Weight—At least 112 lbs
Chest measurement—At least 33"
Sound physique and good eyesight
Medical standard required—Grade 1
Must be able to read and write correctly

CONDITIONS OF SERVICE

Men when enlisted will be paid at the following rate:

1st year of enlistment—2 shillings per day.

2nd year of enlistment—2 shillings and threepence per day and threepence per day, Military Proficiency Pay. Free board, housing, bed, blanket, uniform and kit, upon enlistment, will be provided.

Men enlisted in Newfoundland will have full opportunity of promotion to NonCommissioned, Warrant and Commissioned rank, equally with all other soldiers.

Single men will be accepted first, then married men.

Single men with any one dependent on them will not be accepted for the present.

Recruits will be provided with food and accommodation as from the day upon which they are called for enlistment. Also transportation from their homes to St. John's.

MARRIAGE ALLOWANCES

In the case of married men, Marriage (or separation) Allowances will be paid at the following rates:
Wife only—17 shillings /week.
Wife and one child—22 shillings /week.
Wife and two children—26 shillings /week.
3 shillings /week for each additional child.
The foregoing applies to children under the age of 14 years.
Before Marriage Allowances will be paid a man will be required to contribute a portion of his pay to his wife and family.

CERTIFICATES

In order to qualify for any pay, unmarried men will be required to produce their Birth Certificates.

Married men will be required to produce their Birth Certificates, Marriage Certificates, and the Birth Certificates of their children (if any).

GENERAL

Men residing in the St. John's area (which comprises the Districts of St. John's, East and West; that portion of the District of Harbour Main from Avondale to St. John's inclusive; and that portion of the District of Ferryland from Bay Bulls to St. John's inclusive), should apply in person if possible or otherwise in writing to the Recruiting Officer, King George the Fifth Seaman's Institute, Water Street East, St. John's. The Office will be open for the purpose of interviewing applicants between the hours of 10 a.m. and noon, and 3 p.m. and 5 p.m. daily. Sundays and holidays excepted. Men residing outside of the St. John's area who wish to offer their services should do so either in person, if convenient, or otherwise in writing, to the Magistrate within whose jurisdiction they reside. If the Magistrate is satisfied that the applicant possesses the required qualifications, he will arrange for a medical examination. These qualifications and examinations are subject to review upon the arrival of the recruit at St. John's or any other Recruiting Centre. If for any reason the man is found not to be up to the standard required either by the Recruiting or Medical authorities, he will be returned to his home. These examinations will be strict. Applicants should consult the Magistrate or the Recruiting Officer on any points on which they are in doubt.

Recruits will be attested before sailing. The first draft will probably embark for England early in April.

GOD SAVE THE KING

Given under my Hand and Seal at the Government House, St. John's, this 6th day of February, A.D. 1940.

By His Excellency's Command,
(Sgd.) J. A. WINTER,
Commissioner for
Home Affairs and Education.

The Chance of Your Lifetime
Compiled by Fred Adams

The following advertisement appeared in a newspaper in St. John's in 1940 and an immediate response was the result. The last line in the advertisement is very provocative.

Young men of Newfoundland

HAVE YOU

Daring - Skill - Initiative?

IF SO, JOIN THE

Royal Air Force-Air Craft Crews

Pilots

Observers

Wireless Operators-Air Gunners

Serve your King and Country

In This Great Adventure

The Chance of YOUR Lifetime!

A Letter to Will

Stephen Walsh

During this century, Canada has sent young men and women overseas for World War I, World War II, the Korean Conflict, and numerous United Nations Peacekeeping actions. Some left home, never to return. Others came home disabled for life. Those who returned were profoundly affected by their experiences. On November 11th, we remember the men and women who were killed in our nation's wars and think about their supreme sacrifice.

For the soldiers the mail call was a precious respite from the alternating horrors of war and the boredom of waiting. It was a special time; with family and loved ones. It was a time to catch up on family events, to learn what life on the home front was like, and to give loved ones a glimpse into the everyday reality of war. Many of these letters have become treasured mementos of those who never came home. For those who were writing overseas, the letters were equally important.

The following is a fictional letter from home. It is similar to thousands of letters written to loved ones overseas. It was written by a 16 year old to his older brother serving in France.

> Box 33
> Topsail, Nfld.
> January 4, 1945
>
> Dear Will,
>
> Hello. How are things at the front? Things here haven't changed since the last letter. We still have to line up for most of our food. Having a farm will help next summer, though.
>
> Dad's still doing construction work at Fort Pepperrell. He likes working with the Americans. The ones I've met are really nice. They're very, very friendly.
>
> Mary's dating an American soldier now. I think he's from Iowa. His name's Rick and he's coming for dinner next Sunday. Even though Dad likes Americans, he isn't sure if he wants his only daughter to marry someone from the U.S.A.
>
> I want your advice on whether I should enlist or not. I want to join the army like you did and sign up with the artillery, but Dad wants me to join the Navy and Mom wants me to stay in school.
>
> I want to go. I want to be like you. I don't want to miss the war. I don't want to die like Johnny Soper from school did, but I feel I have to do my duty for England, and I don't want to disappoint you.

This essay was chosen by the Royal Canadian Legion, Newfoundland Command, for First Place in the 1990 Essay Contest for high school students. [Eds.]

I forgot to tell you in my last letter that Liz Farrell and I are dating now. I'm not sure if she wants me to go. She says I'd look the world in a uniform. One of her brothers died when his ship was torpedoed, so she's probably afraid that someone else she knows will die.

I saw your girl Betty in the store yesterday. She said that she misses you a lot. She also said she's being true to you, even though you are in France. She said she writes you every week so I guess you know all that.

Mom says she misses you. She wants you to be careful and come home safe and sound. She says don't be a hero, just come home.

Dad wants you to come home so you can help him around the farm. He says he is very proud of you. I want you to come home, too.

I've kept you long enough, so write home soon.

So long.

Your little brother,
Robert

TELEGRAM

From: Allied Command, London
To: Mr. and Mrs. Joseph Neville, Topsail, Newfoundland

WE REGRET TO INFORM YOU THAT PRIVATE WILLIAM JOSEPH NEVILLE HAS BEEN KILLED IN ACTION IN FRANCE ON JANUARY 4 STOP HE HAS RECEIVED A MILITARY BURIAL STOP HIS PERSONAL EFFECTS WILL BE SENT TO YOU SHORTLY STOP

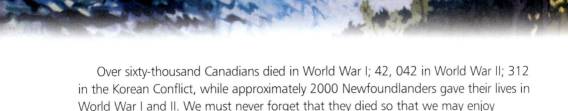

Over sixty-thousand Canadians died in World War I; 42, 042 in World War II; 312 in the Korean Conflict, while approximately 2000 Newfoundlanders gave their lives in World War I and II. We must never forget that they died so that we may enjoy everything we have today. Our prosperity and freedom were secured by the service personnel who paid the ultimate price.

We must never forget those who were wounded or taken prisoner. We cannot forget those who are still listed as missing. We must not forget all the veterans who travelled to foreign lands to protect Canada and her allies. Every person who served our country deserves our respect and on November 11th we pay tribute to those who did not return. We pause to remember and think.

Inscription

Robert G. MacDonald

> Because they rest in grim Gallipoli;
> Because they sleep on Beaumont Hamel's plain;
> Because beneath the ever-flowing main
> Their bodies find a grave eternally
> Till the Last Call: in memory of them we,
> Whose Land and theirs they saved, that not in vain
> Their lives were given, have reared this fitting fane
> For many generations yet to be.
> Here shall the ancient lore of Rome and Greece,
> The learning and science and the art
> Of England, Flanders, Italy and France,
> Flow in a stream that plays its generous part
> To fertilize the mind of youth, to advance
> And foster progress in a world at peace.

This poem was written for the opening of Memorial College, dedicated to the memory of those who gave their lives during the Great War, so that through higher learning the youth of Newfoundland and Labrador might progress "in a world at peace." [Eds.]

Snaps from the war in Nurse Cluett's album

Excerpt from a Letter

Written by Frances Cluett, Nurse World War I, Rouen,
to her Mother, Martha Cluett, Beloram, Newfoundland, October 26th, 1917

Nearly all the patients we have got lately on the Medical Lines are gassed; that means their eyes have to be bathed and inhalations of boiling water and Friars balsam, a teaspoonful of balsam to a pint of boiling water. Many of them are burned but not blistered: that is with they say mustard gas; we do the burns with Baking Soda and Borasic Powder which heals them very quickly.

Sometimes I relieve on the Surgical Lines; it is there the horrible sights are: you would not believe me mother if I tell you about what I have seen and gone through. I always think of what Lil told me about not being able to stay in a ward with the dead. Tell her, I have stood by many a bedside in the middle of the night, with lights darkened, watching for the last breath, the[y] put screws about him, and in addition to that, the rats would rush underneath the beds with a swish. I do not think about them mother; but I shall never forget some of the most piteous sights that ever could possibly be.

I don't think I ever told you I did night duty in the German Compound for Prisoners of War. I had five German wards to look after and one of the wards was an acute surgical, where amputated legs and arms had to be watched for hemorrhages.

I think had you known that was where I was doing night duty you would have felt a bit uneasy. Of course there was an English night orderly also. It was funny, I did not feel at all scared; but perhaps I did feel a bit nervous sometimes.

I knew they could not harm me there, or at least I suppose they couldn't: I have passed through their wards with them lying on either side: sometimes I used to think, if they would jump up; but then on the whole I had nothing whatever to complain about; they were always very respectful to me. The Colonel came to me one night and asked me if I had any complaints to make against them. I could speak quite a bit of German while I was there; but I have forgotten most of it now, not having reason to speak it. I could tell you heaps of things but I dare not. One night in the German Compound I was stopped by the English Sentry outside the barbed wire who wanted to know about one of the German orderlies; he said he was carrying a light in his hand which he would revolve at intervals: of course I knew nothing about it; but had to go through the wards and imagine if either of them had been using an electric torch; but they hadn't; I think it must have been a cigarette the sentry saw; being a VAD is not all sunshine mother.

We were awakened the other night by the air raid. Oh the awful noise of the guns.

I used to stand by the barbed wire Compound when I was on night duty and listen to the guns on the battlefield. About 2 pm they would be at their loudest.

We always know after a rush at the front, that our wards will soon be full again.

Sat. 8 pm

The patient I was telling you about that was so badly gassed died at 1:30 pm. last night: I knew he was dead before I went for duty this morning; for mother I thought he called me during the night. However I woke up, and of course when I went on duty, the first thing I saw was the empty bed: poor chap, he suffered terribly; out of all we did for him, we could not save him.

Letter Written by Frances Cluett

Nurse, World War I, Rouen, to her Mother, Martha Cluett, Beloram, Newfoundland, December 29th, 1917

Rouen
Sunday night   B. E. F.
Dec. 29-12-17

Dear Mother,

Xmas is over; but I do wish you all a Merry one and a Happy New Year; but I suppose it is a bit difficult to be joyous under present circumstances; still these are things one must cope with daily: I can imagine poor Aunt Sarah and Uncle Walt; I cannot yet realize Vince is dead: I did think we were going to meet some day in France: I even went so far as to think he would be getting "leave" somewhere about my time then we should spend it together.

I received a letter written by him before he was wounded: but it did not reach me until days after his death: it gave me a weird feeling to read that letter, knowing the writer had passed away; but I shall visit the grave before leaving France; it is not far from here.

I received two boxes from home. Will you thank the Seuders mother; for I cannot write them all, although I may drop each one a postal.

The cake wasn't hashed at all this time, but a bit dried. The tea Aunt Emily sent me, I took it to the ward on Xmas day to make tea for Nurse Parker, Owen-Davies, Wilcox and Sister Lucas. We had our tea together on the ward table; but it was so draughty all around, that the tea party was nearly a failure. I went into town a few days before Xmas with "Sister" to purchase cakes, etc, for the boys tea on Xmas day. We went to the E.F.C—Expeditionary Force Canteen—for there, things are ever so much cheaper than elsewhere: the French charge us abominably for everything.

However, we bought tinned damsons, dried prunes, potted salmon, potted meat, nuts, apples, cake etc. With the cake we made "trifle"; that is, you put the cake in slices on the bottom of a bowl or pan, then a layer of fruit, then custard or jelly or Blanc Mange, it is very good. Sister made the "trifle" for her four wards.

Out of the fruit we made fruit salad: that is we put all the different kinds of fruit we had into our bowl; of course there was a lot of syrup with them as we had tinned fruit to mix with it. Three of our wards did their fruit that way: but I didn't, for one of my up patients told me it would be much better to keep the fruit separately; as some of the patients may not like all the different kinds of fruit.

This up patient was such a help to me in decorating the wards; he helped me with one half of the ward, and practically did the second half all by himself; he was a splendid decorator; he has done quite a bit of work in that line in pre-war days.

Matron gave us some coloured paper decorations; but not enough; so with some tissue paper we made some ourselves, and hung in festoons from the ceiling of the tents; of course we had no hammering to do, for we could easily pin through the canvas.

(I must put this letter up, for one of the nurses has a talking ticket: she has not ceased talking for the past couple of hours); however, I am having a day off to-morrow: oh! mother won't it be ripping to stay in bed; I shall have my breakfast brought to the cubicle. Good night mother.

Monday 30-12.

It is now 9 p.m. I have had my day off. I stayed in bed until 12 a.m: got up and dressed for lunch, after which I tidied my room, as I was absolutely ashamed of it, then at 3 p.m. I went into Rouen to get some knitting needles: I started to knit myself a pair of stockings, I expect to finish them about June.

I am preparing for my leave: I don't know where I shall go until I hear Clare who is at St. Omer. She wrote me saying her leave would be due in a month's time, so I shall wait for her. I have suggested that we should go to the South of France. "Sister," who has just come back, is in ecstasy over it, and strongly [urged] me to go there. I have also written Gallishaw about our leave, as I know hers will be due very soon. I think also she is going home in January. Poor old Gallishaw, I would give worlds to see her.

I shall not write any more tonight mother. My knitting is waiting; and I am just longing to get at it. "A new broom sweeps clean." Good night.

Give my love to Aunt Suse.

From Fannie.

Three O'Clock, 1968
Oil on board, 15 1/2" x 18"

I remember the tranquillity of childhood afternoons, when the dishes were done and the men were still away from the house. More than the description of a kettle or a clock or a kitchen stove, this painting is about a mood and a time of day. I try to create rooms, both physical and philosophical, in which the mind can wander and play.

— *Christopher Pratt*

The Master

Herbert Pottle

He smote the keyboard into rapturous being,
And the mortality of man
He transposed to the evermore of music.
And no one stayed the magic moment to inquire
Into his pedigree,
His ideology,
Or what his salary;
Whether African or Asian,
Croat or Caucasian.
For all who heard him in that moment
Took on immortality;
His symphony awoke
Responsive chording in their common kind,
And in that moment all were excellent,
Moved to a nobler humanhood.
And he who had composed this wondrous while,
Poring over his cascades of harmony,
The necessary dissonance,
By his right hand the finger-shafts of lightning,
And by his left the echoing roll of thunder—
In that creation's moment
He was very God;
And, brooding there upon his handiwork,
Lo!
It was very good.

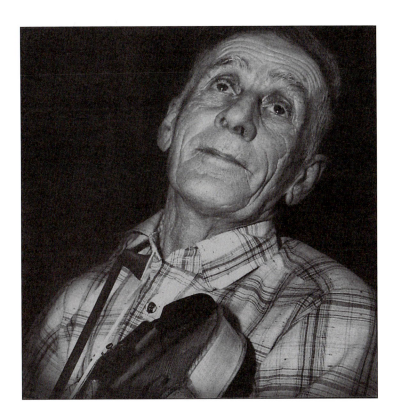

Emile Benoit (top) and Rufus Guinchard—friends and fiddlers

Facing the Gale

Geoff Meeker

Ron Hynes writes music that will stop you in your tracks. Ironically, he may just be a victim of his own talent. The Newfoundland-born singer-songwriter, who was nominated in four East Coast Music Award categories this year (but didn't win), writes powerful, evocative pieces that lend new meaning to the term "hurtin' music."

Often tagged as a country singer, Hynes is more a folk-rock performer. His compositions, especially those on his latest album, are populated by intriguing, believable characters tormented by the loss of life, love or home. The precisely crafted songs and vividly drawn characters elevate Hynes to grand-master status in an industry where the term "artist" is used too loosely.

Hynes' poetic gift is evident in this verse from "St. John's Waltz":

> Oh, the harbour lights are gleamin'
> And the evening's still and dark
> And the seagulls are all dreamin'
> Seagull dreams on Amherst Rock
> And the mist is slowly driftin'
> As the storefront lights go dim
> And the moon is gently liftin'
> As the last ship's comin' in

However, just as the most arresting pieces of visual art in a gallery are often the last to sell, Hynes' solo recordings have not been commercial successes. Last August, Hynes was dropped by his label, Capitol-EMI, after recording just two albums in a six-album deal.

"I really don't want to discuss it," Hynes said in an interview. "I was told in August that I have no further responsibilities to the label. That's as much as I was told."

However, industry sources suggest Hynes was dropped due to disappointing sales. His first album, *Cryer's Paradise*, was leavened by the inclusion of several upbeat numbers. It sold just 10,000 copies. But Hynes' second release, the dark, disturbing *Face to the Gale*, apparently sold even less.

From opening to closing track, *Face to the Gale* features a parade of anguished characters and themes. There's the cab driver who picks up a man who confesses to having just murdered someone ("Killer Cab"); the electrifying tribute to Maritime songwriter Gene MacLellan ("Godspeed"); a man who pines for his lover while shackled in a prison cell for killing the "other man" ("Constance"); and the saga of generation after generation who must leave their home towns in search of work ("Leaving on the Evening Tide").

The lyrics are stirring and poetic, but they don't mask the fact that this is an album about loss and leaving.

"Yeah, the whole album was kind of centred around those themes," Hynes said. "I had to set the album in a kind of space and time that we've all grown up in here, that we've all experienced. What happened to us? Who the hell are we? Where did we come from? How did we get here? I wanted to tackle those questions without getting really specific. The way I see it, we're a dysfunctional nation…and a dysfunctional province within Canada, the country that we were sold into."

And Hynes has no apologies for the poor sales of his albums.

"I have no regrets about it. I think I did two really good records. I can't call them 'failures' in any way or put any kinds of negatives on them as a result of success or failure at retail. What determines good work for me is the dedication of the artist, and the amount of honesty and integrity you are willing to bring to your work."

Hynes' face-to-the-gale pride in his work is not surprising, given that the loss of the recording contract is the only sour note he's endured in recent years. If anything, Hynes is on a career high.

One high point happened two weeks ago in Halifax, when Hynes performed onstage with the Nova Scotia Symphony Orchestra, as part of the Symphony Concert Series at the Rebecca Cohen (he performed "Godspeed," "Constance" and "Leaving on the Evening Tide"). The orchestra then moved to the Metro Centre, to perform at the 10th Annual East Coast Music Awards (ECMA), where Hynes again performed "Godspeed" with orchestral accompaniment, to a hushed ECMA audience who showed their appreciation with a standing ovation.

"I didn't expect the ovation and I was taken by surprise. I felt very grateful. Most of it was for Gene, I know, and it shows the fondness with which he's remembered…but I like to think some of it was for me."

There have also been recording and songwriting successes. *11:11*, an independently produced album featuring 11 Newfoundland women singing 11 songs penned by Hynes and his wife Connie, was a critical and commercial success. It was the biggest selling CD in St. John's during the Christmas season, and is already into a third pressing.

The pair began working on the album—quite unknowingly—in 1991, when Joan Kennedy scored a hit with their "Never Met A Liar I Didn't Like."

"We started writing all these songs and waiting around for the next hit…and waiting and waiting and waiting," Hynes laughed. "So we reached a point where we said, 'OK, that was a once-in-a-lifetime thing. So let's just get some songs covered ourselves.' As we wrote tunes, we invited people to sing them, and it turned into this project…a real labour of love."

The two are currently writing a television special that builds upon the *11:11* album, featuring music video-style performances of the music interwoven with interview clips about the songs and the people who sing them. A major television network and a potential corporate sponsor have already expressed interest in the production.

Hynes has co-written new material with Canuck folk hero Murray McLauchlan and Joan Besen of Prairie Oyster. "No Change in Me" appeared on McLauchlan's *Gulliver's Taxi* album, and has been covered by Newfoundland's up-and-coming Ennis Sisters, and John McDermott, who also covered Hynes' "Sonny's Dream."

"People are still covering Sonny," Hynes said. "I've kinda lost count of how many acts have covered it. The last time I checked, it was about 48. The biggest success anyone has had from the song is Mary Black in Ireland. The song still makes more money per year from that part of the world than the rest of the catalogue makes in Canada altogether."

Hynes has been invited to perform later this year at the Newport Folk Festival, and has finally managed to participate in the lesser-known Kerrville Songwriters Festival in Texas.

"It's a very prestigious festival. It takes a long time to get on—you can audition for years trying to get into Kerrville, so I'm really looking forward to that."

Hynes will also reprise his acting role as the seedy Johnny Shea in the offbeat comedy *Dooley Gardens*, which was piloted last year and has been renewed for six more episodes this fall. Shooting starts in April.

Also in the works is an album of songs by Johnny Burke, a talented and influential "town crier" who was famous in St. John's at the turn of the century, and a new independent album of Hynes' own material, tentatively titled *Hard Rock and Water*.

Hynes is making no predictions about the content of that album, or whether it will be less disturbing than the previous outing.

"I'm not interested in writing any one kind of song, dark or whatever, and I don't think that all of my stuff is dark," he said. "But whatever moves you, moves you, and you write what you have to write. I've never been a fan of novelty songs or sing-along kind of stuff. I'd rather use the musical arrangement to bring out the bright side of a very dark lyric, than present a bright lyric just for the sake of not being perceived as dark and depressing…. There's a balance in all of it, and I try to have a lyric retain some sense of humour."

Many of his lyrics do invoke humorous scenes, and he says humour often plays a role in his live performances.

"I'm always trying to be funny on stage because the songs, for the most part, have a bit of a dark side to them…I'm not afraid to fall flat on my face once in a while just to lighten the moment."

Humour comes naturally, Hynes adds, when one works closely with artists like Greg Malone and Tommy Sexton. He played and toured with the comics for six years with the Wonderful Grand Band, a group that has had an enormous influence on both trad-rock and comedy performers in Newfoundland.

"You can't come out of that and not have some kind of humour. It becomes part of the lifestyle and it's not such a bad attitude to have because the music industry is a fool's game at best. You've got to be able to laugh at it all—especially yourself. I think humour is essential, and that music shouldn't get too big for its boots."

The secret to writing memorable music, Hynes explained, is simply to write what you know.

"If you write about something that happened in your own backyard, it will strike a universal chord, because everybody has a backyard."

Too many budding songwriters internalize what they see, then write about it in the first person, Hynes said.

"The hardest part was to get outside of yourself. For me, 'Sonny's Dream' was that kind of breakthrough. I was writing about somebody else, or a bunch of people, or a generation of people. But I knew that I was a part of it and that people would understand. And it was the first time that I got outside of 'me.'"

Hynes has reached a point in his career where Sonny's Dream and other songs in his catalogue are providing a reasonable source of income.

"Yes, I am making a living at it," he said. "I'm not getting rich. But I am paying the cable and the rent. Sometimes the payments are late, but I manage to pull it off. I look back on it now and wonder how the hell did I ever get through some of those years, but we seem to be kind of at the end of it, alive, still writing and still doing it.

"In terms of being alive in the music industry, I still feel really young. I feel like it's all still an adventure. There's always new songs to be written, new records to be done, and I hope that I can get to write for the rest of my life."

Sonny's Dream

Ron Hynes

Sonny carries a load, though he's barely a man;
there ain't all that to do, still he does what he can,
and he watches the sea from a room by the stairs,
and the waves keep on rolling, they've done that for years.

Chorus

And it's a hundred miles from town; Sonny's never been there,
and he goes to the highway, and stands there and stares,
and the mail comes at four, and the mailman is old,
oh, and he still dreams his dreams full of silver and gold.

Chorus

Sonny's dreams can't be real; they're just stories he's read;
they're just stars in his eyes; they're just dreams in his head;
and he's hungry inside for the wild world outside,
and I know I can't hold him, though I've tried and I've tried.

Chorus

A Bouquet for Emily

Al Pittman

These frail flowers will not last
the length of your journey.
They'll not stay in bloom long enough
to decorate your destination
or bless your destiny with blossoms.

They are buttercups given only
to lament the gladness of your going.

As you always have, you will go
on tip-toe, summer-saulting
and cart-wheeling all the way.

These fragile flowers will wilt
long before this beginning begins.

But whatever awaits you (wherever
you go) won't matter as long
as what fate rains down on you
is as golden as these petals are now
and as you have been in all seasons
beneath the meadows in the sky
lighting the fields with love and laughter
upsidedown and homeward bound
ever brighter than the brightest light.

I shall be forever fond of those fields
and the flowers blooming there wild
(with you within) as I walk among them
bending the long grass in the shadow
of your green and golden glow.
Because there's little else to offer
(now as you depart) I pass you
this fistful of flowers, wish you
heaps and leaps of love, lots of luck
and quiet smiles all the way home.
Always with buttercups growing
from the ground up and the sky down.

Author Index

Adams, Fred 247, 250
Andersen, Torsten 210
Andrews, Frederick 240
Baggs, Jeff 203
Barbour, Capt. Carl 102
Bouzane, Lillian 27
Blackwood, David 103, 151
Brooks, B. 39
Browne, Nadine 222
Bryan, Tara T. 1
Burke, Johnny 132, 134
Burt, Robert 2
Butt, Grace 222
Byrne, Pat 53, 43
Camacho, Jorge Luis 9
Chubbs, Boyd 18, 52, 149, 169, 223
Churchill, Stewart 191
Clark, Brenda 104
Cluett, Frances 254, 255, 256
Cook, Michael 6
Crummey, Michael 75
Dalton, Mary 222, 223
Davidge, Bud 150
Dawe, Tom 46, 148
de Leon, Lisa 135
Duley, Margaret 117, 135
Elliott, David 195
Fidler, Jim 241
Fillier, Scott 29
Fogwill, Irving 182, 243
Fowler, Rosalie 159
Fulford, Don 116
Goldie, Terry 225
Goudie, Scott 112, 113
Greene, Richard 13
Grenfell, Wilfred 177
Hall, Pam 220, 221
Hay, Gilbert 162
Hayman, Robert 7
Heather, H. M. 212
Horwood, Harold 35
Horwood, R. F. 134, 137
Hynes, Ron 266
Inuit Art Quarterly 162
Jackman, Dianne C. 20
Kearley, Wade 2
Kelland, Otto 90
Kent, W. J. 204
Leggo, Carl 24
Loranger, Danielle 12
Lowell, Robert 16
Macdonald, Alastair 174, 224

MacDonald, Robert 242, 253
Major, Kevin 236
Mason, John 8
Mars, P. C. 95
Martin, Harry 176
Martin, Martin 114, 209
McFarlane, Lucy 140
McGrath, Carmelita 166
Meeker, Geoff 262
Mercer, Angela 76
Moakler, Leo 22
Minty, Dennis 268
Mobilewords Ltd. 38
Montague, Shirley 164
Moore, Tom 7
Newfoundland Ancestor 23
Obed, Enoch 108
O'Dell, Catherine 211
O'Mara, John F. 19
Peacock, F. W. 34
Pinsent, Walt 37
Pitt, David 196
Pitt, Janet Miller 17
Pittman, Al 3, 6, 45, 55, 269
Porter, Helen 32
Pottle, Herbert 192, 260
Pratt, Christopher 258, 259
Pratt, E. J. 1
Puddester, Sharon 184, 185
Reid, Brad 171
Ritchie, William B. 160, 161
Rubia, Geraldine 40
Russell, Ted 85
Saunders, Gary 186, 193
Scammell, Art (A. R.) 98, 217
Schwall, Mary 223
Smith, Warrick 8
Sparkes, R. F. 10, 152
Story, George 124
Tizzard, Aubrey M. 170
Traditional 81, 83
Tuck, T. E. 87
Tucker, Otto 21
Turner, Jack 244
Walker, Mark 14
Walsh, Agnes 168
Walsh, Stephen 251
Wareham, Wilfred 80
Watts, Enos D. 44
Wellman, Jim 33
Withers, Jack 97
Wright, Don 30

Title Index

Alder Music 193
Al Pittman and Tom Dawe: Island Poets 225
The All 'Round Newfoundlander 95
Ancestors 7
Any Mummers Allowed In? 150
Avery's Mill 37
The Ballad of Beaumont Hamel 241
Barrens (for three Dylans) 203
Beaumont Hamel 240
Beneath the Dust and Stars 169
Betsy Brennan's Blue Hen 132
Beyond the Obvious 19
Bill 244
Birthday Voyage (for B. W.) 53
A Bouquet for Emily 268
Brick's Tasteless Advertisement 216
Buttercups 268
Camay Soap Advertisement 26
Captain Carl Barbour 103
The Chance of Your Lifetime 250
The Cliffs of Baccalieu 97
Cocomalt Advertisement 51
Cod-Liver Oil Advertisement 147
The Coil that Binds 220
Come-In 222
Common Threads in Inuit Culture 108
Cover of 11:11 Newfoundland Women Sing 265
The Death of a Tree 186
The Death of an Elm 192
Depiction of Inuit Hunters 110
Depictions of the Coil 221
E. & S. Barbour Store, Newtown 102
Epitaphs or Tombstone Inscriptions 21
Erosion 1
Evelyn (story) 3
Evelyn (poem) 6
Eye 222
Excerpt/Letter/Cluett/Mother 255
Excerpt/Letter/Cluett/Mother/Martha 256
Excerpt/Letter/Warrick Smith 8
Facing the Gale 262
Finos Mapas / Fine Maps 9
First Fruit of the Tree 182
foremother 27
The Founding of The Geological Society 17
The Foure Elements in Newfound-land 7
Full Circle 222
Fumigating the Map 35
Genealogy Motif 18

Genealogy One-Liners 23
Gilbert Hay 162
Good Times 12
Goudie (Artist's Statement) 113
The Great Fire of '92 204
Grandmother Figure I 29
Halfway up the Mountain 176
High Water, Eagle River 112
Highway to Valour (summary) 135
Highway to Valour (excerpts) 135
Independence 13
Inscription 253
Inuit Family in Summer Camp 111
Inuit in Labrador: The Old Way of Life 104
It's A Glacial Sound The Quiets the House 52
Jim Wilson's Chum 177
Julie-Ann 196
The "Kimatullivik Exhibit" 107
Kraken or Giant Squid Advertisement 89
Kyle 158
Last Words of a Dying Man 134
A Letter to Will 251
Letter/O'Dell/Daughter/Mary Jane 211
Letter/Andersen/Makkovik 210
Letter/Lake/Earthquake Committee 137
Lies for Tourists 223
Lighthouse—Cabot Island 102
The Little Girl Learns to Swim I, II, III 184
The Lobster Salad 81
Looking Back 44
Map of Newfoundland 8
Martin Martin and Family 115
The Master 260
Miniskirt 174
The Monologue in Newfoundland 80
Mother Boggan (story) 117
The Mummer (poem) 148
The Mummer (illustration) 149
My Grandmother and Knowlton Nash 24
My Political Career 98
Names and Souls 34
New facts for old 2
Newfoundland 16
Newfoundland Paper Money 219
Newfoundland Name Frequency List 38
A New Name 33
The Northern Lights of Labrador 116
No Man's Land (publisher's blurb) 236
No Man's Land (excerpts) 236

Nuikkusemajak 162
An Off-Shore Wind 46
One-room Schoolhouse Scene 143
Paddy with the Maul 30
Percy Janes Boarding the Bus 168
Photograph of Brigus c. 1915 223
Photograph of Emile Benoit 261
Photograph of Rufus Guinchard 261
Photograph of a Tree 191
Places That Were 40
Pleasant Afternoon 171
Praise 223
Pratt (Artist's Statement) 259
Prelude to Doom 243
The Prince of Wales 83
Puddester (Artist's Statement) 185
Quoth the Raven 76
The Recitation 140
Relocating from Silver Fox Island 39
Report of South Coast Disaster Committee 134
Researching Your Family History 20
Ritchie (Artist's Statement) 161
The Road Home 75
Romance in the Twentieth Century 242
Seeking Recruits 247
Smokeroom on the Kyle 85
Snaps from the War 254
Sonny's Dream 266
Squarin' Up 217
The St. John's Balladeers 124

St. John's After the Fire 1892 208
St. Leonard's Revisited 45
A Tall Tale: Giant Squid 87
Talking to Trees 195
The Tangled Forest 160
Teenagers 170
The 1921 Fire at Nain 209
The Terror of Quidi Vidi Lake 90
There is This Photograph 166
The Tidal Wave Disaster 139
Tickle Cove Pond 14
Three Mummers at Winsor Point 151
Three O'Clock 258
Troubled Waters 212
Tuckamore Festival of the Arts 164
untitled - Cook 6
untitled - Fowler 159
Violet Hovering 1
Vocabulary 224
Wanderings 2
Walking 32
West Moon 43
West Moon (cover illustration) 54
West Moon (excerpts) 55
The Winds Softly Sigh (Introduction) 10
The Winds Softly Sigh (Excerpts) 152
We, The Inuit Are Changing 114
Wright (A Profile) 31
Yaffling Fish on a Rooftop 197

273

Text Credits

A BOUQUET FOR EMILY by Al Pittman. From *Thirty for Sixty* by Al Pittman (1999). Reprinted by permission of the publisher.

A LETTER TO WILL by Stephen Walsh. Reprinted by permission of Patrick and Stephen Walsh.

A NEW NAME by Jim Wellman. Reprinted by permission Creative Publishers.

A TALL TALE: MY ADVENTURE WITH A GIANT SQUID by T. E. Tuck. Reprinted by permission of Edna White.

AL PITTMAN AND TOM DAWE: ISLAND POEMS by Terry Goldie. Reprinted by kind permission of the author.

ALDER MUSIC by Gary Saunders. From *Alder Music: A Celebration of Our Environment*, Breakwater, 1989. Reprinted by permission of the author.

AN OFF-SHORE WIND by Tom Dawe. Reprinted by permission of the author.

ANCESTORS by Tom Moore. Reprinted by permission of the author.

ANY MUMMERS ALLOWED IN? by Bud Davidge. Music and lyrics by Bud Davidge, English Harbour West, NF. Reprinted by permission of the author.

ARTIST'S STATEMENT by William B. Ritchie. Used by permission of the author.

ARTIST'S STATEMENT by Christopher Pratt. Reprinted by permission of the author.

ARTIST'S STATEMENT by Scott Goudie. Reprinted by permission of the author.

ARTIST'S STATEMENT by Sharon Puddester. Reprinted by permission of the author.

BARRENS (FOR THREE DYLANS) by Jeff Baggs. © Jeff Baggs, 1997. Reprinted by permission of the author.

BENEATH THE DUST AND STARS by Boyd Chubbs. From *The Birth and Burial Grounds* by Boyd Warren Chubbs (1999). Reprinted by permission of the author.

BEYOND THE OBVIOUS by John F. O'Mara. Reprinted by permission of the author.

BIRTHDAY VOYAGE (FOR B. W.) by Pat Byrne. Reprinted by permission of the author.

CAPTAIN CARL BARBOUR (1908-1990) by David Blackwood. Originally published in *Captain Carl Barbour: Painting the Past*, AGNL exhibition catalogue, 1992. Reprinted by permission of the author.

COME IN by Grace Butt. Reprinted by permission of the author.

COMMON THREADS IN INUIT CULTURE by Enoch Obed. Used by permission of Newfoundland and Labrador Human Rights Association.

EROSION by E. J. Pratt. Copyright University of Toronto Press Incorporated, 1989. Reprinted by permission of University of Toronto Press Incorporated.

EVELYN (poem) by Al Pittman. Reprinted by permission of the publisher.

EVELYN (short story) by Al Pittman. Reprinted by permission of the publisher.

EXCERPT FROM HIGHWAY TO VALOUR by Margaret Duley. Reprinted by permission of Margot Duley.

EXCERPT FROM WEST MOON by Al Pittman. Reprinted by permission of the publisher.

EXCERPTS FROM NO MAN'S LAND by Kevin Major. Reprinted by permission of Doubleday Canada Ltd.

EXCERPTS FROM THE WINDS SOFTLY SIGH by R. F. Sparkes. Reprinted by permission of Paul Sparkes.

EYE by Mary Dalton. First appeared in *TickleAce* and subsequently published in *The Time of Icicles* (Breakwater). Reprinted by permission of the author.

FACING THE GALE by Geoff Meeker. Reprinted by permission of the author.

FIRST FRUIT OF THE TREE by Irving Fogwill. Reprinted with permission of Sylvia Thomas.

FOREMOTHER by Lillian Bouzane. © Lillian Bouzane. From *Back to Back* by Lillian Bouzane and Harold Paddock, published by MAKM Productions Ltd. Reprinted by permission of the author.

FULL CIRCLE by Nadine Browne. Reprinted by permission of the author.

FUMIGATING THE MAP by Harold Horwood. Reprinted by permission of the author.

GENEALOGY ONE-LINERS. Reprinted by permission of *The Newfoundland Ancestor* – a publication of the Newfoundland and Labrador Genealogical Society Inc.

GILBERT HAY—A PROFILE by Inuit Art Quarterly. Reprinted with permission of Inuit Art Quarterly.

GRANDMOTHER FIGURE I by Scott Fillier. Reprinted by permission of the author.

HALFWAY UP THE MOUNTAIN by Harry Martin. Written by Harry Martin (SOCAN), Sound Kitchen Music. Reprinted by permission of the author.

INDEPENDENCE by Richard Greene. Reprinted by permission of the publisher.

INTRODUCTION TO THE WINDS SOFTLY SIGH by R. F. Sparkes. Reprinted by permission of Paul Sparkes.

INUIT IN LABRADOR: THE OLD WAY OF LIFE by Brenda Clark. Courtesy of the Newfoundland Museum.

IT'S A GLACIAL SOUND THAT QUIETS THE HOUSE by Boyd Chubbs. Reprinted by permission of the author.

JULIE-ANN by David Pitt. Reprinted by permission of Jesperson Publishing. Originally published in *Tales from the Outer Fringe*, © 1990, David Pitt.

KRAKEN OR GIANT SQUID ADVERTISEMENT by Memorial University. Reprinted by permission of Memorial University.

LETTER WRITTEN by Catherine O'Dell. From *Them Days*, Vol 9 No. 1, 1983, submitted by Gertrude Hawco, 1983 – Pinware. Reprinted by permission of *Them Days*.

LETTERS by Frances Cluett. Held at the Centre for Newfoundland Studies, Memorial University of Newfoundland Libraries. Reprinted by permission of CNS.

LETTER WRITTEN BY TORSTEN ANDERSEN, 1901 by Torsten Andersen. From *Them Days*, Vol 3 No. 3, 1978, submitted by Curtis McNeil. Used by kind permission of *Them Days*.

LIES FOR THE TOURISTS by Mary Dalton. First appeared in *TickleAce* and subsequently published in *Allowing the Light* (Breakwater, 1989). Reprinted by permission of the author.

LOOKING BACK by Enos D. Watts. Reprinted by permission of the publisher.

MINISKIRT by Alastair Macdonald. Published in the collection *Landscapes of Time: New, Uncollected, and Selected Poems* (by Alastair Macdonald), Breakwater Books Ltd., St. John's, 1994; a volume of *Newfoundland Poetry Series* by Breakwater, 1993. Reprinted by permission of the publisher.

MOTHER BOGGAN by Margaret Duley. Reprinted by permission of Creative Publishers.

MY GRANDMOTHER AND KNOWLTON NASH by Carl Leggo. Reprinted by permission of Creative Publishers.

MY POLITICAL CAREER by Art Scammell. Reprinted by permission of Carrie Scammell.

NAMES & SOULS by F. W. Peacock. Reprinted by permission of Stephanie Smith.

NEW FACTS FOR OLD by Wade Kearley. Reprinted by permission of Creative Publishers.

NEWFOUNDLAND NAME FREQUENCY LIST IN GAZETTEER by Mobilewords Ltd. Reprinted by permission of Tor Fosnaes.

PERCY JANES BOARDING THE BUS by Agnes Walsh. Reprinted by permission of Creative Publishers.

PLACES THAT WERE by Geraldine Rubia. Reprinted by permission of Creative Publishers.

PRAISE by Boyd Chubbs. Reprinted by permission of the author.

PRELUDE TO DOOM by Irving Fogwill. Reprinted by permission of Syliva Thomas.

QUOTH THE RAVEN by Angela Mercer. Reprinted by permission of the author.

RESEARCHING YOUR FAMILY HISTORY IN NEWFOUNDLAND by Dianne C. Jackman. Reprinted by permission of the author.

SMOKEROOM ON THE KYLE by Ted Russell. Reprinted by permission of Kelly Russell, Pigeon Inlet Productions.

SONNY'S DREAM by Ron Hynes. Composed by: Ron Hynes. Courtesy of TMP - The Music Publisher. © 1977 Wonderful Grand Music/Sold For A Song/MCA Music Canada (SOCAN).

ST. LEONARD'S REVISITED by Al Pittman. Reprinted by permission of the publisher.

SQUARIN' UP by A. R. Scammell. Reprinted by permission of Carrie Scammell.

SUMMARY OF HIGHWAY TO VALOUR by Lisa de Leon. Reprinted by permission of Jesperson Publishing. Originally published in *Writers of Newfoundland and Labrador*, © 1985, Lisa de Leon.

TALKING TO TREES by David Elliott. From *The Edge of Beulah* (Breakwater, 1988). Reprinted by permission of Rosalie Fowler.

TEENAGERS by Aubrey M. Tizzard. Reprinted by permission of Garry Tizzard, in respect of, *On Sloping Ground* by Aubrey M. Tizzard.

1921 FIRE AT NAIN by Martin Martin. Reprinted by permission of Susan Martin

THE BALLAD OF BEAUMONT HAMEL by Jim Fidler. Reprinted by permission of the author.

THE COIL THAT BENDS, THE LINE THAT BINDS by Pam Hall. Reprinted by permission of the author.

THE DEATH OF A TREE by Gary Saunders. Reprinted by permission of the author.

THE DEATH OF AN ELM by Herbert Pottle. Reprinted by permission of Helen Wesanko.

THE FOUNDING OF THE NEWFOUNDLAND GENEALOGICAL SOCIETY by Janet Miller Pitt. Used by permission of *The Newfoundland Ancestor* – a publication of the Newfoundland and Labrador Genealogical Society Inc. and the author.

THE GREAT FIRE OF '92 by W. J. Kent. From *The Book of Newfoundland*. Reprinted by permission of William Smallwood.

THE MASTER by Herbert Pottle. Reprinted by permission.of Helen Wesanko.

THE MONOLOGUE IN NEWFOUNDLAND by Wilfred W. Wareham. Reprinted by permission of the author.

THE MUMMER by Tom Dawe. Reprinted by permission of the author.

THE NORTHERN LIGHTS OF LABRADOR by Don Fulford. Reprinted by permission of the author.

THE RECITATION by Lucy Fitzpatrick-McFarlane. Reprinted by permission of the author, Lucy Fitzpatrick McFarlane.

THE ROAD HOME by Michael Crummey. Reprinted from Michael Crummey's *Arguments with Gravity*, by permission of Quarry Press, Inc.

THE ST. JOHN'S BALLADEERS by George Story. Reprinted by permission of Alice Story.

THE TERROR OF QUIDI VIDI LAKE by Otto Kelland.Reprinted by permission of the author. © Otto Kelland, C.M., 66 Deermarsh Road, Flatrock, NF A1K 1C8.

THERE IS THIS PHOTOGRAPH by Carmelita McGrath from *Poems on Land and on Water* (Killick Press, 1992). Reprinted by permission of the publisher.

TROUBLED WATERS by H. M. Heather. Reprinted by permission of Creative Publishers.

TUCKAMORE FESTIVAL OF THE ARTS: SONGWRITING by Shirley Montague. Reprinted by kind permission of the author.

UNTITLED by Rosalie Fowler. Reprinted by permission of the author.

UNTITLED by Michael Cook. Reprinted by permission of Madonna Decker Cook.

VOCABULARY by Alastair Macdonald. Published in the collection *Landscapes of Time: New, Uncollected, and Selected Poems* (by Alastair Macdonald), Breakwater Books Ltd., 1994; *Newfoundland Poetry Series* Breakwater, 1993. Reprinted by permission of the publisher.

WANDERINGS by Robert Burt. Reprinted by kind permission of the author.

WALKING by Helen Porter. Reprinted by permission of the author.

WE, THE INUIT, ARE CHANGING by Martin Martin. Reprinted by permission of the Susan Martin.

WEST MOON by Pat Byrne. Reprinted by permission of the author.

Visual Credits

Scanning services by Ray Fennelley.

Music prepared by Fergus O'Byrne.

Illustrations on the following pages custom created by Boyd Warren Chubbs: 3, 5, 7, 9, 18, 23, 32, 46, 50, 52, 64, 65, 67, 68, 69, 72, 76, 79, 101, 117, 123, 140, 146, 149, 156, 157, 169, 177, 182, 196, 212, 218.

1: Photography by Ned Pratt; courtesy of Christina Parker Fine Art; **8**: Association of Canadian Map Librairies and Archives; **12**: Danielle Loranger; **30**: Photography by Ned Pratt; courtesy of Christina Parker Fine Art; **37**: Walt Pincent **39**: B. Brooks (August 1961), courtesy of the National Archives of Canada, Serial II, PA154123; **42**: Breakwater Archives; **48**: Clyde Rose; **54**: Breakwater; **89**: Glen Loates, created for Dr. F. Aldrich, Department of Biology, Memorial Univeristy of Newfoundland, August 24, 1988; **102**: Courtesy of Estate/Art Gallery of Newfoundland and Labrador; **107**: Courtesy of the Newfoundland Museum; **110**: Keld Hansen, from *Salik and Arnaluk* (Breakwater, 1981); **111**: Joan Steadman Photo, courtesy of *Them Days*; **112**: Courtesy of Christina Parker Fine Art; **115**: Joan Steadman Photo, courtesy of *Them Days*; **139**: Provincial Archives of Newfoundland and Labrador; **143**: Breakwater Archives; **151**: Courtesy of David Blackwood; **158**: Tom Ronayne, from *Part of the Main* (Breakwater, 1983); **160**: Lithograph by William B. Ritchie; **162**: William B. Ritchie; **163**: Art Procurement Program, Government of Newfoundland and Labrador; **167**: Clyde Rose; **171**: Courtesy of Christina Parker Fine Art; **184**: Courtesy of Sharon Puddester; **191**: Stewart Churchill; **194**: Gary Saunders, from *Alder Music* (Breakwater); **197**: Breakwater Archives; **208**: Provincial Archives of Newfoundland and Labrador; **219**: Breakwater Archives; **221**: Pam Hall; **223**: courtesy of CNS; **235**: Clyde Rose; **254**: Held in the Centre for Newfoundland Studies, Memorial University of Newfoundland; **258-259**: By permission of Christopher Pratt; **261**: (top) Breakwater Archives, (bottom) *The Telegram*; **265**: Connie Hynes; **267**: Vinland Music; **268**: © Dennis Minty.